THE POLITICS
OF ETHICS

THE
RUFFIN SERIES IN BUSINESS ETHICS
R. Edward Freeman, *Editor*

Forthcoming titles to be announced

THE POLITICS OF ETHICS

Methods for Acting, Learning, and Sometimes Fighting with Others in Addressing Ethics Problems in Organizational Life

RICHARD P. NIELSEN

New York   Oxford
Oxford University Press
1996

Oxford University Press

Oxford   New York
Athens   Auckland   Bangkok   Bogota   Bombay
Buenos Aires   Calcutta   Cape Town   Dar es Salaam
Delhi   Florence   Hong Kong   Istanbul   Karachi
Kuala Lumpur   Madras   Madrid   Melbourne
Mexico City   Nairobi   Paris   Singapore
Taipei   Tokyo   Toronto

and associated companies in
Berlin   Ibadan

Library of Congress Cataloging-in-Publication Data
Nielsen, Richard P.
The Politics of ethics : methods for acting, learning, and
sometimes fighting with others in addressing ethics problems in
organizational life / Richard P. Nielsen.
p.   cm.
Includes bibliographical references and index.
ISBN 0–19–509665–7; ISBN 0–19–509666–5 (pbk.)
1. Business ethics.   2. Interpersonal communication.
3. Persuasion.   4. Negotiation.   I. Title.
HF5387.N537   1996
174'.4—dc20   96–7928

9 8 7 6 5 4 3 2 1

Printed in the United States of America
on acid-free paper

Earlier versions of some chapters, as well as parts of chapters, in this volume first appeared as articles in the following journals. Permission to use this material is gratefully acknowledged.

"Arendt's Action Philosophy and the Manager as Eichmann, Richard III, Faust, or Institution Citizen," Copyright 1984 by The Regents of the University of California. Reprinted from the *California Management Review*, vol. 26, no. 3, by permission of the Regents.

"Changing Unethical Organizational Behavior," *Academy of Management EXECUTIVE*, vol. 3, no. 2. Copyright 1989 by the Academy of Management. Reprinted by permission of the Academy of Management.

"Woolman's 'I Am We' Triple-Loop, Action-Learning: Origin and Application in Organization Ethics," *Journal of Applied Behavioral Science*, vol. 29, no. 1, pp. 117–138. Copyright 1993 by NTL Institute, Inc. Reprinted by permission of Sage Publications, Inc.

"Varieties of Postmodernism as Moments in Ethics Action-Learning," *Business Ethics Quarterly*, vol. 3, no. 3. Copyright 1993 by the Society for Business Ethics. Reprinted by permission of the Society for Business Ethics.

"Varieties of Dialectic Change Processes," *Journal of Management Inquiry*, vol. 5, no. 3. Copyright 1996 by Sage Publications, Inc. Reprinted by permission of Sage Publications, Inc.

The figure in chapter 3 is adapted from C. Argyris, *Overcoming Organizational Defenses: Facilitating Organizational Learning*, © 1990, p. 94. Adapted by permission of Prentice-Hall, Upper Saddle River, New Jersey.

For my parents, Placide and Lilyan Nielsen, my wife, Angela, and our daughters, Lara and Anna, whose love, sense of humor, and support brings joy to my life. In addition, this book is dedicated to the students and alumni of Boston College and the Athens Laboratory of Business Administration.

FOREWORD

R. Edward Freeman

The hallmark of recent work in business ethics is the integration of thinking in the humanities with sound business theory and practice. No longer is it useful to make the "business ethics is an oxymoron" joke, nor is it helpful to separate out "business" from "ethics." The scholars who have published books in this series have without exception contributed to the deeper and more integrated understanding of how business and ethics go together.

Richard Nielsen has taken this line of thinking a giant step forward by opening up a dialogue between business thinkers, literary figures and corporate managers trying to act ethically. In doing so, he has written at once a very practical and a very theoretical book. *The Politics of Ethics,* is just what it says: an exploration of the difficult human problems of thinking and acting ethically in large organizations. Ethics cannot be separated from politics, just as it cannot be separated from the day-to-day life of business.

By juxtaposing Faust and Socrates with Eichman and Richard III and by showing how understanding these figures is relevent to the ethical situation of the modern corporate manager, Nielsen has written a book that is both action-guiding and literary. Scores of cases are intertwined with the best thinking from the "action learning" school of social sciences and Nielsen's reading of our literary figures to offer a rich source of insight for managers and scholars.

The anchor of Nielsen's work with many organizations around the world has always been dialogue. In this book he shows us how to have better conversations about acting ethically, and he points out the difficulties that such conversations yield. Nielsen has given us the benefit of his wisdom and experience which is unique in a world where most books, even those about ethics, simply ask us to conceive of corporations as athletes, capable of being leaner, meaner, and stronge, rather than wiser.

The purpose of the Ruffin Series in Business Ethics is to publish the best thinking about the role of ethics in business. In a world in which there are daily reports of questionable business practices, from financial scandals to environmental disasters, we need to step back from the fray and understand the large issues of how business and ethics are and ought to be connected. The books in this series are aimed at three audiences: management scholars, ethicists, and business executives. There is a growing consensus among these groups that business and ethics must be integrated as a vital part of the teaching and practice of management.

Richard Nielsen has given us a book that will repay the close reading that it deserves. He connects many new threads and weaves them together into a tapestry that will open up some novel ways of thinking about the connection of business and ethical action. It is a privilege to publish this book in the Ruffin Series, for it challenges us to act as well as to think more carefully about the processes that ultimately yield ethical action.

ACKNOWLEDGEMENTS

To a large extent, this book is an integration and summary of my work over the past twenty-five years. I would like to acknowledge several people and institutions for their help, support, and friendship: my friends and colleagues at Boston College in the Carroll School of Management and the Organization Studies department, as well as some friends in the Philosophy and Theology departments.

Most of the ideas presented in this book have been tested and re-fined through the critical, patient, and good-humored comments of colleagues at conferences of the Society for Business Ethics, the Academy of Management, and the International Association for Business and Society. I would also like to acknowledge the work of two pioneers in this field: David Ewing, whose work has been pathbreaking in identifying the very substantial practical problems involved in bringing ethics and civil liberties to the workplace; and Chris Argyris, whose work has provided a conceptual framework for considering different types of action-learning feedback loops and methods. I have tried to build upon and extend the work of both to achieve a practical politics of organizational ethics.

I am particularly grateful to Professor R. Edward Freeman, the editor of the Ruffin Series in Business Ethics, for his continuing encouragement, which began fifteen years ago, to persevere in this type of work even though it was not very mainstream. At Oxford University Press I received wonderful help from editors Herb Addison and Henry Krawitz. I especially wish to thank Martha Ramsey for her very careful, patient, and insightful editing of the manuscript.

Students, alumni, and managers in Boston, Greece, Indonesia, Ireland, Italy, Latin America, and Pakistan have helped me better understand the structural and cross-cultural differences and difficulties involved in applying oneself to a practical politics of ethics. I thank them for their illustrative examples of ethical inquiry, practical method, and courage, which provide continuing inspiration and hope for ethical organizational life.

Finally, I wish to thank the members of the Society of Friends (Quakers) for their inspiring history of trying to "Speak truth to power" and to "Walk cheerfully over the world answering that of Go(o)d in every one." To some extent, this book also represents a limited and contingent evolution from the win-lose method to the win-win method to interpersonal dialog to dialog with and within different traditions. While there are some situations where the win-lose method and minimal peaceful coexistence may be the only practical alternatives, there are often many more hopeful possibilities than seeing everything in terms of winning and losing.

CONTENTS

THE POLITICS
OF ETHICS

The student of ethics must apply himself to politics.

Aristotle

Politics prolongs ethics by giving it a sphere in which to operate.

Paul Ricoeur

1

Introduction

Applying ethics to organizational life may be a bit like driving in a big city. While there are many periods of pleasant driving and other times when, with careful planning, we can avoid traffic jams, there are also difficult traffic conditions that must be driven through. Sooner or later, whether we are good drivers or bad, we will get into an accident. Similarly, in our organizational lives sooner or later we, or people we care about, will encounter serious ethics problems that will have to be dealt with. Effectively addressing ethics problems and conflicts is not the same as understanding an ethics issue.

This book presents a wide range of methods for addressing ethics conflicts and problems. Many people are not very aware of the methods available for doing so in our organizational lives. A wide range of methods suggests a wide range of alternatives and, consequently, increased individual and organizational degrees of freedom—or, as Ricoeur (1991) observed, a greater civic space for ethics to operate.

As people with hard-won organization ethics experience know, the obstacles to maintaining ethics in organizations can be quite formidable and even intimidating. Individuals initiating or cooperating with unethical behavior can be very intelligent, strong, relentless, nasty, and even courageous—as well as unthinking, weak, timid, and conformist. In addition, external environments and internal organization traditions can encourage unethical behavior. Understanding the severity and complexity of the problems can lead to the conclusion that it is only practical to "go along and get along."

3

This is why Aristotle suggested long ago that "the student of ethics must apply himself to politics." It can be practical to do ethics in organizations. As Paul Ricoeur has observed, "Politics prolongs ethics by giving it a sphere in which to operate" (1991, p. 334). While the difficulties and dangers are quite substantial and can be intimidating, things are far from hopeless. There is no need to be fatalistic even in the most difficult of environments. This is not to suggest that the ethical will always triumph, but neither is the reverse true.

As this book illustrates, there is a wide range of methods that people can use in order to effect positive, ethical changes in both the external socio-political world of their organizations and developmentally within themselves. Most of these methods involve acting, learning, and sometimes fighting, with others. A few of the methods are essentially individual and self-contained.

In the chapters that follow I consider the strengths and limitations of these different methods. Different methods are more or less appropriate depending upon the situation and the people involved. As the last chapter demonstrates, a citizen of the modern organization may have to be like the Greek sea god Proteus, who could and would change his shape as the situation required. We may need to be conversant with a wide variety of methods in order to realize our responsibilities and opportunities as ethical citizens of organizations.

The obstacles and dangers are very real; fights are often possible and sometimes unavoidable. Practicing ethics in organizations does require some courage, and method is not a substitute for it. Technique cannot eliminate danger. Nor is technique a substitute for the classical Greek concepts of practical wisdom combining technical proficiency with appropriate action (*phronesis*) and love of honor (*philotimo*). But technique can work in tandem with courage and practical wisdom to be both effective and substantially reduce personal risks.

A problem for many of us is that while we are concerned about ethics, we do not always know methods to overcome powerful obstacles, to building ethical community and to care for own personal ethical development. Understanding ethics issues is not the same as the behavioral process of acting and learning—and sometimes fighting—with others in adddressing them. When we do not know how to act appropriately, we may not act at all, or we may act counterproductively. Method can help us practice Aristotle's concepts of *poiesis* (action that changes the external world) and *praxis* (action that also developmentally changes the individual).

This book focuses on methods for practicing ethics with others in organizational contexts. The appropriateness and effectiveness of the following different types of combined action and learning methods are considered:

- top-down forcing methods, such as punishment-based ethics compliance codes
- bottom-up forcing methods, such as secretly blowing the whistle outside the organization
- persuasion, win-lose negotiating, and win-win negotiating
- classical, modern, and postmodern dialog
- internal due process systems

THEORETICAL FRAMEWORK

An understanding of the strengths and limitations of the various methods can increase our freedom, political space, and opportunities for ethical development. A behavioral science-based action-learning theoretical framework is used to understand more precisely how the various methods are interrelated, their relative strengths and limitations, their civic appropriateness, and the obstacles they are designed to address.

Action-learning methods combine elements of acting with elements of learning with others. That is, one can learn while acting and one can act while learning. action-learning theory and method offer a framework for considering the behavioral and political processes operating within organizations that underly organization ethics. In addition, certain archetypes of action-learning behaviors, drawn from literature and political philosophy, can help to evoke the human dramas involved.

Relatively few articles and no books have approached organization ethics from either a behavioral science-based action-learning perspective or a philosophy-based perspective that combines praxis (action) and epistemology (learning). This book makes four contributions in this area. First, it presents a wide range of practical methods for doing ethics in organizations. Second, the behavioral science-based action-learning approach may be combined with the use of evocative archetypes in such a way as to offer us choices that are both technically practical and evocatively meaningful. Third, the book considers several new methods, such as triple-loop action-learning dialog, that combine elements of behavioral science and postmodernist philosophy. Fourth, it helps bridge the theoretical literatures of behavioral science-based action-learning, philosophy-based praxis epistemology, and archetypes drawn from literature and political philosophy.

OVERVIEW

The book is organized as follows. Following this introductory chapter, chapter 2 explores different types of individual and organizational obstacles to doing ethics, and introduces the archetypes that will be used throughout the book. These include: Shakespeare's Richard III, who intentionally commits unethical acts for personal gain; Goethe's Faust, who uses unethical means for ethical ends; Socrates' Jailer (in the *Phaedo*), who obeys orders he believes are unethical because of fear; and Dr. Suguro, who cooperates with unethical behavior out of a belief that it is impractical to be ethical (Endo, 1972).

The Eichmann archetype takes unethical behavior to a different qualitative level, facilitating it administratively and impersonally on a very large scale, apparently without thinking about any ethical ramifications (Arendt, 1964). A more subtle type of character is Socrates' Phaedo—sometimes called Socrates' "beloved disciple"—a friendly, intelligent, good person who does think and talk about the ethical, but does not understand it unless he discusses it with a wise leader or teacher, who is not always around.

Also considered in this chapter are problematical organization traditions and external environments. For example, an environment of pervasive political corruption can make it difficult to do organization ethics where large-scale bribes or extortions are required and the competition is permitted to act unethically. Internally, organization traditions of rewarding unethical behavior and punishing ethical behavior are also problematic. In addition, differing traditions can make it difficult for people to agree on solutions.

In chapter 3 relevant aspects of the behavioral science-based literatures are reviewed and extended, including theories of "exit, voice and loyalty" (Hirschman, 1970), "reciprocal interactions" (Bateson, 1972; Weick, 1979) and "action-learning" (Argyris and Schon, 1974, 1988; Argyris, 1990, 1992, Argyris, Putnam, and Smith, 1985).

In chapters 4 and 5 various types of single-loop feedback methods are considered. In single-loop politics one is open to learning about more effective actions for achieving one's driving values, but is not open to reconsideration of those driving values. Chapter 4 considers the single-loop forcing politics of proethical, top-down Ethics Generals, bottom-up Ethics Guerillas, and win-lose negotiators. The Ethics General is the high-level manager who orders, and through threat and punishment, forces compliance with what he considers ethical organizational behavior. He permits no challenge or discussion of what he considers ethical. His mirror image is the Ethics Guerilla, who also forces what he believes is ethical but, having less organizational power, uses different forcing techniques such as secret whistle blowing and sabotage. Both Ethics Generals and Ethics Guerillas practice single-loop feedback politics in that they are open to learning about more effective techniques for forcing compliance with their ethical values, but they do not engage in open conversation about ethics issues. Often, unethical organization behavior for both is less a problem of understanding than a perceived contest between good and evil.

Chapter 5 considers the nonforcing, single-loop feedback politics of Sophists, persuaders, and win-win negotiators. The Sophist uses manipulative language instead of force to foster ethical organization behavior. His politics are single-loop in that while he engages in conversation, he is not open to reconsidering his driving values. Sophists might be litigators, political debaters, advertisers, some behavioral scientists, some motivators, and some salespeople. The persuader, unlike the Sophist, tries to use what he considers honest arguments rather than manipulative language to convince others. The win-win negotiator, instead of relying upon manipulative or persuasive language is willing to make a real deal. He asks questions and listens to others in search of what he can offer the other in exchange for the other adopting what he considers ethical behavior.

The key strength of win-win politics is that it retains much of the effectiveness of forcing while encouraging productive cooperation. However, there can be little mutual learning, development or belief conversion toward the ethical. People change behaviors because of rewards but may not change opinions or values. If the specific and explicit rewards for ethical behavior stop, the ethical behavior may stop. If there is a shift to rewarding unethical behavior, behavior may follow the rewards. Furthermore, the person offering the rewards may have incomplete or wrong information about what is ethical.

In chapter 6 three different types of double-loop dialog methods are examined. In double-loop politics one is open to both changes in one's instrumental actions and changes in the values that drive them. A key benefit of having different types of individuals with different types of skills, experiences, and specializations in an organization is that different pieces of information, truth, and insight can come together to solve an ethical problem or make a decision. Through dialog, we can learn from each other and help each other and our organizations develop ethically.

Double-loop politics can be especially useful in situations where the problems are located primarily at the level of individuals. But sometimes individuals are not the problem so much as the biased traditions, systems, and environments they work within. Such systems and traditions can shape choices so that ethical outcomes are very difficult or unlikely. In chapters 7 and 8 I consider how two types of triple-loop dialog can address such problems.

In triple-loop politics we question not only the effectiveness of instrumental actions and the appropriateness of driving values, but also the tradition system within which these are shaped and embedded.

The tradition system is treated critically as a partner and ally in mutual action-learning.

Other methods may be called for in situations where the key participants believe that they are part of very different and even antagonistic traditions. Chapter 9 describes how a postmodernist dialog method was used effectively to address such a situation. The method incorporates, as moments in a continuous process, three postmodernist approaches—Gadamer reconstruction, Derrida deconstruction, and Rorty experimental neopragmatism. (Some scholars within the deconstruction stream consider the latter two more late modernist than postmodernist. For lack of better terminology, I refer to these three branches as friendly reconstruction, adversarial deconstruction, and civil experimentation.) Strengths and limitations of the method are discussed. This chapter demonstrates how it can be beneficial to build bridges between and within the literatures of postmodernism and organization ethics, and how postmodernism can be positively ethical and not necessarily aethical or nihilistic.

A fundamental idea of postmodernist philosophy is that tradition systems (the potential triple-loop) usually shape our ideas about the ethical in the particular case. Our ideas and behaviors concerning ethics evolve with interactive changes between our traditions and particular cases, as we frame questions less about what is objectively right or wrong than about what is better or worse.

Chapters 4 through 9 consider how individuals within organizations can act and learn with each other, their tradition systems, and their environments. Chapter 10 considers internal due process systems, which are somewhat different: they are best described as ethics processing machines. These systems, not necessarily designed solely to address ethics issues, do process them. There are single-, double-, and triple-loop types of due process systems. The two major forms of single-loop systems are investigation-punishment and grievance arbitration systems. The two major forms of double- and triple-loop systems are mediator-counselor and employee board systems.

Chapter 2 considers various obstacles to ethical behavior and development in organizations at the levels of the individual, tradition, and environment. Chapters 4 through 10 analyze the strengths and limitations of the different types of single-, double-, and triple-loop politics. Chapter 11 circles back and links the methods to the obstacles, examining how well the different forms of politics can address the obstacles considered in chapter 2.

In conclusion, Chapter 12 offers the suggestion that to be an organization citizen who acts ethically, appropriately, and effectively in different types of organizational worlds may require something of the transformational ability of Proteus.

It is my hope that this book will provide a better understanding of the strengths, limitations, and civic appropriateness of the various types of single-, double-, and triple-loop politics and thereby increase our freedom, political space, and opportunities to be ethical citizens within ethical organizations.

Both physicists and economists tell us that there is no long-term equilibrium. Things get better or worse; they constantly change. The obstacles within organizations can be complex and intimidating. Technique is no substitute for courage and practical wisdom. Nonetheless, as the many examples in the book illustrate, an intelligent method combined with some degree of courage can make a positive ethical difference in a continuing and changing process.

2

Obstacles to Ethical Organization Behavior

It is important to be realistic and understand the nature of the difficulties of ethics problems in order to develop effective politics for overcoming and transcending them. In this chapter, different types of problematical individuals and environments are considered.

ARCHETYPES

Max Weber constructed archetypes, evocative representative models, designed to reveal essential features of human behavior. His most well-known archetype was the "Protestant Capitalist," presented in his *Protestant Ethic and the Spirit of Capitalism* (1904, 1930). Weber contrasted aspects of "Protestant" and "Catholic" philosophy that he saw embodied in different types of work-related behavior. While he recognized that there were Catholic Florentines and Venetians who were capitalists long before there were Protestants, he used the archetype of the "Protestant Capitalist," with his "Protestant Ethic," to illumine key aspects of capitalist behavior that had new significance.

Emerson in his *Representative Men* presented the exemplary archetypes of "The Philosopher," "The Mystic," "The Skeptic," "The Poet," "The Man Of The World," and "The Writer" (1850, 1895). Long before Emerson were Plato's "Philosopher-Leader" and "Sophist," and Machiavelli's modernist "Prince."

More recently, and within organization studies broadly construed, have been Mayo's (1933) "Manager-Diagnostic Healer," Barnard's

(1938) "Executive," Camus' (1946) "Outsider," Miller's (1949) "Sales-man," Wilson's (1955) "Man in the Gray Flannel Suit," Whyte's (1956) "Organization Man," Marcuse's (1964) "One-Dimensional Man," Mac-coby's (1976) "Gamesman–Company Man–Jungle Fighter–Crafts-man" typology, Argyris and Schon's (1974) "Action-Scientist," Chandler's (1977) "Visible Hand," Greenleaf's (1977b) "Servant Leader," Schon's (1983) "Reflective Practitioner," and my own "Faust," "Richard III," "Eichmann," and "Institution Citizen" (Nielsen, 1984).

In this chapter I present six archetypes of people who initiate and cooperate with unethical organizational behavior. Archetypes illumi-nate particularly important and meaningful aspects of a behavior, they are not mutually exclusive categories that all or even any people can be neatly placed into.

THE EICHMANN

Hannah Arendt was a philosopher and political theorist who died in 1975. One of her most noted works was *Eichmann in Jerusalem: A Report On The Banality of Evil* (1964), originally commissioned and published by *The New Yorker* and later expanded into a book. Her analysis of Eichmann and his organizational situation, while an ex-treme case, is a valuable example of a certain type of cooperation with unethical behavior in organizations.

From Arendt (1964, 1978) we learn that Eichmann was an upper-middle-level manager in a Nazi institution engaged in, as Arendt phrases it, the "administrative massacre" of millions of people. Eichmann never belonged to the higher Nazi Party circles and did not participate in policy decisions. He was a manager in an organization where obeying authority was valued, expected, and required.

According to Arendt, Eichmann believed that he was practicing the virtue of obedience when he did his work. He obeyed orders without thinking about ethical implications. Hitler ordered Goering, Goering ordered Himmler, Himmler ordered Heydrich, Heydrich ordered Eichmann, and Eichmann obeyed. Arendt explains what she thinks Eichmann thought: "His guilt came from his obedience, and obe-dience is praised as a virtue. His virtue had been abused by the Nazi leaders. But he was not one of the ruling clique, he was a victim, and only the leaders deserved punishment" (1964, p. 247).

Arendt concludes with the judgment that Eichmann was guilty, but that instead of being insane or monstrously evil, Eichmann was, per-haps more horribly, well within the range of sanity and normality. He was a "thoughtless" and "banal" man who did not think about distinguishing right from wrong in his role as a manager in an organization that harmed people. His job was not, as he saw it, to think about the ethics of policies or decisions made by higher authority. His thinking was narrowly directed toward efficient implementation.

Arendt explains: "Despite all the efforts of the prosecution, everybody could see that this man was not a monster . . . he certainly would never have murdered his superior in order to inherit his post. He merely, to put the matter colloquially, never realized what he was doing. . . . He was not stupid. It was sheer thoughtlessness—something by no means identical with stupidity . . ." (1964, p. 287).

Eichmann was a good technical manager, but was very narrow, "ignorant of everything that was not directly, technically and bureaucratically connected with his job" (p. 287).

The key characteristic of the Eichmann archetype is a narrow, routinized, "in the box" mentality that does not recognize ethical dimensions—as Arendt phrased it, "the banality of evil." Are there such unthinking managers and employees in modern business, government, and nonprofit organizations? Many examples could be cited; a few will suffice.

Ford Pinto (Gioia, 1992) The Ford automobile company had a field recall coordinator at the time Ford Pinto gas tanks were exploding and passengers were burning and dying from rear-end collisions at speeds as low as twenty-five miles per hour. The recall coordinator later asked himself the question, "Why didn't I see the gravity of the problem and its ethical overtones?" (Gioia, 1992, p. 383). He answered his own question as follows: "Before I went to Ford I would have argued strongly that Ford had an ethical obligation to recall. After I left Ford I now argue and teach that Ford had an ethical obligation to recall. But while I was there, I perceived no strong obligation to recall and I remember no strong ethical overtones to the case whatsoever" (Gioia, 1992, p. 388).

On a different scale from Eichmann, but in a similar way, the recall coordinator did not think about the ethical dimensions of the decision. Sometimes people use schemata that are too narrow (Bartunek and Moch, 1987; Bartunek, 1993a). In the case of the recall coordinator, he explained:

> Most models of ethical decision making in organizations implicitly assume that people recognize and think about a moral or ethical dilemma when they are confronted with one. I call this seemingly fundamental assumption into question. The unexplored ethical issue for me is the arguably prevalent case where organizational representatives are not aware that they are dealing with a problem that might have ethical overtones. If the case involves a familiar class of problems or issues, it is likely to be handled via existing cognitive structures or scripts—scripts that typically include no ethical com-

ponent in their cognitive content. . . . Scripts are built out of situations that are normal, not those that are abnormal, ill-structured, or unusual (which often can characterize ethical domains). The ambiguities associated with most ethical dilemmas imply that such situations demand a "custom" decision, which means that the inclusion of an ethical dimension as a component of an evolving script is not easy to accomplish. (Gioia, 1992, p. 388)

The Eichmann phenomenon may be more common than we would like it to be.

C. R. Bard, Inc., and faulty heart catheters (Zuckoff and Kennedy, 1993) In 1993, C. R. Bard, Inc., one of the largest medical equipment manufacturers in the world, pleaded guilty to 391 counts of conspiracy, mail fraud, lying to government regulators, and selling "adulterated products" for human experimentation. Individuals within the company knew that the heart catheters it was selling for use in balloon angioplassty surgery were faulty. Sometimes the tips of catheters inserted into heart arteries broke off inside the artery. Sometimes the balloon did not deflate, causing heart attacks, emergency bypass surgery, and deaths.

Perhaps as many as fifty Bard managers and technicians, at the upper-middle, middle, and lower levels, knew for about three years that the products being sold were faulty. Apparently, none thought that they had any personal ethical responsibilities. They didn't make the decisions, they were just obeying orders and implementing policy decisions. The ethics issues were not part of their narrowly defined in-the-box thinking.

United Fruit Company (McCann, 1976, 1984)   The United Fruit Company in the early 1950s decided to improve local business conditions by helping to overthrow the government of Guatemala. According to an assistant vice president of United Fruit, who later became a vice-president, "At the time, I identified so closely with the company and my job that I didn't think about it as a moral or ethical issue" (McCann, 1984).

This manager was narrowly focused on improving the market share and profitability positions of United Fruit. It did not occur to him to think about the people who would be disenfranchised or killed in the government overthrow that United Fruit was financing and that he as communications assistant vice president was covering up.

RICHARD III

Arendt recognized that some people do act from directly base motives. She termed this phenomenon "calculated wickedness" and distinguished it from the banal, unthinking efficiency of an Eichmann. The archetype she used to illustrate "calculated wickedness" was Richard III, who in Shakespeare's play knowingly and intentionally commits unethical acts. Both the Eichmann and the Richard III types are guilty, according to Arendt. The key difference is that the Richard III archetype can tell the difference between good and evil in his specific organizational context. He knows a behavior is unethical, but does it anyway for personal gain. The following cases illustrate this archetype.

French National Health Service (Kramer, 1996)   According to the French government prosecutors, the top managers and officials within the French National Health Service, the Pasteur Institute, and the Ministry knew that the Pasteur Institute's AIDS blood testing equipment was faulty. They knew that blood would be contaminated. They knew that people would die. They knew it was unethical to knowingly contaminate people.

   Then why did they approve the faulty Pasteur Institute testing equipment? Apparently, they did it, in large part, for financial and technological gain. Approval of the Pasteur Institute equipment would help the Pasteur Institute gain greater sales and financial resources to expand its share of the high-technology medical testing market in Europe and the world. Financial aid to French high-technology organizations was also consistent with France's industrial policy of expanding in this type of industry. Unethical behavior was considered an effective means to these ends.

Bard company (Zuckoff and Kennedy, 1993)   Five top managers of the Bard company have been indicted for intentionally and deceptively selling the unsafe heart catheters that caused deaths, suffering, disability, and emergency bypass operations. According to the U.S. government prosecutors, these managers knew both that injuries and deaths would occur and that it was illegal to release such unsafe products.

   Why did they do it? According to the prosecutors, they did it in large part for financial gain. They had the largest share of the market and did not want to lose ground to the competition. By maintaining market share with their faulty products, they intended to gain the time they needed to develop and introduce safer products, maintain market share, and increase sales and profitability.

General Electric   The Richard III archetype is not a new phenomenon. In 1946, Charles E. Wilson, president of General Electric, noted that several of his predecessors and other top management executives had intentionally and knowingly violated the Sherman Antitrust Act through price fixing and market allocations with competitors.

Why did they do it? Wilson, in criticizing their behavior, noted that one of the key motivations for such intentionally unethical and illegal behavior was personal, individual career advancement and the accumulation of personal wealth and power. Previous CEOs and top managers had learned that price fixing and market allocation increased profitability, which in turn facilitated their personal career advancements. They were concerned with material benefits to themselves (Herling, 1962, pp. 23–38).

SOCRATES' JAILER

> Soon the jailer, who was the servant of the Eleven, entered and stood by him, saying: To you, Socrates, whom I know to be the noblest and gentlest and best of all who ever came to this place, I will not impute the angry feelings of other men, who rage and swear at me, when, in obedience to the authorities, I bid them drink the poison—indeed, I am sure that you will not be angry with me; for others, as you are aware, and not I, are to blame. And so fare you well, and try to bear lightly what must needs be—you know my errand. Then bursting into tears he turned away and went out. (Plato, *Phaedo: The Death of Socrates;* quoted in Jowett, 1903, p. 271)

This may be the most common archetype of all. Socrates' Jailer was under the power and orders of "the Eleven." If he did not obey, he knew he would be punished. He may have had a family, responsibilities, obligations. Plato gives him no name in the dialog. None may be needed, since we have so many already. Many of us have experienced similar pressures. The following cases illustrate this archetype.

Raymond Smith and General Electric   Almost all employees who knew about the price fixing and market allocations at General Electric went along with them. Raymond Smith, a G.E. vice president and general manager of the transformer division, told the U.S. Department of Justice and the Kefauver Senate Subcommittee on Antitrust and Monopoly that throughout his career he and all the other managers in the relevant areas went along with the unethical and illegal behavior because it was condoned by higher authority.

And at G.E. one obeyed orders or suffered the consequences. He "readily acknowledged that he had met with competitors," in violation of the antitrust laws and internal organization ethics codes, because, as Smith explained,

> to my knowledge . . . during the entire period from 1940 through 1956, it was common practice . . . to discuss prices and other competitive mat-

ters with competitors. . . . I was also aware that similar practices were being followed not only in other areas of the company, but also in other companies in the electrical manufacturing industry . . . although the General Electric Policy . . . regarding antitrust practices had been issued in 1946, it had been constantly disregarded in major areas of the company with . . . the tacit approval and agreement of the managers and the officers of the company at the time responsible for those areas. (Herling, 1962, pp. 30–31)

John Geary and U.S. Steel John Geary was a salesman for U.S. Steel when the company decided to enter a new market with a new product, deep oil well casings. Geary protested to several groups of managers that the casings the company was producing and asking him to sell had what the engineers indicated was too high a failure rate and were therefore unsafe.

According to Geary, even though the managers, engineers, and salesmen believed him and the test results, "the only desire of everyone associated with the project was to satisfy the instructions of Henry Wallace [then sales vice president]. No one was about to buck this man for fear of his job" (Ewing, 1983b, p. 86). Geary was fired, and other employees did the work.

Radiation experiments During the late 1940s and early 1950s the United States Department of Defense conducted radiation experiments on people, both civilians and soldiers. Several hundred experiments were undertaken. According to the *New York Times* "Most experiments involved exposing troops to varying amounts of radiation, usually without informing them of the risks or seeking their consent" (Hilts, 1994, p. A14). A lot of debate and opposition to the practice took place among many of the scientists conducting the experiments. For example, Dr. Shields Warren, the chief medical officer of the Atomic Energy Commission, stated in July 1949 that he was "taking an increasingly dim view of human experimentation" (Hilts, 1994, p. A14).

In a 1947 document the Atomic Energy Commission stated, "It is desired that no document be released which refers to experiments with humans and might have an adverse effect on public opinion or result in legal suits. Documents covering such work in this field should be classified 'secret'" (Hilts, 1994, p. A14). Both the ethical debates about the experiments and the experiments were classified secret by the Department of Defense.

Despite their ethical opposition, several of the scientists and doctors obeyed orders, cooperated, and did not blow the whistle. They did so largely because of fear of the penalties for violating the military "secret" classification, which in the late 1940s and early 1950s were quite severe. The experiments continued until at least 1953.

PHAEDO

Phaedo is sometimes referred to as the "beloved disciple" of Socrates. He was an intelligent, good person who cared about the ethical, but he was unable to get it right without Socrates' help. Unlike Eichmann, Phaedo did think about the ethical, but, like Eichmann, he would behave unethically.

Phaedo would come to wrong conclusions about the ethical because of faulty reasoning. However, with Socrates' help, he was able to come to the right conclusions. This type is an obstacle to ethical organization behavior because a Socrates is not always around to help.

In addition, when people doing unethical actions apparently are ethical, nice, well-intentioned people, there is sometimes a tendency to let the unethical behavior go. After all, the person doing it is a good person. Sometimes it can be difficult to oppose the problem without opposing the person, whom we may like and respect and don't want to hurt. The following cases illustrate this archetype.

Forensic medicine agency (Bronner, 1995)   In Turkey, forensic physicians were asked to be "team players" in the fight against terrorism. In this country the government's security forces sometimes torture suspected terrorists to death (Amnesty International, 1995). The government asked the physicians not to report the physical evidence of torture. Only official government forensic reports are allowed into court records.

The head of the psychiatric department of the country's highest forensic agency was a well-respected, well-educated, intelligent, and caring physician. He thought about the ethical and decided it was ethical to be as good team player with the government and not record evidence of torture. In part, because he was such a well-respected and apparently ethical person, criticism of him, his office, and the issue of a forensic coverup was muted. Apparently, he did not question his reasoning until he attended a seminar on forensic evidence of torture and discussed it with the seminar leader.

Preferential lending at a state bank (State Banker, 1994)   On less than life-and-death issues there are many other instances of this archetype. For example, the regional lending officer of a large state bank in a Mediterranean country appeared to be a good man who thought about the ethical and even gave lectures about ethics in banking. He was very helpful to students who graduated from his university. He was very kind to coworkers. After thinking about it, he concluded that it is ethical to help one's friends with loans even when it is unlikely that they will be able to repay them. Bad loans are less of a solvency problem for this state bank than for private commercial banks, since the state bank's financial resources are partly subsidized by tax revenues.

For many years, this man approved bad loans to friends and relatives. In part because he was considered such a good and kind person, other people who knew about the bad loans did not oppose them. After many years of this practice, another manager did discuss the issue with him, pointing out that some of his friends were hurt by overextending themselves with debt they could not repay. In addition, it was pointed out that other good people who needed loans sometimes could not get them because of his preferential lending decisions.

Since this conversation he has reduced these decisions. There are several other apparently good, caring lending officers who believe that it is ethical to similarly help their friends and relatives, and apparently have not participated in similar conversations about the negative aspects of this behavior.

Conflict of interest on a university board of trustees (Nicklin, 1995)   The president of Ashland University was concerned about the ethics of hiring a trustee's company to manage the construction of a seven-million-dollar student center without considering bids from other companies. The trustee involved told the other board members that they were getting a very good deal.

The president thought about the ethical issue and concluded "It's all above board. . . . But I'd like to have done it open bid" (Nicklin, 1995, p. 39). His rethinking of the conflict of interest issue and the university's policy came in response to and with the help of criticism from others. He was reluctant to push the issue too hard. "If we challenge" the awarding of contracts to trustees without open bid, he said, "then in a sense, we're questioning their integrity" (Nicklin, 1995, p. 40). Nonetheless, he said he hoped that eventually the board members would adopt a policy of requiring trustees' companies to go through an open bid process before being hired.

Like Phaedo, the president cared about and thought about the ethical. However, without the continuing help and support of critical discussion, it is not clear that he will be able on his own initiative to adopt a strong conflict of interest policy.

FAUST

In Goethe's *Faust* the hero exchanges his soul for what he considers other goods:

> FAUST: I am too old to treat it as a jest,
>   Too young to have given up the game

> What satisfaction can this world bestow? . . .
> Poor devil. What hath thou to give?

MEPHISTOPHELES: One day you'll want to sit
>   O'er some good thing.

FAUST: If e'er I cry to the passing hour
>   "Thou are so beautiful; Oh, linger yet" . . .
>   Then I will go down gladly to the pit.
>   (Mann, 1948, p. 69)

The goods Mephistopheles offered and Faust accepted were knowledge and love of another person. Faust believed that to make a pact with a devil was wrong, but he considered these goods worth the exchange of his soul. Unlike the Richard III archetype, Faust has ends in mind that are not base. Knowledge and love are good for Faust and for the world. To him, the good ends justified the bad means.

This phenomenon is not uncommon. A manager may identify so closely with the mission of his organization that he is willing to act illegally and unethically to further it. He may decide that it is "worth it" if a few employees die of cancer from working in a factory that produces a drug that can improve the lives of thousands of people. He might allow a product to be sold that he knows will harm people because to recall, redesign, and remarket it might be so expensive as to seriously damage the financial health of the organization.

A related phenomenon is a situation where a policymaker is willing to do a lesser rather than a greater evil. Arendt found three problems with this approach. First, it is morally wrong because the people hurt by the less evil act are not consulted and do not agree to be hurt. Second, those who use the less evil means are slowly or quickly transformed into the "larger evil" they think they are resisting. Third, Arendt lacked confidence in our ability to correctly predict the possibility that we might be exchanging present and certain lesser evils for greater future evils rather than goods. The following cases illustrate this archetype.

Procter and Gamble, the Cincinnati police department, and Cincinnati Bell (Hirsch, 1991; Swasy, 1993) Alecia Swasy, a staff reporter for the *Wall Street Journal,* reported in 1990 and 1991 that several Procter and Gamble employees from the Cincinnati area, where the corporate headquarters of Procter and Gamble are located, had secretly blown the whistle to her about possible illegal and unethical behavior, as well as upcoming changes in management personnel, at Procter and Gamble.

According to Swasy, "P & G enlisted the police department to comb through millions of business and home phone records to identify sources of the leaks. Those who dared to call me at *The Wall Street Journal* or at home were being questioned at the police station. . . . A complaint from P & G was enough to prompt the Hamilton County prosecutor's office to open a grand jury investigation. . . . At Cincinnati Bell, there was no delay in turning over the phone records" (1993, p. 291, 295). The chief investigator for the police department was also a part-time security employee of Procter and Gamble, and the police chief had also worked part-time for the company.

When what Procter and Gamble, the prosecutor's office, the police, and Cincinnati Bell were doing became known, there was a general outcry in both the national press, such as the *New York Times,* the *Washington Post,* and the local Cincinnati press (Rawe, 1991). The *Cincinnati Post* editorialized, "After years of working to improve its reputation as a corporate bully and impenetrable fortress, this incident paints that picture all over again" (Swasy, 1991, p. 300). The Cincinnati chapter of the Society of Professional Journalists wrote, "The misguided action Procter and Gamble is taking threatens to trample the First Amendment and obviously reflects more concern in identifying a possible leak within the company rather than protecting any trade secrets" (Swasy, 1991, p. 300).

Why did so many different people, public utility officials, and government officials cooperate with what was generally considered after the fact an inappropriate invasion of privacy and abuse of the First Amendment protection of the press? Part of the explanation has to do with the Faust phenomenon. Procter and Gamble was a very large employer in the Cincinnati area and had made many important contributions to the Cincinnati community. Many people genuinely liked, respected, and were grateful to Procter and Gamble. Protecting Procter and Gamble was considered good for the community. Many people in Cincinnati believed that what was good for Procter and Gamble was good for Cincinnati even if it required cooperation with unethical and illegal behavior.

Roche Holding and Stanley Adams (Adams, 1984) In 1972 Stanley Adams was promoted to the position of world product manager for the Roche Swiss pharmaceutical company. In this new position, he discovered that the company was involved in several illegal and unethical practices. For example, it would make payments to smaller manufacturers, who in turn would agree to stop production, buy its products at discounted prices, then resell them at regular prices under their own names. The company also colluded with other major manufacturers to set prices and production levels, producing less than estimated demand, so that prices would stay high. Artificial shortages in times of heightened need were also used.

In December 1972 Switzerland signed a free-trade agreement with the then European Economic Community. This meant that Swiss companies trading in the EEC would be bound by the EEC rules of competition, spelled out in the Treaty of Rome and restated in this new agreement. Adams noted that Article 86 of this treaty stated that it was illegal for a firm to "abuse a dominant position" in the market. In February 1973 he wrote a letter to Albert Borschette, commissioner for competition at the EEC Commission in Brussels, informing the EEC about Roche's violations of Article 86 in the sale of bulk vitamins and chemicals in Europe.

The following year Adams left Roche and moved to Italy, where he started a business in pig farming. Meanwhile the EEC Commission conducted raids at several of the company's facilities and found further evidence of their violations. The EEC began to take legal action against the company and to prepare their formal case for presentation before the commission and the European parliament.

On December 31, 1974, Adams went with his family to Switzerland to celebrate New Year's Eve with his wife's sister. He was stopped at the border and asked if he had given any information to the EEC. He admitted that he had. He was arrested for giving trade secrets to a foreign power. Roche had initiated the arrest.

Adams was put in prison and was not allowed to speak with a lawyer. Later, he was put in solitary confinement in a Basel prison. Before being put in solitary confinement, he asked his cellmates, who were young men arrested for minor offenses, for help. He asked that whoever got out first contact the EEC. Adams gave them the address, phone number, and a short message to pass on, which they all wrote on the inside of their shoes.

The EEC received the message and contacted the Swiss government. Adams was permitted to talk with a lawyer, but the lawyer was not permitted to be present when the police continued their company-directed questioning of Adams. Adams was held in prison for three and a half months.

Roche's violation of the free-trade agreement became a major issue among the EEC Commission, the European Parliament, and the Swiss government. The agreement stated that any involved party must report any violations, yet Mr. Adams had been arrested for doing so. In June 1976 the EEC found the company guilty of violating Article 86 of the Treaty of Rome. They were fined and ordered to stop all illegal activities.

On July 1, 1976, a Swiss court in closed session found Adams guilty

of "persistent economic espionage." In May 1978 the Swiss federal
supreme court upheld Adams' conviction, stating, "National legal provisions continue to apply, even if the principles of competition of the
Free Trade Agreement are infringed. . . . Business secrets count as
a factor of economic life and maintenance of their secrecy, in the Swiss
view, is a legitimate interest and they therefore are to be protected vis-
a-vis other countries. . . . Their disclosure violates not only private,
but indirectly also national economic, i.e. State interests" (Adams,
1994, pp. 106–7). Even when "business secrets" were illegal and violated the treaty, they were still protected under Swiss law. Anyone who
attacked Swiss business was deemed to be attacking the Swiss state.
The economic end, the good of the company and the country, justified
illegal and unethical means.

In 1980 the European Parliament took its first unanimous vote in
supporting Adams against the Swiss court's decision.

General Electric and Bill Wiggins (Stricharchuk, 1988)   The unit manager in G.E.'s Cincinnati jet engine factory admitted to the FBI that he
had told foremen to falsify the time cards of workers on some government contracts. Some contracts were underbilled and some were over-
billed.

He said he did it because he did not want the workers to lose their
jobs. He was concerned that if it was revealed what the real costs were
on some projects, there would be layoffs and the plant might close. He
said his motivations were good and, at the time, he thought that helping the workers keep their jobs justified falsifying the time cards.

DR. SUGURO

The Japanese novelist Shusaku Endo, in his book *The Sea and Poison*
(1972), describes the true story of Dr. Suguro, who participated in
what he believed were unethical medical experiments on American
POWs. The experiments were cooperatively performed by the Japanese army, a medical hospital, and a team of doctors. The purpose of
one experiment was to determine scientifically how much blood people can lose before they die.

He cooperated with activities he considered unethical in significant
part because he believed it was impractical not to cooperate with the
Japanese military government that his hospital organization was subordinate to. He believed that his environment was corrupt and that it
was impractical for him not to cooperate. Unlike the Nazi doctors who
were forced to perform similar experiments on civilians and prisoners

of war, the Japanese doctors were not forced to cooperate (Lifton, 1987). Instead, they believed that it was impractical not to cooperate.

Endo describes the reasoning and feelings of Dr. Suguro as he looked back at his behavior. "At the time nothing could be done. . . . If I were caught in the same way, I might, I might just do the same thing again. . . . We felt that getting on good terms ourselves with the Western Command medical people, with whom Second (section) is so cosy, wouldn't be a bad idea at all. Therefore, we felt there's no need to ill-temperedly refuse their friendly proposal and hurt their feelings. . . . Five doctors from Kando's section most likely will be glad to get the chance" (Endo, 1972, p. 75).

Errol Marshall and Hydraulic Parts and Components, Inc. (Pound, 1985)   On a much less serious issue, but on the basis of similar reasoning, Errol Marshall paid kickbacks. As an employee of Hydraulic Parts and Components he helped negotiate a subcontractor's sale of heavy equipment to the United States Navy while giving seventy thousand dollars in kickbacks to two materials managers of Brown and Root, Inc., the project's prime contractor.

According to Marshall, the prime contractor "demanded the kickbacks. . . . It was cut and dried. We would not get the business otherwise" (Pound, 1985, p. 25). He believed that the kickbacks were unethical, but that was the way the industry worked. It was not practical to not pay the kickbacks. His company needed the business now. A few years later, one of the upper-level Brown and Root managers, William Callan, was convicted of extorting kickbacks, and another manager, Frank DiDomenico, pled guilty to extorting kickbacks from Hydraulic Parts and Components as well as several other firms. None of the people who paid the kickbacks were charged with any illegal behavior, even though it was illegal to pay kickbacks.

Carlo De Benedetti and Olivetti (Cowell, 1993a, 1993b)   On a larger scale, Carlo De Benedetti, the CEO of Olivetti, was indicted for paying bribes to Italian government officials.

From at least the 1950s through 1992, almost all businesses that did business with the Italian government were required to pay bribes to Italian government officials. In the 1950s the bribes were as little as one or two percent. The contracts were generally given to the bid that best combined quality and price. That is, the bribe did not gain the contract, but had to be paid after the contract was awarded in order to keep it. By the early 1990s things had gotten much worse. Often the contracts went to the contractor paying the highest bribe rather than the best bid. Bribes had grown to as much as 25 percent of the value of the contract. The money was divided among the leading political parties according to their percentage of the vote.

De Benedetti acknowledged that he and his company paid tens of millions of dollars in such extortions to Italian government officials. However, he argued that while it was illegal and unethical, it was also impractical not to pay the bribes. He claimed that Olivetti would have been forced out of business in Italy if it did not cooperate.

Tax auditors in a Latin American country   It is a common practice in a certain Latin American country for tax auditors to extort bribes from businesses (personal interview, Latin American banker, 1993). For example, if the legitimate tax bill is five million dollars, the tax auditor tells the business that they can either pay a tax bill of seven million, or three million with a payment of one hundred thousand dollars to the tax auditor. The auditor also tells the business that if the business tries to go to court they will lose, since some of the judges, including some supreme court judges, also receive bribes. The auditors and judges receiving money have been from the leading political parties of both the left and the right.

For the most part the businesses pay bribes. They know it is illegal and unethical to require such payments but they pay anyway. It is the shared belief that it is impractical to oppose such payments because political parties and some judges are part of the corruption.

PROBLEMS WITH CORRUPT AND/OR DESTRUCTIVE EXTERNAL ENVIRONMENTS

Were Dr. Suguro, Olivetti CEO De Benedetti, and the Italian businesspeople correct in their judgment that it was impractical not to cooperate with unethical behavior in an unethical environment? Was Marshall correct in his judgment that "it was cut and dried. We would not get the business otherwise" in his industry environment of systematic, pervasive corruption? Some environments can be very difficult for people and organizations concerned with doing ethics.

Arendt has observed that there are mutually reinforcing and self-fulfilling, unethical interaction relationships between ethically thoughtless people such as Eichmann and systematically corrupt environments. That is, such environments reward such people for cooperating with unethical behavior, and in cooperating, such people help perpetuate such environments. Arendt felt that previous Western social and political philosophy did not adequately include these mutually reinforcing phenomena.

The example of Eichmann brings into serious question the assumption that all managers and employers naturally think about what is right or wrong in environments where efficient implementation and obeying orders are at a high premium. Arendt explains:

> The judges did not believe him, because they were . . . perhaps too conscious of the very foundations of their profession to admit that an average, "normal" person neither feeble-minded nor indoctrinated nor cynical, could be perfectly incapable of telling right from wrong. They . . . missed the greatest moral and even legal challenge of the whole case. Their case rested on the assumption that the defendant, like all "normal persons," must have been aware of the criminal nature of his acts. . . . However, under the conditions of the Third Reich only "exceptions" could be expected to react normally. (1964, pp. 26–27)

Arendt thought that we need to learn more about thinking, judging, and acting independently of habitual, routinized, historical-theoretical, or ideological banisters that can unconsciously confine people to overly narrow within-the-box thinking.

We might like to think that with respect to the pressure of organizational versus individual conscience, things are very different in modern institutions. However, there are some similarities. Ledvinka and Scarpello have observed that as far as legal protection of employees from arbitrary institutional power, U.S. federal law states that for the most part employers "may dismiss their employees at will . . . for good cause, for no cause, or even for cause morally wrong, without being hereby guilty of legal wrong" (1991, p. 315). Some states, such as California, do have strong state laws that make unjust discharge more difficult.

There are many cases where managers were severely punished for not doing what was illegal or what they considered morally wrong. Ewing has found such courageous managers to be exceptions. Not thinking about illegal or immoral behavior while working hard and creatively for organizational goals is frequently both encouraged and rewarded.

Italian "Partitocracy" (Cowell, 1993c; Forman and Bannon, 1993)
The recent Italian "Partitocracy" scandal provides an example of an environment of systematic, pervasive corruption. The Italian judge Antonio Di Pietro, the chief prosecutor in the scandal, estimated that about forty billion dollars over the previous ten years had been paid in bribes and kickbacks on business-government contracts. This figure represents five to fifteen percent of almost every government contract; apparently, the percent was somewhat negotiable. The Italian political parties divided the money according to their percentage of the popular vote. Literally thousands of top business executives and government officials have been indicted. The Italian situation is more

the rule than the exception in some industrialized countries, many third-world countries, and some industries in developed countries.

The cost of corrupt environments are not limited to the financial. Many of the deaths in the recent Italian and Mexican earthquakes resulted from substandard construction that was permitted because of bribes to government officials and building inspectors. While southern European and many third-world countries have rigorous laws concerning employee safety, consumer safety, and environmental protection, they are systematically ignored as part of the normal, routine corruption.

Many organizations, even if they have safe products, safe working conditions, and safe environmental protections, are still required to pay such bribes. Many managers ask themselves whether it makes sense to pay additional safety costs when their competitors are not paying such costs and when they are required to pay large bribes anyway. In fact, sometimes new safety laws are passed mainly because illegal exceptions to the laws represent new sources of bribes for government officials.

In addition, decisions to do what is ethical, for example to improve safety conditions and not pay bribes, can result in scandals that are very damaging to personal and organization reputations. For example, if a company pays the safety costs and not the bribes, they become the target of government investigation. The government officials investigate until they find some imperfection in safety measures and then bring charges in publicly spectacular language. In many countries it is not admissible defense evidence that most of one's competitors are paying bribes and have far worse safety conditions.

Cadburys and destructive British labor relations (Gardiner, 1923; Emden, 1939; Child, 1964; Windsor, 1980; Nielsen, 1982; Dellheim, 1987; Smith, Child, and Rowlinson, 1990)   While environments can be both corrupt and destructive, as in the last example, they can also be destructive without necessarily being corrupt.

Cadburys has an almost two-hundred-year tradition of cooperative learning, high productivity, and ethical employee relations. In contrast with the general history of British labor relations, there have been very few strikes or other forms of work disruption at Cadburys.

In the early years of the Thatcher administration in England, 1978–1983, management-labor relations at the national level were destructively adversarial. There was an intense adversarial climate between labor and the Conservative Party government (Krieger, 1987). The labor unions perceived that Thatcher was trying to break the unions. The Thatcher government perceived that the unions were trying to sabotage Conservative Party plans to restructure and reinvigorate the economy. Management was generally perceived as being allied with the Thatcher government, and the labor unions were perceived as being allied with the Labor Party opposition. There were a great number of organizational-level strikes and work stoppages in Britain. Productivity in many organizations was declining (Smith, Child, and Rowlinson, 1990).

This destructive environment temporarily spilled over into Cadburys. Their long tradition of good relations between management and labor was temporarily disrupted and overwhelmed by the national-level conflict. Some managers and union leaders lied to each other, threatened each other, and sabotaged each other, and there was a strike. (Chapter 7 considers how this destructive environment was eventually successfully resisted within Cadburys.)

INSIDE PROBLEMS WITH BIASES OF A SHARED TRADITION

In addition to problematical external environments, there can be shared organization traditions with embedded biases that discourage ethical and/or encourage unethical behavior. For example, biases against particular groups of employees, such as women and minorities, can exist within different divisions or vertical levels of an organization. There can be biases against behaviors that are important for ethics, such as open and protected dialog about sensitive issues, including ethics issues. There can be strong punishment-based compliance systems that reward and teach unquestioning obedience more than concern for ethics. There can be an organizational history of top management tolerating or encouraging unethical or illegal behavior. The following examples illustrate these types of internal bias.

American Telephone & Telegraph (Nielsen, 1993e)   As at many American organizations, before the late 1960s there were very few women or minority managers at AT&T, with the exception of a few telephone operator supervisors. An important reason for not hiring women and minorities for managerial positions was that there was an institutional bias within the AT&T tradition system that silently, perhaps subconsciously, but nonetheless systematically didn't consider minorities or women for managerial positions. Many of the managers at AT&T had entered AT&T when this tradition was already established; while they maintained it, they did not create it. Such tradition-system biases can be as important as individual and group prejudices.

Many of the managers implicitly framed the issue in terms of the "unsuitability" of women and minorities for management and leadership roles. Some managers observed that since they didn't see any women or minority managers at AT&T, they just didn't think of them as candidates for managerial positions. The informal tradition of not having women and minority managers led them to not consider the possibility. Other managers observed that it didn't appear that many women or minorities had the training or experience required for managerial consideration. Since it was not expected that women and minorities would become managers, they were not encouraged to pursue the type of training and experience required. Several other managers observed that most women and minorities did not apply for managerial training and managerial positions and that this might be related to a somewhat fatalistic expectation. That is, there was little point in applying for managerial training and managerial positions, since the implicit tradition did not include many women and minority managers.

General Electric (Herling, 1962; Guyon, 1988; Naj, 1992)   Chester Walsh blew the whistle outside the organization on several upper-level managers of G.E. who were defrauding the United States Defense Department (Naj, 1992). William Lytton, general counsel of G.E. Aerospace, suggests that Walsh should have used the G.E. internal ethics compliance system, since the defrauding behavior was a violation of the G.E. ethics code and would have been corrected by G.E.

Walsh responded that it was his perception that it was also part of the tradition within G.E. to selectively ignore the ethics code when convenient for senior management. He explained, "I did a lot of research to see what happened to people who went up the chain of command and reported wrongdoings. All I found was they lost their jobs, their security; they lost everything" (Naj, 1992, p. 1).

General Electric is known for having a strong top-down, bottom-line oriented authoritarian culture. Obeying orders is required, including orders to obey the organization's ethics code. So why did Mr. Walsh feel that he had to go outside rather than inside the organization? His perception of the tradition within G.E. was that senior managers usually looked the other way when rules were disobeyed if it was convenient for them. And internal whistle blowers were in fact often punished. For example, Mr. Salvatore Cimorelli, a G.E. employee for 29 years, who worked in the parts department of G.E.'s Lynn, Massachusetts engine factory, believes that he lost his job because he blew the whistle internally as the G.E. compliance system requires. He concludes, "What it tells me is that Chester Walsh did the right thing" (Naj, 1992, p. 6).

General Electric had an ethics code as early as 1946. Policy Directive 2.35 (later 20.5) declared that it was the policy of G.E. for all employees to act in strict conformance to the antitrust laws. Penalties listed included firing and even criminal prosecution.

This policy was instituted in part because as far back as 1900, G.E. had participated in antitrust violations. In 1956, the year that the ethics code provision was rewritten and updated, "General Electric was involved in three separate large-scale antitrust violations, two of which involved price fixing and market allocations in conspiracy with other electrical manufacturing companies" (Herling, 1962, p. 24). The policy directive requiring antitrust compliance has been regularly reissued since 1900. Nonetheless, during the 1940s and 1950s, G.E., Westinghouse, Allis-Chalmers, the Federal Pacific Electric Company, I-T-E Circuit Breaker, the national Electrical Manufacturers Association, and other companies engaged in illegal and unethical price fixing and market allocation behaviors.

In 1962, shortly after several G.E. managers were convicted and jailed for price fixing in the United States, the director of marketing in the consumer products division for a Latin American division of G.E. received (along with all other domestic and international G.E. personnel) a letter from the chairman of the board specifically instructing all G.E. personnel not to participate in price fixing or collusion "of any kind, direct or implied." His boss in this Latin American country first suggested and then ordered him to continue to participate in collusive biweekly meetings concerning prices, terms, production schedules, and so forth with competitors (Westinghouse, Phillips, Sylvania). He reasoned with his boss that since they both had received direct personal letters from the CEO not to collude, they should not collude and he chose to stop attending the price-fixing meeting. Another manager was sent instead, and business continued as usual. He thinks that his decision to obey the paper order from New York and not the verbal order of his direct line manager essentially ended his opportunities for advancement in G.E. He said, "My future with GE was irrevocably damaged by my refusal to participate in the competitive collusion and, within ten months of the confrontation with my then boss, I was terminated" (personal interview, marketing director, 1986).

Internal bias and Japanese consensus building (Endo, 1972) Just as authoritarian top-down organizational cultures can support unethical behaviors, so can participative, consensus-building cultures. For example, Japanese doctors were not forced to help perform medical experiments on prisoners. They collaborated because they participated in a tradition that encouraged conformity with the larger consensus even if one individually disagreed. Dr. Sugoro said, "For me the pangs of conscience . . . were from childhood equivalent to the fear of disapproval in the eyes of others. . . . To put it quite bluntly,

I am able to remain quite undisturbed in the face of someone else's terrible suffering and death. . . . I am not writing about these experiences as one driven to do so by his conscience . . . all these memories are distasteful to me. But looking upon them as distasteful and suffering because of them are two different matters. Then why do I bother writing? Because I'm strangely ill at ease. I, who fear only the eyes of others. . . . I have no conscience, I suppose. Not just me, though. None of them feel anything at all about what they did here" (Endo, 1972, pp. 118, 123, 157).

CROSS-TRADITION BIASES

In the previous cases people more or less believed that they belonged to the same internal tradition. Where the key participants believe that they belong to very different and even antagonistic traditions, it can be very difficult to address an ethics problem.

For example, a buyer for an American retailer found himself in a situation in an Asian country where there were important cross-tradition differences and biases. The ethics issue involved brain and lung injuries to child workers in an acid-washed clothing factory and the top management of the American company who believed that it was "inappropriate to get involved in the internal affairs of a foreign supplier" (personal interview, Buyer, 1985).

Individuals from several different cultural traditions were involved in the case. The Asian factory manager was a middle-class Muslim from a lower-class family. The American buyer was a middle-class Caucasian Christian. The owners of the factory were wealthy "overseas" Chinese. In addition, the Chinese owners had to give a piece of the ownership in their company to a wealthy Muslim general as part of the cost of doing business in this country, which also allowed the factory to operate independently of many employment and other laws. The American retailer was a publicly owned company with relatively large shared held by a mixed group of top managers and institutional investors.

The buyer knew almost nothing about modern Chinese neo-Confucian ethics, Muslim ethics, the country's public and private life ethics, or ethics within the country's military framework. His previous ethics experiences were important with respect to how he thought about ethics and how he talked about ethics with people who shared similar experiences. However, he thought that the ways he had previously talked about ethics issues might be inappropriate for a very different cross-cultural setting with important cultural differences among the key players. He felt that there was no or very little center that all the different groups shared.

Local businesspeople told him that one reason poor families in that country had large numbers of children was because they realistically expected that not all would survive through childhood. He was also told that these families considered themselves better off with the little money the children earned even if it meant serious injuries and deaths. If a family member could be helped to stay in school through the factory work of other children, the family would be better off. A poor family could not afford to protect or help all its children.

It was part of the implicit ethics tradition of the buyer's company to address working conditions within its own U.S. facilities, but to "not interfere in the internal affairs" of foreign suppliers. With foreign suppliers it would negotiate the design of products, quality of products, reliability of supply, size of shipments, and pricing, but not internal human resources conditions or ethics.

While a foreign noninterference policy has its merits from an international imperialism perspective, such a policy can conflict with other ethics issues, in this case, injuries to the child workers (Donaldson, 1989, 1992).

The American buyer discussed the issue with the Asian factory manager. Both recognized that it was likely that there was no mutual center amidst all the parties' different cultural, social, political, and economic backgrounds and the different pressures that were impacting each party. Each recognized biases in the other's tradition that contributed to the problem. The American buyer was able to see and talk about the negative impacts of the corruption in that society, where it was common for generals to extort shared ownership; overseas Chinese owners who appeared to have more concern for profitability than child workers; and a political system that did not permit full citizenship participation for either the Chinese minority or the majority lower- and middle-class Muslims.

The Asian factory manager was able to see and talk about the history of his country's exploitation by European and Japanese colonizers, as well as American multinationals, and the irony of children from his country suffering injury and death while producing acid-washed jeans for American children. The buyer and the factory manager recognized that there was very likely no ethical center among these entangled tradition-system factors. Further, these macro-level factors were not controllable by them or perhaps anyone else.

Buyer colleagues from the buyer's own company and other American and European companies knew about the injuries and deaths but didn't try to address the issue. Their common perception was that when "we" (the buyers) were in this country, we were in a "different" world that was not "our" world. While the unhealthy working conditions were unfortunate, they were not particularly unusual and were "none of our business."

The international buyers were able to see biases within this Asian country's tradition. The Asian managers were able to see biases within what they considered European, American, and Japanese neocolonial practices and attitudes. Each party blamed the other, and each only partially understood the other's tradition and biases. The actual biases in the different traditions, as well as misunderstandings of each other's traditions, can greatly reduce the common space needed to address shared problems jointly.

CONCLUSION

As the preceding cases illustrate, the obstacles to doing ethics in organizations can be quite formidable and intimidating. Individuals initiating and cooperating with unethical behavior can be very intelligent, strong, relentless, and even courageous, as well as sometimes unthinking, weak, timid, and conforming.

An understanding of the severity of the obstacles can lead one to the conclusion of Socrates' Jailer or Dr. Suguro that it is only practical to "go along and get along." However, as the following chapters illustrate, there are many cases where different types of people in various types of organizations and environments using a wide range of methods have been able to act and learn and make positive, ethical differences.

It can be practical to do ethics in organizations if the organization citizen can be like Proteus, able to change shapes and methods as the situation requires. We may need to be competent with a wide variety of politics and methods in order to realize our responsibilities and opportunities as ethical citizens of organizations.

3

A Politics of Ethics Framework
Based on Action-Learning

In this chapter I develop a behavioral science-based action-learning theoretical framework for considering the methods of doing ethics in organizations. This theoretical framework helps to understand how various methods are interrelated, their relative strengths and limitations, and their civic appropriateness.

Hirschman (1970) in his classic book *Exit, Voice, and Loyalty* framed organizational ethics action theory in terms of three individual strategies for resisting organizational and bureaucratic abuses: exit, voice, or loyalty. This analysis has become a foundation for behavioral science-based ethics action theory. Argyris and Schon implicitly recognize the foundational nature of Hirschman's framework, but in their critical deconstruction of it they point out that Hirschman "shares with much of the contemporary literature a particular way of framing relations between individuals and their organizations. He treats exit and voice as measures by which individuals may resist organizational tyranny" (1988, p. 199). That is, he implicitly frames problems in win-lose, adversarial terms.

RECIPROCAL INTERACTIONS

Within a generalized individual-to-individual interaction frame, but without specific reference to ethics phenomena, Bateson (1972) ob-

33

served that well-intentioned individual actions, including "voice," can be escalatingly negative, destructive, self-defeating, and ineffective. In a generalized framework without specific reference to organization ethics, Weick (1979) also observed such escalating processes, but found that individuals' interactions can also be escalatingly positive and effective. He further observed (1979) that we can sometimes choose whether to work with positively escalating processes or negative ones.

Weick (1979) found that organizing processes contain individual behaviors that are reciprocal. That is, the behaviors of one person are contingent on the behaviors of another person(s). Individuals understand that their ability to achieve their own organizational objectives depends on others performing instrumental acts. He refers to these contingencies as "interacts." In turn, others will perform instrumental acts in exchange for instrumental acts from others. There is an implicit social contract. Weick calls these intraorganization exchanges "double interacts" and suggests that they are the foundation of organizing and organizations: As sets of interlocking behaviors are continued, a collective structure is developed. Weick further suggests that we can cocreate organization change by identifying and working with these positive, productive reciprocal relationships.

SINGLE- AND DOUBLE-LOOP POLITICS

Weick's (1979) reciprocal double interacts and Argyris and Schon's (1974, 1988) reciprocal double-loop action-learning are similar concepts. Argyris, Putnam, and Smith (1985) offer the following example of single-loop action-learning. An agent has a governing value of short-run conflict suppression. He uses an action strategy of not saying anything controversial as a means for realizing this value. However, other people start to say controversial things. In order to realize his value, the agent now has to try a different action strategy. He then talks a lot about issues that the people present are likely to agree on. According to Argyris, Putnam, and Smith, in such a situation, where a new action strategy is used to realize the same governing value, there is single-loop action-learning.

Argyris and Schon do not distinguish between win-lose and win-win single-loop action-learning. Their example, the agent unilaterally talking a lot about issues that the people present are likely to agree on, illustrates win-win, single-loop action-learning. For example, the agent might interrupt the conversation and ask people what they wanted for dessert. He would win in that the conversation on the controversial topic is stopped. The other people win in that they engage in an enjoyable conversation about dessert alternatives. He might ask if people would mind postponing discussion of the controversial topic until an unspecified later time and instead discuss what he would describe as a more immediate issue they were also interested in, such as new employee benefits.

More win-lose examples would be for him to say he did not want to discuss this subject, or that the topic was inappropriate. He might adjourn the meeting before the controversial topic could be continued or clear the table to stop the conversation. All these win-lose and win-win methods are single-loop, in that the driving value of conflict suppression is not held open to questioning and learning.

These processes are illustrated in the following figure, which is an adaptation of Argyris' (1990, p. 94) diagram.* I have added the following to the single and double-loop Argyris framework: embedded social tradition-system, win-lose single-loop, win-win single-loop, and triple-loop action-learning politics.

In double-loop action-learning, both governing values and action strategies are held open to questioning and learning. Continuing with the example, instead of trying to suppress conflict in the short term, the agent instead would choose both to hold open to inquiry the governing value of conflict suppression and to discuss the conflicts.

Argyris and Schon (1988) suggest that single-loop methods can be ineffective as an expression of ethical integrity, because it encourages the type of escalating, noncooperative interactions that Bateson focused on. A double-loop dialog can be more effective because it encourages the type of positive, escalating behavior that Weick values.

While Bateson and Weick do not specifically refer to organization ethics, Argyris and Schon do. They suggest that action methods are

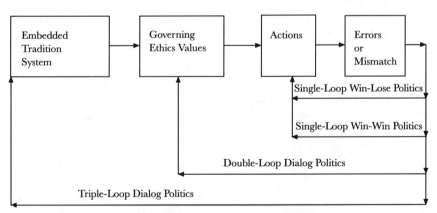

*This figure is adapted from C. Argyris, *Overcoming Organizational Defenses: Facilitating Organizational Learning*, 1990, p. 94, adapted by permission of Prentice-Hall, Upper Saddle River, New Jersey. I have added the following to the single- and double-loop Argyris framework: embedded social tradition-system, win-lose single-loop, win-win single-loop, and the triple-loop.

often ineffective as expressions of ethical concern because they assume "an adversarial relationship between the organization and individual ethical integrity where more cooperative and mutually reinforcing relationships are also possible and may be operating simultaneously" (1988, p. 205).

For example, in their deconstruction of Hirschman's (1970) *Exit, Voice, and Loyalty,* they point out that in Hirschman's terms, integrity can be redescribed as a social virtue whereby a person dissents from a behavior he considers unethical by means of voice or exit. Ethical relations between individuals and organizations are framed in an adversarial manner. Building upon Bateson's (1972) observation that there can be escalating, destructive interactions within organizations, Argyris and Schon point out that there can be similarly destructive and self-defeating conversational methods for expressing ethical concern (1988, p. 205).

When individuals express integrity in a win-lose sense, they voice and frame their expression as the ethical individual against unethical individuals or the unethical organization. If the targets respond with defensive confrontation, they are also acting in a single-loop, win-lose fashion. In turn, their win-lose response is not acceptable to the originators because it limits the expression of their integrity. Negative, adversarial escalation results that is not effective in exploring the ethical dimensions of the driving values.

Win-lose action-learning can be effective, however, in a narrow political sense, even with little or no learning about driving values. In narrow, top-down, win-lose politics, powerful people can suppress conversation and force cooperation with either ethical or unethical behavior. Less powerful people may submit because of fear rather than any learning about the ethical. This issue is explored in the chapter 4 discussion of the single-loop archetype, of the Ethics General.

Less powerful people also adopt single-loop win-lose politics when they use techniques such as secret whistle blowing to force ethical behavior. In such cases behavior may change toward the ethical not because of any learning but because of fear of getting caught. (This issue is explored in the chapter 4 discussion of the Ethics Guerilla.)

Single-loop win-win methods can also be quite effective in either suppressing or encouraging ethical behavior with little or no learning about driving values. One effective win-win method for both maintaining financial corruption and reducing effective opposition to it is to give potential opponents parts of the corruption. This strategy has been successful for organized crime and is common in the public sectors of many countries.

For example, in Italy the Christian Democratic Party, the Socialist

Party, several other smaller political parties, and literally thousands of business executives have been sharing the corruption for over thirty-five years. Illegal bribes and kickbacks from businesses are allocated among the political parties according to their proportions of the vote. The people who value the financial corruption do not question that value, but can be quite flexible and open to learning with respect to who they need to share the corruption with and how much. Single-loop escalating cooperation, when it supports unethical behavior, can be just as damaging to ethical organization development as escalating conflict.

Of course, single-loop win-win politics can be effective in developing ethical organizations. Many people cooperate with ethical behavior simply because they have learned that they are rewarded for doing so. This issue is explored in the chapter 5 discussion of single-loop win-win negotiators.

Argyris and Schon (1988) observe that Hirschman wrote very little about the concrete methods individuals can use in carrying out the strategy of voice. They ask the important question, "What way of expressing integrity would be likely to achieve its manifest purposes while also reducing its unintended, paradoxical outcomes (i.e., negative escalations)?" (1988, p. 207). They recommend double-loop action-learning, in which the partners in the conversation are open to questioning not only instrumental actions but also their driving values.

Argyris and Schon make two important advances in this area. First, they build upon Hirschman by developing a politically practical way for individuals to enact the voice strategy. Second, they build upon Bateson and Weick by developing their double-loop action-learning method, which is a positively escalating, inquiring, open, less adversarial, and reciprocally interactive.

The key strengths of a politics of double-loop dialog are that it retains much of the cooperative effectiveness of win-win method while encouraging mutual ethical learning, mutual ethical belief conversion, and mutual ethical development among individuals. This can be very important, especially in situations where the ethical problems are located primarily at the level of individuals. However, the double-loop method still frames organization ethics and integrity issues as individual phenomena while generally ignoring, or at least not explicitly considering, embedded social traditions.

TRIPLE-LOOP POLITICS

In triple-loop politics, the embedded tradition system can be both criticized and treated as a partner in mutual action-learning. Continuing with and extending the Argyris, Putnam, and Smith (1985) example, the agent would open for learning and change (a) the effectiveness of the action strategy of not talking about controversial issues (single-loop), (b) the appropriateness of the governing value of short-term conflict suppression (double-loop), and (c) positive and/or negative biases in the embedded social tradition that may be causing individuals inappropriately to accept that governing value (triple-loop). For example, one might inquire about whether there is something about one's family's, department's, or organization's tradition that makes it easier to discuss some topics and difficult to discuss other controversial topics. Or one might refer to past cases where one's organization tradition was able to address and adapt to new problems, and ask whether and how it could help address the present problem, or how it might have to change in order to address a different type of problem or opportunity.

While not recognizing the phenomenon of triple-loop action-learning, Dianne Argyris (1985) has found a few cases where people have been able to call into question dysfunctional aspects of another's social tradition. However, she concludes that there is little record of people being able to reframe an issue as a problem with respect to their own social tradition and then engage in reform-directed action-learning with respect to that social tradition.

This point is key. Double-loop method is still understood, at least in practice, to be substantially interactions that can be described as individual to individual—I–ther, or at best I–Other–Other's dysfunctional social tradition. Within much of conventional organization ethics action-learning theory, including double-loop theory, which has been with us for more than a generation, ethical problems are considered as ones of competing, conflicting moral values, and the solution has appeared to lie—necessarily, but also uneasily—with individuals. The politics of double-loop action-learning for the most part ignores embedded social tradition as a potential partner and/or obstacle.

As societies have become more industrial, bureaucratic, and culturally diverse, our understanding of the importance of embedded social tradition has grown substantially. Historical experiments in dialog have been extended beyond a solely individual focus. Later experiments have carried dialogic action-learning beyond the confining contexts of solely individual dyadic interactions. Examples of this type of triple-loop action-learning are considered in chapters 7, 8, and 9.

4

Single-Loop, Win-Lose Forcing Methods

Ethics Generals, top managers who unilaterally write ethics rules and then use punishments to force compliance, and Ethics Guerillas, who use methods such as secretly blowing the whistle outside the organization, both practice a politics of forcing. Its key strength is its short-run effectiveness, which can be particularly important in emergency situations. An important limitation of forcing is its destructiveness, particularly with respect to internal organization cooperation. The basic function of organization is to enable us to do more through cooperation than we can do atomistically. Therefore, it is important to maintain and encourage cooperation. However, there are times when the only practical alternative is forcing. We may need to at least keep in reserve the methods of single-loop forcing for those circumstances where more peaceful, cooperative, constructive, and sophisticated methods are ineffective.

TOP-DOWN ETHICS GENERALS

Before 1920, before psychology, before Hawthorne, before human relations, before the organizational behavior period of management thought and practice, the boss typically wrote the rules and punished those who didn't obey them. This included the boss's ethics rules. Top management often assumed that most employees were naturally lazy,

not very intellignet, and if not tightly supervised, watched, and disci-
plined, also ethically corrupt. McGregor (1960) termed this type of
management Theory X. In many countries and industries it is still the
typical style of management.

This approach was and is sometimes entangled with religious beliefs
concerning human nature as "fallen," nasty, brutish, and corrupt.
Harsh discipline is considered the best way to instill ethical behavior.
Within organization ethics and even within generally participative organizations, top-down forcing continues to be one of the most common approaches (Benson, 1989).

The boss, or a small staff appointed by the boss, writes an ethics
code. Employees are required to obey and comply with it. If subordinates are caught disobeying the rules, they are punished and made
examples. Types of punishments used to force compliance with the
boss's ethics rules include firing, denial of unemployment benefits
after firing, criminal and civil prosecution, demotion, transfer, loss of
promotion opportunities, suspension, reduction in pay, lower salary
increments, public embarrassment, and so on. In some countries, such
as South Korea, it is not uncommon to also physically abuse employees
publicly for violating the rules.

In 1985 the CEO of Wang, a Boston area computer company, announced a rule that sexual harassment was against company ethics
policy. This was several years before the supreme court decision and
1991 Civil Rights Act that made sexual harassment illegal. In addition,
the human resources vice president announced that in each ethics case
brought to the attention of top management, if the accused was found
guilty he would be fired, and if he was found not guilty, the accuser
would be fired.

In G.E. as early as 1946, a company policies code that included
many ethics items was written by a small staff appointed by the CEO.
Today, G.E. employees are given a copy of the updated code and
required to read it once a year and to sign a statement saying that they
have read it, understand it, promise to obey it, and promise to report
internally colleagues who violate it.

Similarly, Xerox Corporation has "Guides for Xerox Employees,"
with a matrix of references to company policy statements, brief sum-
maries of the policies, a list of policy violations with severity ratings
ranging from serious to extremely serious, and a "commitment of
understanding," which the employee must sign. The employee ac-
knowledges that he or she has read and understands the "policy understanding," will never knowingly violate Xerox policies, and will
promptly report knowledge of any violations (Ethics Resource Center,
1988, p. 134).

Small organizations can also have top-down, punishment-based ethics codes. For example, the CEO and entrepreneurial founder of a Boston-area research and consulting organization decided that he wanted to develop an ethically as well as economically and technically strong organizational community. He instructed a staff member to draft an ethics code. The draft, written with the help of an external ethics consultant, was revised slightly and approved by the organization's management committee, composed of the CEO, four vice presidents, the general counsel, and the comptroller. The code specified general policies and penalties, for example, that it was not permitted to deceive potential telephone interview respondents (personal interview, Research Manager, 1986).

Many Ethics Generals appear to believe sincerely that the best way to develop ethical employees and organizations is through tight discipline. Many also appear to believe that most of their subordinates are naturally weak when faced with temptations to behave unethically, and that the best antidote is character-building, tight, harsh discipline.

Not all organization ethics codes are solely single-loop, top-down, force-based approaches. A few organizations, such as Champion International, have bottom-up, double-loop aspects incorporated into their top-down, punishment-based codes. For example, work groups, departments, and even divisions of the organization are allowed to present and justify to top management revisions that would be more applicable to their situations (McCoy and Twining, 1988; Vanesse, 1991). (These more participative types of systems are discussed in later chapters.)

Ethics Generals use a form of single-loop politics. The boss does not hold his driving ethical values open to discussion with subordinates. What he is willing to learn about are what enforcement mechanisms may be more and less effective.

BOTTOM-UP ETHICS GUERILLAS

The Ethics Guerilla, the mirror image of the Ethics General, has assumptions about a particular boss or bosses in general that are as negative as those the Ethics General has about employees. But there are also important differences. While the Ethics General's assumptions about employees are generalized, the Ethics Guerilla's tend to be more particular with respect to a specific boss. Sometimes such negative assumptions and opinions can be quite correct, as in the examples in the discussion of the Richard III, Faust, Eichmann, and Dr. Suguro archetypes.

The politics of the Ethics Guerilla are single-loop; he typically does not think it possible to discuss ethics with the boss he thinks is initiating or permitting unethical behavior. And he may believe that it is not possible to have an open discussion with an Ethics General who has stereotypical negative opinions of employees' ethics.

Several different types of bottom-up forcing methods are worth examining, for three reasons. First, there is a great deal of variation in the types of bottom-up forcing methods that is not generally understood. Second, sometimes bottom-up forcing methods are necessary and unavoidable. Third, I have found that when employees are aware that they are not powerless with respect to forcing methods, then they are more able and willing to use the more dialogic methods.

There are a wide variety of possible bottom-up forcing methods. Examples of each follow.

Secretly blow the whistle inside the organization   A purchasing analyst for a Boston-area industrial company secretly wrote an anonymous letter to an upper-level manager stating that his boss, a purchasing manager, was soliciting and accepting bribes from subcontractors (Neuffer, 1988). On the basis of the letter, the corporation notified the FBI that there might be a problem. The FBI investigated and found that the tip was correct. The company fired the purchasing manager and worked with the Department of Justice to prosecute him. He was convicted of a felony and was sentenced to six months imprisonment for taking a hundred thousand dollars in bribes in exchange for granting favorable treatment on defense contracts.

Quietly blow the whistle to a responsible higher-level manager (Toffler, 1986)   When Evelyn Grant was first hired by the company at which she is now a personnel manager, part of her job was to administer a battery of tests that would in part determine which employees would be promoted to supervisory positions. She explained:

> There have been cases where people will do something wrong because they think they have no choice. Their boss tells them to do it and so they do it, knowing it's wrong. They don't realize there are ways around the boss. . . . When I went over his [the chief psychologist's] data and analysis, I found errors both in assumptions regarding the data, as well as actual errors of computation. . . . I had two choices: I could do nothing, or I could report my findings to my supervisor. If I did nothing, the only persons possibly hurt were the ones who "failed" the test. To report my findings on the other hand, could hurt several people, possibly myself. (Toffler, 1986, p. 157)

She quietly told her boss about the problem. He quietly arranged for a meeting to discuss the discrepancies with the chief psychologist, who did not show up for the meeting. The test battery was dropped, and no one beside her immediate boss knew that she blew the whistle.

Secretly threaten the offender with blowing the whistle (personal interview, Insurance Company Manager, 1986)   A salesman for a very large Boston-area insurance company attended a weekly sales meeting with other salespeople at which the sales manager instructed, both verbally and in writing, his salespeople to use a sales technique that the salesman considered unethical. He wrote the sales manager an anonymous letter threatening to write a letter to the Massachusetts Insurance Commissioner and the *Boston Globe,* with a copy of the unethical sales instructions, if the sales manager did not retract his instructions at the next sales meeting. The sales manager retracted the instructions. The salesman still works for this insurance company, and it is not known within the company who threatened to blow the whistle.

Secretly threaten an ethically responsible manager with blowing the whistle outside the organization (personal interview, Real Estate Manager, 1986)   In San Francisco, a recently hired manager found that the construction company his real estate development company had contracted with to construct a building was systematically not giving minorities opportunities for foreman training. He wrote an anonymous letter to a higher-level manager who he thought was ethically responsible. He threatened to blow the whistle to the press and government if the situation was not corrected. The real estate manager intervened and the contractor did then hire minorities for foreman training positions.

Publicly threaten a responsible manager with blowing the whistle (personal interview, University Administrator, 1986)   A woman in a business office of a large Boston-area university observed that a middle-level male manager was sexually harassing several women in the office. She tried to reason with the office boss to get him to do something about the offensive manager. The boss would not do anything, and she thought he was afraid of the lower-level manager. A few days later she observed the same manager again harassing women in the office in front of several people, including the boss. She became quite angry and yelled at her boss in front of the whole office that if he didn't do something about the harassing behavior, she would blow the whistle to the personnel office. The boss then told the offender that he had to stop the harassing behavior because this emotional woman was going to get everyone in trouble. The manager stopped his unethical behavior, but he and several other employees refused to talk with her. She then left that job and the university.

Sabotage the implementation of the unethical behavior (personal interview, Program Manager, 1986)   A program manager for a Boston-area social welfare agency was told by her superior to remove a significant percentage of her clients receiving disability benefits through her program and replace them with Soviet emigrants. The manager said that there must be cheaters and it was her job to find them and kick them out of the program. She thought it was good to help both the emigrants and her current clients, but unethical to drop current clients. She knew most of them very well and did not believe they were cheaters. However, for a while she gave in to her boss's pressure and dropped people from the rolls.

One of the people she dropped subsequently committed suicide, because he did not want to force his family to sell their home in order to pay for the medical care he needed and to qualify for poverty programs. After trying unsuccessfully to reason with her boss about why this case failed, she sabotaged him. She worked with the secretaries to delay his work, not give him messages, and not notify him of meetings. In addition, she instituted a paperwork chain with a federal funding agency that prevented her local office from dropping people for nine months, at which time they were eligible for a different funding program. Both her old clients and the new emigrees received benefits. To her boss she blamed the federal bureaucracy for making it impossible to drop people quickly. Her boss, a political appointee who didn't understand the system very well, also blamed the federal agency. Soon thereafter he quit his job and went back to the private sector. The next boss did not order her to drop people for the disability rolls.

Publicly blow the whistle inside the organization (Reinhold, 1986) John W. Young, the chief of NASA's astronaut office, wrote a twelve-page internal memorandum to ninety-seven people after the Challenger explosion that killed seven crew members. The memo listed a large number of safety-related problems that he said had endangered crews since October 1984, and stated, "If the management system is not big enough to stop the space shuttle program whenever necessary to make flight safety correction, it will not survive and neither will our three space shuttles or their flight crews." The memo was key to widening the safety investigation throughout the total NASA system and beyond just the space shuttle program.

Quietly not implement an unethical order/policy (Ladwig, 1986) A top salesman and branch manager for over forty years for a Boston-area computer company at times had trouble balancing his responsibilities (Ladwig, 1986). He was trained to sell solutions to customer problems. He had order and revenue quotas to make. He was responsible for getting and keeping important customers with annual revenues of two hundred fifty to five hundred thousand dollars. He was responsible for aggressively and conscientiously representing new products that had required large investments in research and development. He was required to sell the full line of products and services.

Sometimes he had quotas to sell products which in his opinion were not a good match for the customer or to him looked marginal in performance. He would quietly not sell those products and concentrate on selling those he believed in. Or he would quietly explain the characteristics of the questionable products to his knowledgeable customers and get their reactions, rather than make an all-out sales effort. Then when occasionally his sales managers asked him why this product was not moving, he would explain what customers objected to and why. He stated that this type of solution strategy to ethical conflicts is very difficult for a salesman or manager with an average or poor performance record to get away with.

Indicate uncertainty or refusal to support a cover-up if the individual and/or the organization gets caught (Broker, 1986)   In the Boston office of a brokerage company four brokers informally worked together as a group. One had been successfully trading on insider information provided by a mole within Lotus Corporation. He invited the other three members of his group to do the same. One night a fifth broker was working late and, unseen by the other brokers, overheard them discussing their insider trading. When he revealed himself from behind his cubicle, they invited him to participate. He indicated to them that if there ever was an investigation he wasn't sure whether he would be able to help cover up the insider trading. The other brokers decided not to participate in further insider trading, at least on the Lotus stock. (Coincidentally, Lotus had begun tracing trades it believed were based on insider trading. Just before the tracing reached the brokerage office, the insider trading stopped.)

Secretly blow the whistle outside the organization (Pasztor, 1985)   William Schwartzkopf anonymously wrote a letter to the Justice Department alleging large-scale, long-time bid rigging among many of the largest American electrical contractors. The secret letter accused the contractors of rigging bids and conspiring to divide billions of dollars of contracts since 1970. Companies in the industry have already paid more than twenty million dollars in fines.

Publicly blow the whistle outside the organization (Fitzgerald, 1977)
A. Earnest Fitzgerald was a high-level civilian manager in the Air Force and a former corporate CEO. He revealed to Congress and the press that the Air Force had allowed Lockheed to underbid in order to

gain Air Force contracts and then to bill and receive payments for cost overruns on the contracts. While Fitzgerald was fired for his trouble, through Congressional intervention he eventually received his job back, and the underbidding and cost overruns on at least the C-5A cargo plane were stopped.

WIN-LOSE NEGOTIATORS

Win-lose negotiating techniques do not always result in win-lose outcomes. In a win-lose outcome, if one of the players wants ethical organization behavior and wins, the player trying to do the unethical behavior loses. For example, one player might want more money spent to improve worker safety conditions, but the increased costs might reduce the other player's salary increment reward that is tied to reducing costs. A win-win outcome would be for the safety conditions to be improved without increasing costs. Or the safety conditions to be improved and the criteria for salary increment rewards expanded to include safety improvements.

Sometimes win-win outcomes are possible, other times they are not, or not in the short or medium term. For example, it may not be physically possible with current technology to improve safety conditions without increasing costs. Because of intense competition top management might refuse to discuss changing the salary increment reward system to include safety improvements.

Depending upon the situation, both win-lose techniques and win-win techniques can produce either win-lose outcomes or win-win outcomes. What we think we know about negotiating is that generally, win-lose techniques generate win-lose outcomes and win-win techniques produce win-win outcomes, but not always (Fisher and Ury, 1991; Raiffa, 1982). For example, while one player might use win-win technique, the other might refuse to play a win-win game and use a win-lose technique in response.

Three examples follow of win-lose techniques in organization ethics contexts: extreme demands, good guy–bad guy, and leverage building. There are many more. While such techniques are not necessarily recommended, they can be effective and are sometimes necessary, at least in the short term, to achieve an ethical outcome. As in the Faust situation discussed in chapter 2, there can also be ethical problems with using win-lose techniques, which will be discussed later.

Leverage building. In leverage building one builds a type of power that another is vulnerable to and then explicitly or implicitly threatens to use that power against him unless he gives in to what one wants.

Leverage building was a key technique used by lawyers from the Equal Employment Opportunity Commission and the Federal Communications Commission in negotiating with AT&T to agree to seven years of hiring and promotion quotas. The EEOC and FCC lawyers recognized that AT&T had one of the highest levels of minority employment levels of any large corporation. The civil rights lawyers explained that they wanted to make an example of AT&T: If a company with such a good record as AT&T had to greatly increase its hiring and promotion of minorities through quotas, then other companies would probably follow AT&T's example "voluntarily." After AT&T objected to the quotas, the EEOC and the FCC lawyers threatened to deny telephone rate increases if AT&T did not consent to the quotas. AT&T thought that it would take several years to win in court against the FCC and the EEOC, during which time AT&T would lose tens of millions of dollars if rate increases were denied or reduced. In 1973 AT&T signed a consent decree with the EEOC for seven years of quotas, and the FCC moved forward with permitting rate increases. The lawyers from the EEOC and FCC described their motivations as ethical in the service of the civil rights movement (Northrup and Larson, 1979). The increase in minority employment under the consent decree was about the same, 4.3 percent, as the increase attained in the ten-year period without quotas (Nielsen, 1993e).

Good guy–bad guy. With this technique, two people on the same negotiating side pretend to a person on a different side that one is a reasonable and calm person while the other is an extreme, emotional, and aggressive person. The "bad guy" makes extreme demands while acting threateningly. When he is not present, the "good guy" offers to make a deal that the "good guy" can get the "bad guy" to accept. For example, an internal company affirmative action officer secretly teamed with an EEOC lawyer against the CEO of an electronics corporation (Ackerman and Bauer, 1976; Bauer, 1973). The company was not making as much affirmative action progress as the internal affirmative action officer wanted, so he asked the EEOC lawyer to help him. The EEOC lawyer demanded large changes in an extreme, unreasonable, and aggressive manner. The affirmative action officer then went to the CEO and said that he could get the EEOC lawyer to back off if the CEO would do more to push internal affirmative action. The CEO agreed. The affirmative action officer said that he acted this way because of the ethical importance of greater affirmative action results; he did not think the CEO would move strongly enough without it.

Extreme demands. With this technique one aggressively demands much more than is reasonable and then appears to compromise. For example, if one was buying a used car and the price for a particular car was between seven and eight thousand dollars, one would make an extremely low offer of four thousand and then "compromise" at six.

This technique can be applied to ethics situations, as in the following example. An automobile product safety engineer was concerned about a model's safety (personal interview, Automobile Engineer, 1985). The company standard for auto crash safety was no damage in a fifteen mile-per-hour collision. The engineer had seen reports that with the particular design of the car his factory was producing, there were some gas tank explosions at fifteen miles per hour. He made the judgment that the company standard of fifteen miles per hour was too low for this car. He aggressively demanded a redesign and retooling of the chassis, which would cost fifty million dollars, but "compromised" at an increased bumper strength to twenty-five miles per hour that would cost less than three million.

STRENGTHS AND LIMITATIONS OF A POLITICS OF SINGLE-LOOP FORCING

Strengths of Single-Loop Forcing Methods

Single-loop forcing can have quick behavioral effectiveness. As the cases illustrate, when single-loop forcing methods are used, they are often quickly effective. Short-run effectiveness can be very important. In some ethics situations, the issues can be quite clear, as in embezzlement, emergency health and safety issues, physical sexual abuse, and so on. In such situations, learning which action methods are instrumentally more effective in achieving the driving ethical value can be more appropriate than more sophisticated and time-consuming double- or triple-loop action-learning. More sophisticated is not necessarily better or more appropriate. Such methods can take a substantial amount of time, which can mean that employees or consumers are hurt or killed while these processes play out.

For example, when G.E. decided to enforce its ethics code rules concerning antitrust activities and kickbacks with punishments such as demotions and firings, the unethical activities stopped, at least for a while. Similarly, when the purchasing analyst secretly blew the whistle internally on his boss, the kickbacks quickly stopped. When Evelyn Grant quietly blew the whistle to a responsible higher-level manager about the invalid test that had been used for fifteen years, the test was discontinued within three months. When the insurance salesman secretly threatened his boss that he would blow the whistle to the *Boston*

Globe and the Massachusetts insurance commissioner, the practice was discontinued within two weeks. When the female employee publicly threatened her manager with blowing the whistle to human resources about the sexual harassment by the male employee, the harassing behavior stopped immediately. When the computer salesman quietly did not implement what he believed were unethical instructions to sell inappropriate products to his clients, the products were not sold to his clients. When the stockbroker indicated uncertainty about whether he could support a cover-up of the insider trading, the insider trading stopped, at least on that stock. When William Schwartzkopf secretly blew the whistle about the electrical industry bid-rigging that had been going on for over ten years, the unethical practice was stopped within a year—at least for a while. When Earnest Fitzgerald blew the whistle on the Lockheed-Air Force cost overrun collusion, those activities, at least on the C-5A cargo plane, stopped. When the EEOC lawyer used rate-setting leverage with the FCC against AT&T, AT&T gave in. When the affirmative action officer used the good guy–bad guy technique with the EEOC lawyer against his own CEO, the CEO gave in. When the automobile product safety engineer made extreme demands, the safety measure he wanted was achieved.

Single-loop forcing focuses on behavior, and lack of understanding is not always the problem. Perpetrators of unethical behavior sometimes understand perfectly well that what they are doing is unethical. In such situations the key factor is behavior, not understanding. The Richard III archetype understands that his is unethical. The problem is how to stop him. Single-loop forcing can force ethical behavior, at least for a while. Similarly, the Socrates' Jailer archetype understands that his behavior is unethical, but does it out of fear. Single-loop forcing gives him something to fear on the side of ethics. The Faust understands that his means are unethical, and single-loop forcing can block those means, at least for a while. And for the Dr. Suguro, who behaves unethically because he believes it is impractical not to, force can change the equation and make it less practical to cooperate.

Some single-loop forcing methods are relatively safe for users. Trying to do something about organizational ethics can be dangerous for the ethically concerned actor. Punishment is not uncommon. Powerful people in an organization who gain from unethical behavior often use their power against those who would threaten those gains. Punishments can include being fired, laid off, passed over for promotion, lower salary increments, transfers, shunning, industry blackballing, legal prosecution, and sometimes even physical violence to one's friends, family, and self. There are good reasons to be afraid.

Several single-loop forcing methods are relatively safe for users. These include: secretly blowing the whistle inside the organization; quietly blowing the whistle to a responsible higher-level manager; secretly threatening the offender with blowing the whistle; secretly threatening an ethically responsible manager with blowing the whistle; secretly sabotaging implementation of the unethical behavior; quietly not implementing an unethical order or policy; and secretly blowing the whistle outside the organization.

There can be exceptions. If only a few people are in a position to know about the unethical behavior, those who try to stop it can sometimes be tracked down and punished. For example, Chester Walsh chose to secretly blow the whistle externally rather than use the G.E. 800 number for secretly blowing the whistle internally because "the call would have been easily traced back to me. . . . I did a lot of research to see what happened to people who went up the chain of command and reported wrongdoings, all I found was they lost their jobs, their security; they lost everything" (Naj, 1992, pp. 1, 6).

Secret external whistle-blowing can also be dangerous. For example, the sanitation industry in New York city has been infiltrated by the Mafia for many years (Bailey, 1993). Employees are afraid to secretly blow the whistle both internally and externally. On occasion the police department and the newspapers have also been infiltrated by the Mafia. It appears that at times the Mafia has been able to use police and newspaper information to track down and assassinate secret whistle-blowers and members of their families. When the press and the justice system are part of the corruption, there may be no one to secretly blow the whistle to. This situation is common in many developing countries where the press, the police, the military, and the government are all part of the corruption.

Limitations of Single-Loop Forcing Methods

A politics of single-loop forcing has the following important limitations.

Single-loop forcing does not give us the opportunity to learn with others about what is more or less ethical. With both top-down and bottom-up forcing, people can be mistaken and try to force behavior that is in fact unethical. We can be wrong in thinking that others will act unethically or are acting unethically. We can force people to behave when it is unnecessary to force them. If we are wrong about the ethics of a particular issue, we may be unintentionally forcing people into unethical behavior.

Single-loop forcing does not give us the opportunity to reexamine inappropriate governing values or to learn from others' experiences and perspectives. Others may have information or insights that would suggest a different, more appropriate direction than the one we are trying to force. Instead, we focus on the relative effectiveness of behavior-change methods. This may not be as large a problem with the more clear-cut ethics situations such as physical sexual harassment or an emergency worker safety issue, it can be an important problem with the more subtle, gray-area situations.

For example, in the computer company sexual harassment case, the human resources vice president, under orders from the CEO, would fire either the employee found guilty of sexual harassment or the employee making the charge if the accused was found not guilty. While such decisive action might be applauded at one level, one might disagree with both the severity of the penalty and the chilling effect of the penalties on both accuser and accused. Single-loop forcing did not give people or the organization the chance to explore the issue and learn about what more and less appropriate sexually related behaviors might be in the organization. For example, it was not unusual for technical employees to work seventy-two hours a week. For many of them their work was the main or only opportunity for social relations. There was some confusion about what was appropriate behavior with respect to approaching another, having a relationship with another, and a relationship breaking up. (This "either the accused or the ac-cuser must go" practice was stopped by another single-loop forcing technique, the threat of a lawsuit.)

Similarly, in the AT&T employment quotas example, where AT&T agreed to quotas for seven years, apparently the EEOC lawyers re-fused to discuss with the AT&T managers the ethics of quotas relative to alternative affirmative action methods such as better recruitment, technical training, and management development methods. Later, se-rious conflicts among workers as well as accidents caused by inade-quately experienced and trained workers and managers resulted from the quotas. In addition, many of the workers felt that they were being punished for historical problems that they were not responsible for, a resentment that exacerbated negative race relations within AT&T.

Some ethics code provisions may not be ethical. For example, in the Roche example in chapter 2, it was part of the company's code that no employees could reveal any company information to anyone outside the company. When Stanley Adams (1984), testified to the EEC Com-mission that his company initiated and organized price fixing and market allocation agreements and paid bribes to managers of compet-ing companies, he was fired from the company for violating this code. There was no opportunity within the company for most managers and employees to discuss the ethics of such an industrial espionage policy with the company's top management. Not only is such an ethics provision of questionable ethical validity, but the company's reputation in Europe suffered when the violation of EEC rules was discovered, publicized, and prosecuted by the EEC.

Similarly, in a bottom-up forcing situation, an individual can be wrong about the organization acting unethically. It is common for lower-level employees not to have as much or as good information about ethics situations and issues as higher-level managers. Lower-level employees also often do not have as high a quality of experience as higher-level managers concerning specific ethical issues. Quality of experience and information can influence the quality of ethical judgments. To the extent that this is true in any given situation, the use of bottom-up forcing to change organization behavior can be in error. For example, a person in the computer salesperson's situation but with less experience, information, or knowledge, could be wrong about the quality of a computer or a stock that a higher-level manager ordered sold.

Single-loop forcing can teach narrow, routinized, unthinking obedience more than individual or organizational ethical learning. With respect to top-down forcing situations, obeying authority generally, as well as specifically obeying authority that is ordering unethical behavior, is common. As Arendt (1964), Toulmin (1961), Baier (1958), and Gauthier (1986) recognize, some people use authority more than internal ethical reasoning or dialog to arrive at ethical judgments and behaviors.

As discussed in the Eichmann, Ford Pinto, AIDS-contaminated blood, and Bard Company heart catheter cases, pressure to obey and implement orders efficiently can narrowly focus one's attention on the received narrow framework. People can be so well trained to efficiently carry out orders that when an ethics situation occurs that requires some deviation from the standard operating procedure, they are not prepared to think independently.

Even when a behavior might directly violate an ethics code provision, top-down forcing can condition people to think that it is appropriate for higher-level management to unilaterally make exceptions to an ethics code, since "they" wrote it in the first place. In the several G.E. examples, middle-level managers obeyed the orders of higher-level managers to violate G.E.'s own ethics code. The lower-level managers were so used to obeying orders that they did not think of questioning whether higher-level managers should be making exceptions to the ethics code. Since they had not participated in developing the ethics code, it was difficult for them to understand when an exception was being ordered for legitimate or illegitimate reasons. A single-loop forcing type of ethics code required and taught them to obey orders more than it taught them to think independently about ethics issues. (More participative types of ethics codes are considered in later chapters.)

Both cooperative relationships and the organization can be damaged by forcing. Instead of looking at this issue from the point of view of the responsible and courageous individual forcing the organization to act ethically, we can look at it from another perspective. How do we feel when we are forced to change our behavior? Further, how do we feel if we are forced to change our behavior by another, known or unknown, if we think that we have the positional right, the quality of information, or the quality of experience to make the correct decisions? Relationships are probably at least strained, especially if we are ethically right and are being forced to change unnecessarily, but even if we are wrong, and don't understand it at this time, or even if we know we are wrong but still don't like being forced.

As Argyris and Schon (1988) have pointed out, and as discussed in chapter 2, such actions can lead to escalatingly negative and destructive interactions. On the other hand, if the person could ethically justify their behavior to us instead of simply trying to force us, perhaps cooperative relationships could be maintained rather than destroyed.

As Weick (1979) and Argyris and Schon (1988) have pointed out, effective organizations are built upon a structure of interlocking, positively reinforcing, and positively escalating individual interactions. When those individual links are damaged, as the links of a chain might be damaged, the strength of the whole organization can suffer.

In addition, if an organization can learn from its members that what it was doing is inappropriate, it might be able to avoid negative outcomes. For example, when an organization gets caught for doing unethical things, legal penalties and bad publicity can damage it. If it can learn from its employees that its behavior was unethical, it might be able to change direction before the negative consequences were realized.

If we want "wrong" people, who might also be more powerful than we are now or in the future, to exercise self-restraint with respect to the use of force, then we may need to exercise self-restraint ourselves even if we are "right." A problem with using force, as in the law of "an eye for an eye," which many of us still implicitly act upon and believe, is that the other side can have more powerful and effective force that we can lose to now or later. Many people have been punished for trying to do the ethical both when they are right and when they are wrong. Using force can also contribute to an atmosphere or belief culture that the only way to get things done is through force. Gandhi's response to "an eye for an eye" was that if we all carried it out eventually the whole world would be blind. Wrong people can and do use force and win. Do we want to help build an organization culture where forcing plays an important role? We may prefer to exercise self-restraint.

CONCLUSION

Given the severity of the limitations, should a politics of single-loop forcing ever be used? As the following chapters illustrate, there are often alternative methods that are both effective and less destructive. But in some circumstances there may be no alternative. A severe emergency situation may require the quick behavioral effectiveness of a politics of forcing. In situations where others refuse to discuss the issues with at least some openness, then there may be no other effective alternative. We may need to at least keep in reserve the methods of single-loop forcing for those circumstances when more peaceful, cooperative, constructive, and sophisticated methods are ineffective. More sophisticated is not necessarily better or more appropriate.

5

Single-Loop Win-Win Methods

The present chapter examines how win-win politics retains much of the effectiveness of forcing while encouraging productive coopera-tion. With win-win politics, though, there can be no belief conversion toward the ethical. With win-win politics it is possible to adopt ethical behavior without reference to the ethical or even concern for the ethical among all parties to an agreement. This is both a strength and limitation of this type of politics.

As is well known, win-win integrating as general management method was central to the post-1920s management reform efforts. This reform movement adapted psychology and cooperative human relations to management practice and has evolved into the fields of organizational behavior and leadership. Perhaps less well-known is that ethical concern was foundational for some of the leading scholars in this reform movement such as Elton Mayo.

Mayo's formal training was more in ethics, philosophy, and aes-thetics than in psychology. His key teacher as a post-medical student (he withdrew from medical school before receiving a medical degree) at Adelaide University was the philosophy and ethics professor Sir William Mitchell. For Mayo, "the facts of ethics are found in psy-chology" (Trahair, 1984, p. 54). Cooperating, uniting, and integrating were key ethics action-learning principles he developed.

According to Trahair, Mayo's biographer, "For Mayo . . . unity is not governed by simplicity but by well integrated complexity. . . . Mayo was a 'healer' of disease in industrial society. His main task was to help people to cooperate and collaborate, i.e., to bring unity to

conditions that aroused conflict (through integrating complexity).
. . . As a healer, he aimed to unite and integrate divisive elements
within the firm" (1984, pp. 55, 357). For Mayo, accepting and working for these values was motivated by a sense of high ethical purpose.

According to Abraham Zaleznik, a student of two of Mayo's students, Fritz Roethlisberger and George Homans, "The key idea that
caught Mayo's attention, along with most other participants in the
human relations movement of the . . . era, was to change the practices of authority figures to incorporate the efficacy of healing" (1984,
p. 12). Mayo was in part motivated by what he considered the destructive and less-than-ethical labor-management conflicts of the late nineteenth and early twentieth centuries as well as what he and others
considered dehumanizing and unethical working conditions. Much of
the early funding for his work came from efforts to reform these
conditions.

Mayo's efforts at win-win integrating method were resisted not only
by managers with a single-loop forcing orientation, but also by organized labor leaders who believed in labor union forcing as a necessary
response to management forcing. According to Zaleznik, "The intel-
lectual leaders of the labor movement saw in the work of the human
relations practitioners a means of blocking workers' political motives
with the consequence (whether intended or not) of increasing the
dependency of workers on management" (1984, p. 12). Some managers and labor leaders still prefer adversarial instead of cooperative
relationships.

Despite its limitations, single-loop win-win method is an important
organizational ethics action-learning approach. The late Kenneth
Boulding, in his book *Stable Peace,* asked the question, "If we had a
policy for stable peace what would it look like?" (1978, pp. ix–x). His
answer was directly concerned with win-win agreements, in which the
players agree to a "taboo line—the line which divides what we can do
but refrain from doing from what we can do and do" (p. x).

Similarly, Gauthier in his book *Morals By Agreement,* observes,
"For social seekers and strivers morality could be no more than a
needed but unwelcome constraint. But . . . a morality of agreement, although still a source of constraint, makes their shared activity
mutually welcome and so stable" (1986, p. 337). That is, it is possible to
negotiate ethical agreements among players in actual or potential conflict without either force or ethical belief conversion, when satisfaction
of at least some of their self- and shared interests are integrated in a
win-win solution.

There are at least three types of win-win techniques: mutual gain
negotiating, peaceful minimal coexistence, and persuasion. Examples

of these techniques follow. These methods are then discussed as forms of single-loop politics. Finally, the strengths and limitations of win-win politics are considered.

MUTUAL GAIN NEGOTIATING

In mutual gain negotiating, the parties agree to a deal because each gets enough of what they want to make the deal worthwhile for each of them. If at least one party in the negotiation wants something ethical, it is possible to include the ethical as part of the deal even if the ethical issues are never explicitly discussed.

Research company (personal interview, Research Manager, 1986)   A project manager at a research company knew what she wanted—to not misrepresent interview time to potential respondents, and to keep her job. She asked the vice president what he needed with respect to the long interviews. He indicated that what he wanted was a specific project completion date, a minimum response rate of 20 percent, and a minimum number of completed interviews.

The project manager offered a win-win deal where she would meet those targets in exchange for flexibility in how she positioned and carried out the interviews. The vice president agreed. Instead of lying to potential respondents, she told them how long the interview would actually take and that if this was not a convenient time, she would like to arrange for a time to call back. The method exceeded the required response rate and the required number of completed interviews relative to the lying method, but took about 10 percent more time.

The solution was limited in that the boss continued to require the other project managers and analysts to lie to respondents.

General Electric (Herling, 1962)   In 1957 the Department of Justice and the FBI began an investigation of G.E. Shortly thereafter, G.E.'s CEO and chairman of the board, Ralph J. Cordiner, instructed Ray H. Luebbe, G.E.'s general counsel and vice president, to address the issue. He in turn instructed Gerard Swope, Jr., G.E.'s trade regulation counsel and son of a former president of G.E., to "look over," "review compliance," and address the situation.

The instructions were somewhat vague. If they had been more direct, such as to stop the antitrust behavior, that might have implied that Cordiner and Luebbe knew of the antitrust violations and might be personally, criminally liable.

Gerard Swope took something of a win-win negotiating approach, not using ethical language and not framing the conversations as involving ethics issues. He told several G.E. managers that he needed compliance with ethics code policy directive 20.5 concerning compliance with antitrust law, and "a more dynamic pricing policy to get away from the consistent identity of prices which had resulted in so many public criticisms during the years, and which enhanced the exposure of the company to investigation and charges based on circumstantial evidence" (Herling, 1962, p. 15). He also indicated that he needed to know if there were any current or past problems in this regard.

He also asked and listened to what the managers were concerned about and needed. Several managers indicated that what they wanted was to retain their employment with G.E. and to not be held personally responsible by G.E. for past violations of policy 20.5.

He offered the following deal to several managers. If they would not violate 20.5 in the future, and would help him with the information needed to defend G.E. against the current investigations, they would not be punished by G.E. for violations earlier than the last three years. (The legal statute of limitations was five years.) They might be demoted, but not fired.

Several managers accepted the deal. At least for a while, in the United States, such antitrust violations stopped, and Swope received important information about past violations. He stated:

> It was feared that the taking of action against those who had violated the policy (20.5) could have serious legal consequences both for the company and the individuals. The names of many of those involved had not, in all probability, been brought out in grand jury testimony; if it became known by the government that these employees had been disciplined, they might be identified as individuals who possibly had also violated the law, to the obvious prejudice of the individuals and the company. Not only would there be exposure to possible indictment, but the defense of any action which might be brought could also be seriously embarrassed. It was also appreciated that many in the company who knew and liked those whose fate was being weighed, might strongly disagree with the wisdom or fairness of a decision to impose discipline upon them. (Herling, 1962, p. 27)

Polaroid (Polaroid executive, 1986) Polaroid wanted to locate a new facility in the capital district of a Latin American country. About a third of that country's population lives in the capital district, the commercial and government center of the country, which is very crowded and overpolluted. Breathing the air on an average day there has been equated to smoking two or more packs of cigarettes a day.

A group of Polaroid middle managers prepared a proposal for the Ministry of Industry that complied with all the government's requirements for foreign companies locating plants in the country and in the capital district. The Ministry of Industry official indicated that all the requirements had been met and that the ministry would be happy to welcome Polaroid. In addition, the official indicated that he expected the usual 6 percent of the investment to be placed in numbered Swiss bank accounts.

The managers returned to Massachusetts and discussed the matter with upper-level management. The upper-level managers indicated to the middle-level managers that Polaroid would not pay the bribes, and asked them to return to the Latin American country and try to negotiate a solution.

The middle-level managers negotiated the following agreement with the ministry official. Polaroid would not pay the bribe, but instead would locate its plant outside the capital district in an economically disadvantaged area. The matter of the bribe was never discussed as an ethical issue.

The deal was a win for Polaroid in that it was able to locate a plant in the Latin American country near the capital district and not pay the bribe. It was a win for the country in that it received a plant in an area that was economically depressed, also avoiding further pollution of the capital district. It was a win for the ministry official in that he brought employment to an area in great need of it, which was good publicity for himself and the ministry. This solution was not perfect, but it was more or less win-win. The bribe was not made, but the plant's location was not Polaroid's first choice, and the ministry official continued to ask for and receive bribes from other companies.

Gillette (Gillette executive, 1986)   Gillette wanted to locate a razor blade plant in an Asian country, and chose India. Some government officials wanted very large bribes. As in the Polaroid case, Gillette did not want to pay the bribes. After six years of negotiations, part of which implicitly involved the bribe issue, in exchange for not paying the bribes, Gillette (1) accepted a lower equity position in a joint venture than it could have achieved with bribes, and (2) agreed to export product from India. Ethics were never explicitly discussed.

Elkhorn (Bauer, 1973; Ackerman and Bauer, 1976)   The upper-level management of a lumber company adopted a strategy whereby several mills would either have to reduce costs or close down. The plant manager of one of the mills was concerned that cost-cutting at Elkhorn would prevent the mill from meeting government pollution control requirements and that closing the mill could seriously damage the local community. He believed that he had a greater concern for these issues than his immediate, corporate-level superiors who he thought were more concerned with their responsibility for adequate financial return to stockholders.

If he reduced costs, he would not meet pollution control requirements. If he didn't reduce costs, mills would close and communities would be damaged. He adopted a win-win negotiating strategy and persuaded his superiors to extend the time required to meet their cost reduction targets, which then permitted more gradual improvements in productivity and pollution control, which in turn reduced pollution and permitted the mill to remain open. With his superiors he discussed the issues of pollution control and plant closing only in terms of time, cost, and financial return.

Schindler (Keneally, 1982)   Oskar Schindler was the German owner of a confiscated Jewish factory in Poland who rescued about thirteen hundred Jewish prisoner-workers and their families from murder by the Nazis. His key method in dealing with the German SS and army was mutual gain, win-win negotiating. He never discussed the issues in ethical terminology. Instead, he made a series of win-win deals to protect and rescue the Jews.

In exchange for the Jews, Schindler gave SS and army officers black-market cases of cognac, liquor, food, and diamonds, and parties that he paid for with profits from the factory. He would close these deals with the phrase, "And everybody's happy!" These deals were a win for Schindler in that he saved the Jews and perhaps his own mind and soul. They were a win for the Nazis in the sense that they received abundant amounts of black-market cognac, liquor, food, diamonds, and parties. They were a win for the Jewish workers and their families in that they survived and as workers for Schindler experienced relatively humane treatment.

PERSUASION

Persuasion tries to show through language and/or illustration why an idea or a behavior should be adopted. From the perspective of the persuader, he wins if the other person adopts the idea or behavior he is advocating. From the perspective of the persuaded person, he also wins because he now agrees with that idea or behavior.

As with negotiation, both parties can agree to a behavior while not even considering the ethical appropriateness of what the other person wants or the ethical reasons why he wants it. People can be persuaded not to engage in unethical behavior because of the likelihood of getting caught, or the costs associated with the behavior are "not worth it" compared to other opportunities, or there are more material advantages to acting ethically, as well as because the ethical is desirable in and of itself. And messages tailord to the social-psychological characteristics of the receiver can cause him to be persuaded independently of ethical considerations. Examples of win-win persuasion follow.

Bank (personal interview, Bank Board Member, 1993)   The chairman of the board of a medium-sized bank in a Latin American country asked the board members to approve his recommendation to buy a building from himself at the price he said it was worth. While this practice violated banking law, it was not uncommon in this segment of the banking industry. All but one of the board members at first agreed.

One board member then persuaded the others that if they approved the sale without objective assessments, they might get caught, be held personally responsible, have to pay fines, and/or go to jail. There had recently been a great deal of publicity about business leaders going to jail for various types of illegal activity. The board members decided that it was not worth the risk of getting caught and insisted that the purchase price be based on an objective outside assessment.

The board chairman was also the chairman of a much larger bank. He was later implicated in a scandal involving foreign investors accused of paying large bribes to government and banking officials. Following this event and the investigation of the financial affairs of the board chairman, several of the board members thanked the board member who had persuaded them to purchase the building at the higher price recommended by outside assessors instead of the board chairman's price.

Price-Waterhouse (Windsor, 1980)   The Price-Waterhouse public accounting firm was founded in England in the early part of the nineteenth century. At the time, public stock companies were just beginning to become popular. Many of the public companies made exaggerated and false reports about their economic resources and performance in order to attract and retain investors.

Price-Waterhouse was one of several public accounting firms founded by Quakers, who had a reputation for honesty and ethical behavior. Much of the early success of Price-Waterhouse has been attributed to that reputation, which enabled them to greatly increase their market share, growth, and profitability. The partners of the company persuaded investors to hire them because their reports were accurate, which in turn made it easier for their clients to raise and maintain investment funds. Clients hired Price-Waterhouse not solely because Price-Waterhouse was ethical, but because there were impor-

tant economic advantages to being perceived as honest. This remains a key selling point for some public accounting firms. Price-
Waterhouse wins by getting the business. Investors win because they
receive accurate information.

Fatalism project (Nielsen, 1973)   Persuasive messages can be effective
when they are tailored to the social-psychological characteristics of
target audiences, independently of ethical consideration. In 1971 an
experiment was conducted to persuade highly fatalistic, low-income
people to adopt more nutritious meal preparation for their children
and to register to vote. The motivation for the experiment was ethical
in the sense that the researchers believed that low-income parents had
an ethical responsibility to feed their children nutritious food and to
register to vote.

   Highly fatalistic people tended to believe that they would not receive long-term rewards as a result of their own behavior. And they
did not believe that benefits accruing to groups that they were members of would also benefit them as individuals. Because of this characteristic, short-term benefits to them as individuals were emphasized in
the persuasive messages. The highly fatalistic responded more positively to the messages emphasizing short-term rewards to them as
individuals than to messages emphasizing long-term rewards to their
groups.

West Coast bank and sexual orientation (personal interview, West Coast
banker, 1995)   A West Coast bank had a policy of nondiscrimination
concerning sexual orientation. It had for over fifty years made contributions to a national youth organization. The bank's director of community investment learned that this youth organization had a policy of
discrimination according to sexual orientation.

   He concluded that it was unethical for the bank to continue to
contribute to the youth organization since its policy conflicted with the
bank's policy. He made an appointment to talk with the bank's CEO,
intending to persuade him to terminate these contributions.

   The director told the CEO that while he understood that it might
not be in the short- or long-run economic interest of the bank to
terminate the contributions, he believed that it was the ethical thing to
do. The CEO was convinced and agreed to terminate them.

   There was a large public reaction against the bank with an apparent
net loss of deposits and loan assets. The director of community investment was also harassed. Nonetheless, the bank remained firm in its
decision. However, since the bank does not want to relive this very
difficult experience, it prefers to remain anonymous.

MINIMAL PEACEFUL COEXISTENCE

Negotiating minimal peaceful coexistence is different from mutual gain negotiating. The intention of mutual gain negotiating is to achieve positive gains for all the parties. That is, if a scale of outcomes ranged from − 10 through 0 to + 10, mutual gain negotiating tries to move up the positive scale from a zero point or a positive point. For example, if a salesman had no previous relationship with a potential customer, he might try to establish a positive mutual gain relationship. Similarly, if he had a previously good selling-buying relationship with a customer, they both might want to expand the relationship and make the outcomes even more positive.

With minimal peaceful coexistence, the problem is how to move from a − 10 to a − 6 or from a − 6 to 0, that is, to reduce mutual losses rather than achieve mutual gains. After such a reduction the parties might be in a better position to try for mutual gains, but the focus of the negotiation is first to reduce the losses. Examples follow.

Middle East peace negotiations   For the past fifty years the Israelis and the Palestinians have been engaged in mainly negative transactions and relationships, with essentially negative outcomes. Both sides have lost lives, suffered many injuries, and spent enormous economic resources in support of their war and conflict efforts.

Beginning informally and then formally in 1992, they have been negotiating toward more peaceful coexistence. Both sides are trying to reduce the negatives of their interactions and relationships. This is far from trying to negotiate mutual gains or alliances. Nonetheless, more peaceful coexistence can reduce the negative costs of lives lost, injuries, and war expenditures.

During these negotiations, the Israelis and Palestinians often accuse one another of past and present abuses. It is mutually clear that they do not like each other. It is also clear that they have radically different perceptions of identity and history as well as very different perceptions of who is more to blame for the losses both sides have experienced. At least in the formal negotiations, neither side has expressed a desire or an expectation of being friends or allies with the other. Nonetheless, the negotiation process has tried and to some extent succeeded in reducing negatives.

Affirmative-action dispute at a Boston bank (personal interview, Boston Banker, 1992)   A division manager of a Boston bank disagreed with the bank's human resources manager about whether equal opportunity or preferential hiring was the appropriate interpretation of affirmative action. They further disagreed about who should be hired for the bank's next opening for a loan officer.

The human resources manager, a black woman, pointed out that the lending division had very few black male loan officers. The division manager, a white male, responded that there was no evidence of past discrimination in his division. She asked him to hire a black male as the next loan officer. He responded that while he would be happy to go out of his way to search for black male candidates and would give equal opportunity for a black male to be hired, he would hire the most qualified person with the best experience and education. He said that he believed it was racist and unethical to hire a less qualified person because of their race. She told him he was acting like a racist because he was blocking "affirmative action and diversity." He told her that what she was pushing was "reverse discrimination."

The dispute escalated negatively into other areas. The two managers were supposed to be cooperating in normal planning, training, graduate school reimbursement, evaluation, compensation, promotion, employee relations, and employee assistance activities. The dispute spilled over into these areas and they were fighting with each other about many other things besides how to hire the next loan officer. Normal activities were not getting done or being done very poorly.

It became obvious to both the managers and their subordinates that performance in both areas was deteriorating. Another manager suggested to the two managers that they try to negotiate some form of peaceful coexistence while upper-level management was deciding how to resolve the dispute, which might not happen for several months.

The two managers decided to stop meeting with each other because they were mostly fighting at their meetings. They both designated subordinates to handle their other normal negotiations. They further agreed to stop criticizing each other publicly and to stop writing negative memos about each other's divisions to other people in the bank. For the most part, cooperation between the two groups returned to normal.

WIN-WIN METHOD AS SINGLE-LOOP ACTION-LEARNING

As described in chapter 4, Ethics Generals, Ethics Guerillas, and win-lose negotiators use single-loop politics. That is, they do not hold open for potential reframing or change the ethical values they are trying to force others to comply with. Nonetheless, there is single-loop learning in that they are open to learning which techniques for forcing compliance are more effective.

Similarly, the mutual gain negotiator does not hold open for reframing the ethical value he wants to achieve. He is only willing to learn about what the other side wants in exchange for giving him what he wants.

Such single-loop action-learning is illustrated in the negotiating cases just considered. In the research company case, the project director did not want to lie to respondents, and did not hold that ethical value open for reframing, reconsideration, or change. She simply tried to learn what her vice president might want in exchange for giving her the freedom not to lie.

In the G.E. case, the investigating corporate lawyer did not question his driving value of needing to know what type and how many antitrust violations G.E. had been party to. He simply explored various deals for gaining this information, and gave people job security in exchange for information and promises of future compliance.

Polaroid's management, in negotiating with the Latin American government official, was not willing to hold open to change its ethical value of not paying bribes. Instead they offered to locate their plant in a somewhat less desirable location in exchange for not having to pay the bribe.

Oskar Schindler, unlike many others, was not willing to change his ethical value of not killing innocent people. Instead, he traded black-market goods for Jewish lives.

Win-win persuasion was practiced by the Sophists, who were sometimes manipulative, as Socrates and Plato recognized. In modern behavioral science-based organizational terminology, the Sophist is a type of single-loop actor-learner. He is only open to learning in one direction, that is, learning what others need to hear in order to accept what he is advocating. He does not question his own initial governing values. He has already decided, not just tentatively, but definitely, what is appropriate, before acting in conversation with others. He simply tries to learn why the other is resisting him, and tries to construct a more effective message to address that resistance point.

The positions Sophists try to persuade others to adopt are not necessarily unethical. For example, such an approach is not uncommon among litigators, salespeople, and ordinary people trying to persuade other people to support the ethical. Socrates and Plato criticized the Sophists not so much for the positions that they advocated, but for their fundamentally close-minded, single-loop method.

In the Latin American bank example, the board member who persuaded the other board members was not open to violating banking laws. He had on previous occasions used strictly ethical arguments and learned that they were ineffective, because many on the board considered them naive.

The argument stating the likelihood of getting caught, exposed, and going to jail was more persuasive. The other board members considered the position they were persuaded to adopt to be a win. It was single-loop in that the board member did not hold open to change his ethical values with respect to conflicts of interest and not violating banking laws. They adopted it voluntarily, unlike a win-lose whistleblowing threat, because it protected them from risking exposure and jail, and they were able to please the chairman by buying his property, albeit at a lower price.

The Quaker accountants at Price-Waterhouse were not open to changing their value of honest financial reporting. They had consistently refused to certify inaccurate financial reports. However, they learned that strictly ethical arguments were less persuasive than win-win presentations that pointed out economic benefits. It was important for clients to understand that they would raise and maintain more capital, at a lower cost, when investors could trust the validity of the financial reports that Price-Waterhouse certified.

As in the West Coast bank case, there are occasions where more directly ethical arguments are persuasive. The bank's community investment director was not open to reconsidering the bank's policy of nondiscrimination regarding sexual orientation. The bank CEO and director were single-loop in that they were not open to reconsidering their value against discrimination by sexual orientation. He used a very straightforward persuasive syllogism with the CEO: It was the bank's policy to support such nondiscrimination; the youth organization stated that it practiced such discrimination; therefore, the bank should not support the youth organization. The CEO agreed with the first premise, was persuaded by the logic of the argument, and acted on it despite severe criticism and loss of deposits and loan assets. Both people considered the outcome win-win in that both won by choosing to do what they believed was ethical. Some observers might argue that the outcome was also win-lose in that the bank lost money.

Peaceful, minimal coexistence is also a type of single-loop action-learning. In the Boston bank affirmative action case, neither the division manager nor the human resources manager were open to reframing of their different ethical positions.

However, both were willing to consider other ways of handling other joint responsibilities, and their interactions moved upward from negative to zero.

In the Middle East negotiations neither the Israeli or Palestinian negotiators were open to changing their views about their historical origins, historical rights, or relative blame for their conflicts. Nonetheless, the killing and injuries have been reduced since they have been able to negotiate other issues.

STRENGTHS AND LIMITATIONS OF SINGLE-LOOP WIN-WIN METHOD

As discussed in chapter 4, the key strength of a politics of forcing is its short-run effectiveness, particularly in emergency situations, while an important limitation is its destructiveness, particularly of internal organization cooperative relationships. Win-win method retains much of the effectiveness of forcing while encouraging cooperation. However, there can be no belief conversion toward the ethical, as occurs with the dialogic methods considered in the next three chapters.

Strengths of Win-Win Method

Win-win method can be both effective and conducive to organizational cooperation. As mentioned in the discussion of the early work of Mayo (1923, 1930c), one of the foundational findings of organization behavior research is that people can be rewarded and not just threatened or forced into appropriate behavior. As illustrated in the twelve cases considered in this chapter, win-win method was effective in advancing the ethical.

In the research company case, the lying behavior was stopped in the project. In the G.E. case, the antitrust behavior was stopped, at least for a while. In the Polaroid and Gillette cases, they did not pay the bribes. In the Elkhorn case, pollution was reduced and the economic base of the community was saved. Schindler saved thirteen hundred people. The Latin American merchant bank did not pay the chairman an inflated price for his land. Price-Waterhouse helped clients prepare honest financial reports. The low-income people improved their nutrition behavior and registered to vote. The West Coast bank remained consistent with its policy of nondiscrimination on the basis of sexual orientation. The violence in the Middle East has been reduced. The destructive interactions between the Boston bank's division manager and human resources manager were reduced.

Furthermore, win-win method encourages further cooperation, since it pays to cooperate. For example, in the research company case, the project manager and the vice president were able to continue working cooperatively with each other. The manager's call-back method spread throughout the organization and she was promoted with support from the vice president. Similarly, because Price-Waterhouse successfully persuaded and helped clients to prepare honest financial reports, it became one of the world's largest public accounting firms, with long-term cooperative relationships with clients, who in turn received lower-cost capital than they would have otherwise. In the Boston bank affirmative action case, cooperation and productivity between the two departments were restored.

Win-win method can be effective without requiring belief conversion among individuals who hold different driving ethical values. In nine of the twelve cases considered in this chapter, ethics was never discussed among the parties to the win-win agreement. The advocates of the ethical behavior for the most part believed that it was easier to work out a win-win agreement than to achieve belief conversion.

In the research company case, the vice president who ordered the lying behavior had said on previous occasions that he knew it was an unethical practice, but it was the way business was done in their industry. The project manager did not believe that it was possible for her to change his belief that the ethical should be overruled by industry practice. But she did believe, correctly, that she could negotiate a change in behavior based on a win-win deal.

The Polaroid managers did not believe they could change the values of the ministry official toward not asking for bribes because it was unethical. But they were able to negotiate a behavior change in the immediate situation and did not have to pay the bribe.

The Elkhorn mill manager did not try to convince his superiors that they should be concerned about the environment or about community impact of a plant closing. Based on past experience, he did not believe they would respond favorably if he framed the issues as ethical. He worked out a win-win solution within a purely financial and strategic framework.

Schindler never discussed with the SS and army officials the ethics of persecuting and killing innocent men, women, and children. He did not believe that he could successfully discuss the ethics of persecuting Jews with these officials. He did believe that he could negotiate win-win deals with them, and he did so.

The bank board member did not believe that he could persuade his colleagues to oppose the chairman for ethical reasons, but was able to appeal to their short-run interest in not being exposed or going to jail.

The Quaker accountants in the early years of Price-Waterhouse did explicitly use ethical arguments in addition to those of economic self-interest. However, for the most part they found that it was generally easier to convince their clients to do honest financial reporting for the sake of economic self-interest than for the sake of ethics.

Win-win method can be effective cross-culturally in cultures that support unethical behavior and across cultures with different ethical values. Different countries can have different cultures that influence organizational behavior with respect to ethics. For example, in some countries bribes, unsafe working conditions, child labor, and antitrust collusion are a more "normal" and culturally accepted part of business than in other countries.

In the cases just considered, bribes, violation of regulatory laws, and cooperation with human rights violations were for the most part normal and expected practice. Many people did not like these practices, but that is a very long way from being willing to act against unethical behavior on the basis of individual ethical beliefs.

In such environments people often believe simultaneously that the corrupt behavior is unethical, that little or nothing can be done about it, and that in a corrupt world one's primary responsibility is to protect one's family and friends. As illustrated in the examples, instead of trying to turn around culturally supported beliefs, it can be easier to reframe the issues as opportunities for win-win solutions.

There can also be direct conflicts between culturally supported beliefs, which can be solved through reframing as opportunities for win-win solutions. For example, in the Middle East, the Israeli negotiators shared their culture's belief that the primary responsibility for unethical terrorist behavior was on the Palestinian side. In a mirror image, the Palestinian negotiators shared their culture's belief that the Israelis were primarily responsible. Instead of trying to change each other's culturally embedded beliefs about who was the more unethical, the negotiators concentrated on reframing the issues as opportunities to reduce negative costs.

Win-win method can be effective with individuals who learn and know more through personal experience than through analytic reasoning. As Simon (1983) has pointed out, some people learn more from personal experience than from analytic reasoning. Such reasoning is key to methods like double-loop dialog, which is discussed in the next chapter. Win-win method can produce effective experiential experiments for such people.

For example, a sales office manager of a very large Boston-area insurance company tried to hire women salespeople several times, but his boss would not permit it. He inquired about why his boss kept refusing to hire a woman. He learned that his boss had never worked with a woman salesperson and did not believe that women could be good salespeople.

He tried to reason with his boss that statistical data supported women being capable salespeople and even that it was illegal to refuse to hire women as salespeople. Such analytic reasoning was irrelevant for his boss, who based most of his decisions on his own past, personal experience. He had prior experience only of women working in home, school, and minor clerical functions, never in effective sales capacities.

The manager inquired within the company about whether there were any insurance sales areas where there might be an advantage in being a woman. He persuaded his boss to allow him, as a six-month experiment, to hire one woman, on a trial basis, to sell life insurance to married women who were contributing large portions of their salaries to their home mortgages. The woman he hired was not only very successful in selling this type of life insurance, but was also very effective in selling other types of insurance to her targeted women customers, as well as their husbands.

After this experience, the boss changed his discriminatory, unethical, and illegal policy of not hiring women salespeople. This person had to have some personal experience of women as capable salespeople before he could seriously consider or discuss his discriminatory policy. Win-win method constructed the experience for this boss, which was then followed by double-loop discussion and belief conversion (Nielsen, 1989a).

Limitations of Win-Win Single-Loop Method

Win-win, as a single-loop method, may foster little, if any, ethical learning or organization culture development. As Braybrooke has observed about Gauthier's book, *Morals By Agreement,* "To accept 'in effect' is not the same thing as accepting with moral concern" (1987, p. 764). Win-win method as ethics action method may not add very much to the building of a culture that values ethics and ethics dialog. It might even detract from the building of such a culture, if we emphasize too much the making of deals for the sake of agreement and peace at the expense of seeking ethical truth. Such a negative effect does not have to happen, but it can if we are not careful.

In some situations win-win solutions are not possible or have limited effectiveness. Sometimes win-win solutions are simply not possible. For example, in the purchasing manager kickback case considered in chapter 4, there might not have been a win-win solution. The purchasing manager was soliciting and receiving bribes from suppliers. If he were to reduce the size of the bribe he wanted, it would still be a bribe. It is not clear that a supplier could have done anything in a win-win manner that was not some form of bribe. Similarly, in the sexual harassment case, at least at the behavioral level, it might not have been possible to work out an ethical win-win solution. One person was harassing another. The victim wanted it stopped. While the harasser did not necessarily have to be fired, at the behavioral level no win-win or compromise solution appeared possible. In the Commonwealth Electric case, there had been extensive bid rigging, which had to stop. No win-win or compromise solution was possible.

Win-win solutions may not be possible where one party refuses to consider win-win alternatives because they are either very idealistic and/or unreasonable. While there are some techniques for successfully getting people to agree to win-win deals who initially refuse, their effectiveness is limited.

For example, while Schindler was able to save thirteen hundred lives, he was not able to save hundreds of his other worker-prisoners and their families. The SS refused to make win-win deals for as many people as he wanted. Sometimes the SS or the army did not respond favorably to his win-win proposals, and sometimes they would break agreements. Schindler himself was arrested on a number of occasions. And if he had tried to save larger numbers of people, it might have been noticed and stopped by other SS people who did not want to make such win-win deals.

Many people in organizations are not very skilled or experienced with win-win method, particularly where ethics issues are involved. Certain people in organizations, particularly those with careers in relatively isolated clerical, analytical, or technical areas, may have had few opportunities to gain interpersonal win-win experiences and skills. Consequently, they may not know how to do win-win method very well even in ordinary circumstances.

Furthermore, some people are good practitioners of win-win method in their normal specialized work lives where they directly discuss the issues they are developing win-win solutions for. But when it comes to developing win-win solutions to ethical problems without mentioning ethics very much or at all, some people are not able to do such indirect integrating very well.

In addition, if the ethics issues are sensitive and difficult, as they often are, there may be additional physiological difficulties. When we are in difficult conflict situations our blood pressure increases, we sweat, our pulse rate goes up, and chemicals such as adrenalin are released into our systems. These physiological changes trigger fight or flight responses, which are not very helpful for calm, detached, win-win problem solving.

Some win-win solutions can be effective yet unethical. Win-win solutions can be ethically problematical. An American telecommunications corporation negotiated a joint venture agreement with a German telecommunications corporation. As part of the agreement, the German company sold the American company's products and services in Africa and parts of the Mediterranean (telecommunications company executive, 1986). In exchange for receiving and selling the American company's technology and services, the German company paid bribes that the American company did not want to pay. The company won in the sense that it did not pay the bribes and got the business. The African and Mediterranean government officials won because they received the bribes and became wealthier. The German company won in that it increased its sales revenue. Unlike the Polaroid and Gillette cases, where no bribes were paid, in this instance bribes were paid.

Similarly, it is a not uncommon practice for many American corporations to pay commissions to local agents or distributors who are not their employees, so that when government officials or other customers require bribes, the agent or distributor pays the bribe. This solution is a win for the corporation because it does not pay the bribe and gets the sale, and for the customer because he receives the bribe. However the situation is also ethically problematical.

Some people believe that it is unethical to use win-win method in addressing ethical issues. If people think ethical issues are black and white, they may think that to integrate is to compromise, to compromise is to give in, and to give in is unethical. Instead of viewing a situation as multi-dimensional, with opportunities for possible trades of various elements, such as not having to pay a bribe in exchange for a different plant location, they view the situation as one-dimensional—either we pay a bribe or we don't pay a bribe. They view all other solutions as unethical or gradations of the unethical, for example paying larger or smaller amounts of a bribe. While sometimes this is the reality, often it is not, as the examples have illustrated.

Compounding this problem, some people may view the issue in another over-simplified way. They may view the issue as whether one does or does not have "the courage to be as an individual" in opposition to powerful others who prefer the unethical (Tillich, 1952). This view, while of course partly correct, may increase the dysfunctional emotionality of the situation. Nor does this view recognize the simultaneous need in organizational life for the "courage to be as a part" (Tillich, 1952; Nielsen, 1984). The dialogic methods considered in the next three chapters address the problem of how to simultaneous be as an individual and be as a part of an organizational community.

6

Double-Loop Dialog Methods

A key benefit of having different types of individuals with diverse skills, experiences, and specializations in an organization is that there is a potential for multiple pieces of information, truth, and insight to come together in addressing an ethics issue or making a decision. Through dialog within diversity we can learn from each other, learn from the dialogic process, and help each other and our organizations develop ethically.

Such mutual ethical learning and development can then inform our behavior, including win-win behavior. And when we act because we believe it is appropriate ethically and not solely for the purpose of obtaining win-win rewards, ethical behavior can last beyond and independently of win-win rewards.

Tillich (1950) considers dialog and dialogic leadership to be transcendent, that is, a way of being that is beyond oneself and immediate others, and can even be beyond the organizations and communities one is a part of. Such behavior presupposes participation in something that transcends the self and the organization to some extent, regardless of whether the self or the organization "wins" or "loses" in the concrete situational sense. It is a faith in processes that can work through individuals and organizations but also transcend them.

The present chapter examines how dialog between individuals retains much of the cooperative effectiveness of win-win method while encouraging mutual ethical learning, mutual ethical belief conversion, and mutual ethical development.

There are at least three types of such dialog methods: iterative

73

Socratic dialog, action-science dialog, and action-inquiry dialog. These methods are discussed in the order of their historical development, with examples of all three, and a fourth in which all three were used at different times.

The methods are then linked to and interpreted within both behavioral science and philosophy theory, and then compared and distinguished from each other. The comparisons of methods are made after the theoretical discussion because understanding the differences among methods depends to some extent on understanding their different theoretical orientations.

Dialog method is then compared to Theory X leadership, Theory Y leadership, industrial democracy, and participative management. Finally, the strengths and limitations of dialog method are considered, including the differing strengths and limitations of the different types. Questions concerning when to use the different methods are also addressed.

ITERATIVE DIALOG

What is iterative Socratic dialog in concrete practice? In such dialog, the "I" does not try to argue down the "Other" in an adversarial or competitive manner. Instead, the I as a partner in the dialogic process assumes and tries with Others to disentangle, find, and bring out truth, pieces of truths, and appropriate actions that might be found within both the partners and the dialog process itself. Driving values are held open to mutual questioning and inquiry. If, when, and to the extent that we act in this way, we become a different type of leader-manager. Instead of focusing on controlling or mastering others, events, issues, or ethics, we serve a process, a process of searching for potential truth.

There are four parts to iterative Socratic dialog method (Gadamer, 1989a; Lawrence, 1984; Nielsen, 1990, 1993e).

1. The I's first motion toward the Other is respectful and friendly.
2. The I asks the Other(s) for a potential solution and helps to consider the positives of that solution.
3. The I asks the Other(s) to help consider the negatives of the potential solution and to iteratively consider other potential solutions, in an attempt to retain the positives and reduce the negatives of earlier solutions.
4. The process continues iteratively until we can't improve the evolving transformed solution.

Following is an example that illustrates that at least some people, some of the time, to some extent, can act, lead, and be in this way.

Emergency financial aid budgeting   The vice president of an American university formed a committee of administrators and faculty to address the question of whether more money needed to be budgeted for financial aid and, if so, where it should come from. The chairperson of the committee was an administrator who had previously been a professor.

1. I's first motion toward the other is respectful, and friendly. The chairperson personally called all the committee members and thanked them for agreeing to be on the committee and to express his appreciation of their serving. At the first committee meeting he addressed them in a friendly manner and briefly introduced each member to the others, praising his or her abilities and experience and mentioning a personal characteristic he found particularly worthwhile and enjoyable.

Next the chairperson asked the committee member from the financial aid office to review the situation. This administrator pointed out that there was a larger increase than expected in the need for financial aid. The university was a private university with an annual tuition, room and board, and fees cost of more than twenty thousand dollars per year. Most of the students came from two-income families where both parents were working full-time. In the current recession, a larger number of parents than expected had lost their jobs, producing a financial crisis for their families. How could they maintain payments to the university without one of the parent's income? The chairperson and this administrator expressed their concern about whether the university had an ethical responsibility to help the students who were having this type of trouble.

A committee member asked the financial aid administrator to estimate how much more money would be needed this year and the next two years. The administrator indicated that the amount needed was about 5 percent of each year's operating budget. A discussion ensued, followed by a consensus conclusion that the university did have a responsibility to try to help such families. The chairperson asked the committee members to look at their calendars and consider alternative dates for a series of meetings. A schedule of dates and times was agreed upon.

2. The I asks the other(s) for a potential solution and helps consider the positives of the potential solution. Before the committee adjourned for the day, the chairperson gave each member a copy of the operating budget. All of them had previously sat on budgeting committees and were familiar with the format and structure of the operating budget. He asked them to consider, for the next meeting, how the university might meet the additional need for financial aid. He specifically stated that at this stage he was not looking for recommendations but only alternatives to be considered.

At the next meeting, tea, coffee, and cookies were placed in the conference room for the committee members. The chairperson again greeted them in a friendly and respectful manner, and before the meeting began, he personally exchanged a few words with each about how he or she was getting along. Because of these informal conversations and people making themselves cups of tea and coffee, the meeting began about fifteen minutes late. The chairperson sat down in one of four chairs along the long part of a rectangular table, and within a few seconds the others also sat around the table.

After again thanking the committee members for coming, he reviewed what had transpired at the first meeting, and asked whether anyone would be willing to start the discussion with a potential solution. A faculty member suggested that the university could save five percent from the operating budget by laying off about 10 percent of the administrative staff, including clerical, blue collar, and administrative personnel. The committee member added that such downsizing was currently common practice among area businesses. A number of people began to talk at once. The chairperson asked if they wouldn't mind first considering the advantages and then the disadvantages of this alternative before proceeding to the discussion of other alternatives. They agreed.

The committee member from the budgeting office said that it appeared that this action would produce the needed savings. Another committee member pointed out that it would produce them quickly. Another added that if all the cuts came from the administrative side, the academic strengths of the university would not be hurt very much. Another thought such cuts might also give the university opportunities to improve administrative efficiency.

3. The I asks the other(s) to help consider the negatives of the potential solution and iteratively consider other potential solutions in an attempt to retain the positives and reduce the negatives of earlier solutions. The chairperson then asked the committee to consider the disadvantages of this solution and how it might be improved. One committee member said he did not think it was fair that the administrative side should have to absorb all the suffering and that it might not be necessary to lay off anyone if there was a hiring freeze and early retirements were offered. The chairperson asked the representative from the budgeting office how much could be saved in this way. He said he would need a few days to make the estimates. The chairperson suggested that the committee adjourn until the meeting scheduled for the following week when the estimates would be ready.

4. The process continues iteratively until we can't improve the evolving transformed solution. The meetings continued. Several committee members agreed that it was not fair for the administrative side

to absorb all the cuts and that it would also be bad for morale and future cooperation. It was also pointed out that different departments depended on different amounts of services from the administration. Across-the-board cuts would disproportionately effect different academic programs. An across-the-university hiring freeze would produce about 2 of the needed 5 percent. Early retirements might produce additional savings, but would take too long to implement.

The committee agreed to a university-wide hiring freeze, but with some flexibility. Deans, department chairs, and administrative managers would be permitted to make cases for exceptions. Additional cuts were made in nonpersonnel operating expenses such as travel, noncapital building improvements, delayed maintenance, and so forth. Through these iterative improvements, about 4 percent of the savings were made. A suggestion was made to do short-term borrowing to finance the difference, thus avoiding layoffs. The additional resources were transferred to financial aid. The financial aid office concluded that to their knowledge, because of the additional financial aid, no students had to leave the university because a parent lost a job.

ACTION-SCIENCE DIALOG

Argyris, Putnam, and Smith (1985) have developed several behavioral rules that are designed to implement Argyris and Schon's (1974) method of action-science dialog. Unlike iterative Socratic method, the implementation rules of Argyris, Putnam, and Smith (1985) do not necessarily proceed in sequence. They operationalize the method as follows (1985, pp. 258–261):

Rule 1: Combine advocacy with inquiry
Rule 2: Illustrate your inferences with relatively directly observable data
Rule 3: Make your reasoning explicit and publicly test for agreement at each inferential step
Rule 4: Actively seek disconfirming data and alternative explanations
Rule 5: Affirm the making of mistakes in the service of learning
Rule 6: Actively inquire into your impact on the learning context
Rule 7: Design ongoing experiments to test competing views

The following example illustrates the action-science dialog method.

Robert Daniels—Somerdale factory   Robert Daniels was the manufacturing manager of the Somerdale factory of Cadburys during the period 1969–77 and later the manufacturing manager of the confectionary division. He implicitly used the seven rules from Argyris, Putnam, and Smith in his work with the factory's joint production committee (Smith, Child, and Rowlinson, 1990).

Combine advocacy with inquiry. Daniels argued to the joint production committee that productivity at the plant should be improved
through reductions of the number of employees, changes in work
organization, increased capital investment, and rewards to employees
for productivity improvement. Layoffs were considered an ethics issue at Cadburys. Adrian Cadbury, the CEO, considered the issue of
technology displacing workers both an ethics and productivity problem. In referring specifically to business ethics, technological change,
and worker displacement, he has stated:

> The . . . aspect of ethics in business decisions I want to discuss concerns
> our responsibility for the level of employment; what can or should com
> panies do about the provision of jobs? . . . The company's prime respon
> sibility to everyone who has a stake in it is to retain its competitive edge, even
> if this means a loss of jobs in the short run. Where companies do have a
> social responsibility, however, is in how we manage that situation, how we
> smooth the path of technological change. Companies are responsible for
> the timing of such changes and we are in a position to involve those who will
> be affected by the way in which those changes are introduced. (1987, p. 72)

Illustrate your inferences with relatively directly observable data. Daniels
presented to the joint production committee financial data on items
such as the costs of unit hand-packing of chocolates, outputs per
worker per minute, the costs of fixed capital, the costs of redundancy
payments to laid-off workers, savings from past productivity improvements, and increases in wages that were tied to past productivity improvements.

*Make your reasoning explicit and publicly test for agreement at each
inferential step.* Daniels went through each stage of his reasoning with
members of the committee. Areas considered were staff reductions
and changes in work organization that would increase productivity,
increased compensation for remaining workers that would be tied to
productivity gains, and the comparative costs and benefits with automation. At each stage of his presentations he asked the members of
the committee for their perceptions and judgments about whether his
reasoning made sense.

Actively seek disconfirming data and alternative explanations. Daniels
asked production engineers and cost accountants from outside the
committee to check the data and reasoning of different proposals
considered by the committee. For example, the accounts committee
agreed with his numerical analyses, but were concerned that if his plan
worked, then the compensation of the production workers might rise
to as high or higher than the trades (skilled crafts) workers. The

accountants advised Daniels and the joint production committee that this might cause some problems with the trades workers, who were traditionally paid more than the relatively unskilled production workers since they were skilled in such trades as metal working, carpentry, and machine maintenance.

Affirm the making of mistakes in the service of learning. Daniels indicated to the joint production committee as well as higher-level Cadburys management that it was important to take risks at the department level in the service of learning that might benefit the whole plant, the division, and the company. He went over examples where all three had benefitted from taking risks even when the risk-taking turned out less well than hoped for.

Actively inquire into your impact on the learning context. As a member of the joint production committee, Daniels regularly inquired not only about the substantive issues but also the process and his role in it.

Design ongoing experiments to test competing views. The joint production committee that Daniels founded used experimentation for testing proposed changes in production methods and systems. For the most part, the experiments the committee undertook worked well. Productivity rose, staffing was reduced with the agreement of representatives of the production workers, and wage gains tied to productivity improvements brought the compensation of the production workers up to the level of the trades employees.

For the most part, this use of the elements of action-science method worked well. However, there was at least one exception. At one point, after Daniels had been promoted to divisional manufacturing manager, he advocated that instead of a radical labor elimination automation approach advocated by the technical director and the human resources vice president, Cadburys should adopt a labor intensification approach whereby output would gradually be expanded with current or gradually reduced numbers of workers through gradual technological advancement and productivity improvement. In spite of the experimental evidence that such an approach would work, the technical director and the human resources vice president were committed to the radical automation approach and rejected Daniels' experiment-supported alternative. It takes two to dialog. Apparently, while Daniels was able to advocate, inquire, actively seek disconfirming data, and listen to the results of the experiment, his immediate superiors were not so open (Smith, Child, and Rowlinson, 1990).

The technical director, George Piercy, rejected the results of the experiment because it was not supportive of his plan to introduce radical automation. Part of his motivation for this rejection appeared to be his desire to reduce the power of employee participation within

Cadburys. He was later removed from his position. But in this particular case dialogic method was blocked, at least in the short run, by power-backed win-lose adversarial method. This point is further discussed later.

ACTION-INQUIRY DIALOG

Torbert describes action-inquiry method as follows (1987, p. 240):

1. Framing—the frame or purpose of the current endeavor, setting, or conversation; not just the speaker's goal, but the frame or purpose that underlies everyone's participation.
2. Advocating—what the speaker advocates be done within the frame.
3. Illustrating—a concrete example to clarify what the speaker is referring to.
4. Inquiring—a question about how others respond to the speaker's perspective and initiative.

An example follows of how action-inquiry method was effective in addressing an ethics issue.

Tom's of Maine   Tom Chappell is the cofounder and CEO of Tom's of Maine, an "all-natural personal-care products" company. He decided that he wanted his board of directors to incorporate Martin Buber's "I and Thou" spiritual philosophy into the corporation's mission statement, but he also wanted to hold this proposal open to dialog. He considered his motivation as primarily ethical. His company was already successful and growing at a rate greater than 20 percent a year. He explains, "I wanted them all to know that Tom's of Maine could embody an alternative to the soulless, grim, numbers-dominated approach of American business as usual. Since it was Martin Buber who had opened my eyes, I decided to let Buber open theirs" (1993, p. 22). He implicitly used action-inquiry dialog method.

Framing. Chappell explains how he framed the purpose of the next board meeting. "I bought two dozen copes of *I and Thou* and brazenly sent them to every member of the board. . . . I included a note explaining my enthusiasm for the book and an invitation to read it and then join Professor Richard Niebuhr of the Harvard Divinity School and me for a Sunday afternoon discussion. I was so fired up about my little seminar that I actually called around to the secretaries and told them to make sure Buber got into their bosses' briefcases" (1993, p. 23).

Advocating. Chappell advocated to the board that the board adopt a formal mission statement for the company that included elements of Buber's philosophy and then, consistent with that statement, apply

Buber's ideas to the company's business practices and relationships with customers, employees, distributors, suppliers, and the local community.

Illustrating. Chappell offered several concrete examples to both clarify what he had in mind and explain how the application of Buber's ideas had already been successful in maintaining and increasing the productivity and profitability of the company. He also asked Professor Richard Niebuhr of the Harvard Divinity School to help him explain concretely what Buber's ideas were and what those ideas might look like in business contexts.

Inquiring. Chappell asked the board members for their reactions to his and Professor Niebuhr's perspective and initiative. A general discussion was followed by small group discussions. He described the process as follows:

> Against the odds, my Buber strategy was a success. Professor Niebuhr charmed my board and the other hard-liners, and his lecture stimulated a general discussion about relationships in the world of business and about treating customers as more than statistics, as more than objects in one marketing category or another. Then we broke up into groups of four and five . . . to discuss how we might apply Buber's ideas to our lives and business practices. . . . I had actually gotten a group of businesspeople to forget their charts and objectives for a time and reflect on what genuine relationships with each other, with employees, and with customers might look like. (Chappell, 1993, p. 23)

The board accepted Chappell's proposal, agreeing to the following formal mission statements related to Buber's ideas: "We believe that both human beings and nature have inherent worth and deserve our respect. . . . We believe that we have a responsibility to cultivate the best relationships possible with our co-workers, customers, owners, agents, suppliers, and our community . . . to respect, value, and serve not only our customers, but also our co-workers, owners, agents, suppliers, and our community; to be concerned about and contribute to their well-being, and to operate with integrity so as to be deserving of their trust" (Chappell, 1993, pp. 32–33).

A series of meetings over the next few months explored how to translate the mission statement into specific strategies and those strategies into implementation tactics. Action-inquiry as method continued to be used, with the exception of Professor Niebuhr's participation. These meetings were led by Chappell and his senior executives.

The following example illustrates elements of iterative, action-science, and action-inquiry dialog methods.

Challenger Launch Roger Boisjoly successfully used iterative Socratic method within Morton Thiokol, Inc. the night before the Challenger launch, helping the group of Morton Thiokol engineers to understand and recommend to NASA that the Challenger should not be launched. Argyris and Schon also use this example to illustrate how the subsequent communication between Morton Thiokol and NASA was single-loop adversarial rather than double-loop dialogic. The iterative dialog within Morton Thiokol broke down and became adversarial in the subsequent conversation with NASA.

(The direct quotations that follow are from the Report of the Presidential Commission, ABC, and Roger Boisjoly, *Report of the Presidential Commission on the Space Shuttle Challenger Accident*, 1986; McConel, 1987; American Broadcasting Company and George Englund, 1988; Argyris and Schon, 1988; Boisjoly, Curtis, and Mellican, 1989; Nielsen, 1989a, 1990, 1993e.)

The day before the Challenger launch, the Air Force informed J. C. Kilminster, the vice president of the space booster program of Morton Thiokol, that the temperature at the scheduled launch time was expected to be 29 degrees. At a meeting of Morton Thiokol engineers and managers, Kilminster began a Socratic dialog with the question, "Any elements on the solid rocket that this cold will affect?" Using a more iterative Socratic than action-science or action-inquiry method, he did not advocate a position; he asked a question.

Arnie Thompson, the supervisor of rocket motor cases, responded, "The O-rings is the main one." Roger Boisjoly, the senior scientist and rocket seal expert, elaborated, "The O-rings are made of rubber, and rubber is affected by cold, so we know we have some kind of problem." Boisjoly then led an iterative dialog among Morton Thiokol engineers and managers concerning the potential positives and negatives associated with various alternatives such as proceeding as scheduled, recommending against launch, de-icing, delaying for a few hours, and so forth. The consensus conclusion emerged that the launch should be cancelled.

Up to this point, at least in hindsight, through iterative dialog Kilminster, Boisjoly, Thompson, and other team members were successful with respect to both learning and action. Boisjoly and his colleagues learned that there were serious safety dangers involved with the cold-hardened O-rings, and acted to reverse the tentative conclusion to launch.

Boisjoly, Kilminster, and Thompson then used aspects of double-loop action inquiry method and single-loop persuasion/adversarial advocacy in their conversations with NASA. These methods were not effective. They spoke with NASA representatives using action-inquiry, that is, advocacy with inquiry: Kilminster began by saying, "Earlier today we were informed about the extremely low temperatures predicted for tomorrow morning's launch. The main question we're looking at is how the O-rings in the solid rocket booster will be affected. . . . Arnie Thompson and Roger Boisjoly have been doing the research . . . Arnie?" Thompson responds, "We have no data on O-rings operating at temperatures this low, but we have put together a rationale based on the information we do have. . . ." Boisjoly continues, "I'll begin by citing Flight 15 which was launched a year ago. The temperature at that launch was 53 degrees which is the coldest reading experienced to date. . . . Any questions so far? . . . the Air Force estimates 29 degrees at launch tomorrow now. That is far below temperatures we have launched with before, so determining if this extreme cold will effect the O-rings, and if it does, how much, is critical. . . . The indication is that the cold-hardened O-rings will be slower in sealing. Therefore, there could be hot gas leakage past the primary seal and because of that increased danger of the backup O-rings getting eroded." Robert Lund concludes, "So our recommendation is . . . not launching until the temperature is at least 53 degrees."

NASA hears the advocacy part but does not appear to hear the invitation to mutual inquiry. A negative escalation ensues. NASA responds, "Wow! Wait a minute. . . . You are making very serious recommendations." Boisjoly appears to become defensive and to abandon his action-inquiry approach. Rather than with any type of double-loop dialog, he responds adversarily. "Serious recommendations are called for." NASA further objects, somewhat sarcastically, "You now want to base everything on this 53 degrees benchmark. At that rate it could be spring before the shuttle would fly. My God Thiokol! When do you want to launch, next April?"

Lund appears to try to restore some of the inquiring, objective, questioning nature of the conversation, "We're trying to see if it's safe to launch with the O-rings experiencing these severe temperatures." Conversation continues. However, Boisjoly has by now also slipped into an adversarial single-loop approach. "All I'm saying is that launching below freezing is an act away from goodness. . . . It's away from goodness to make any other recommendation." Kilminster supports Boisjoly. "Based on this presentation by Morton Thiokol, I can't recommend the launch." NASA continues in an adversarial manner, "I'm appalled that Morton Thiokol could arrive at the recommendation not to launch . . . especially so late the evening before a launch."

Kilminster tells NASA that Morton Thiokol would like to go off line for five minutes and caucus. Jerry Mason, the Morton Thiokol senior vice president at the caucus, says to the Morton Thiokol engineers and managers, "We have a management decision as much as an engineering decision. . . . It makes an impression on me if George Hardy [NASA] is appalled at something we recommend." Arnie Thompson responds, "Everything we do have shows that we'll be safer lauching at 53 degrees or above." Boisjoly continues, "That's clear! That's absolutely clear!"

Mason asks, "Am I the only one who wants to fly?" According to Boisjoly, "there was not one positive pro launch statement ever made by anybody" at the caucus. Mason tells Bob Lund, the vice president of engineering, "It's time to make a decision . . . take off your engineering [dialogic?] hat and put on your management hat." Back on the line with NASA, Kilminster obeys and says to NASA, "This is Kilminster. We have assessed the data and reviewed our charts. [There does not appear to have been much further review of charts, photographs, or data.] Even though we had some concerns about the low temperatures, we now recommend proceeding with the launch."

The next day the Challenger was launched and exploded, and all the crew members died.

While Socratic iterative dialog as learning method continued to be effective within Morton Thiokol with respect to its way of knowing and learning about what was ethical, it was not effective as action or learning method in withstanding the pressure from NASA. As Argyris and Schon have observed, "The Challenger disaster illustrates both how individuals with power were able to impose their views and how those who lost avoided embarrassment by . . . compliance" (1988, p. 210). In this case Boisjoly, Thompson, and Kilminster were not able to

> break through the . . . defensive routines that discourage the expression of relevant, valid information because it is potentially threatening or embarrassing. For example, some engineers opposed to the launching began to believe that their superiors were closed to further inquiry because . . . these engineers were made to assume the burden of proving that the shuttle should not fly. Indeed, some of them never became explicitly aware of the difference in the stance they were being asked to take [away from dialog] until the investigating commission called it to their attention. (Argyris and Schon, 1988, p. 210)

The earlier consensus recommendation of the company had been to not launch. To this point, Kilminster, Boisjoly, and Thompson were very effective in leading a Socratic type dialog. Emerging from this prior dialog was the consensus conclusion among the dialog participants that the safer and more ethical decision was to not launch.

This case illustrates that there are important differences between the perspectives of organization ethics learning and action, between single- and double-loop action-learning, and among the iterative, action-science, and action-inquiry elements of action-learning. (This is not to suggest that types of conversations were the only important factors in this case. Other contributing factors included individual courage limitations [Boisjoly, Curtis, and Mellican, 1989], analytic problem-solving limitations [Clarke, 1988], and organizational-level flaws in management procedures and technical design [Vaughan, 1990, 1996].)

While this is only speculation, one can wonder whether, if some of the NASA and/or Astronaut people had been brought earlier into the internal Morton Thiokol dialog, the subsequent degeneration into single-loop adversarial conversations could have been mitigated. To further speculate with the benefit of hindsight: Since dialogic ation-learning failed—either because it takes two to dialog, or action-inquiry was heard much more as adversarial advocacy than inquiry, or because Boisjoly and Thompson were not able to implement dialogic method appropriately with NASA—perhaps they should have considered a single-loop "guerilla" approach such as secretly blowing the whistle within NASA to someone like the chief of astronauts or outside NASA to a newspaper or congressperson.

THEORY

Iterative Dialog and Socrates

Plato's *Republic* presents the classical ideal of the "philosopher-leader." A key method of the philosopher-leader, as for example in the *Symposium,* is iterative dialog. The Greek word for dialog was "dialectic." This has since come to represent a wide range of change and transformation processes. Through Socratic dialog we simultaneously learn and act civically with others in social, political contexts.

According to Gadamer, when we use Socratic dialog the achievement of individual ojectives is subordinate. Instead, the realization of two transcendent, transpersonal aims is primary: (1) dialogic action (praxis, not poiesis) as an end in itself and (2) dialog as a way of learning (epistemology) a potentially common and true ethical perspective for a common, transcendent world of meaning (Gadamer, 1989a, pp. 331, 404).

According to Lawrence, "this pursuit, this search, is what saves the partners from manipulativeness as well as from extremes of trivialization and fanaticism" (1984, p. 24). Such an important, independent truth intention is different from what Roethlisberger, in the tradition of Mayo, described—in his discussion of integrative, participative management—as "human controls exercised by the administrator," or the "intelligent exercising of control" (Roethlisberger, 1941, pp. 192–193).

An intense truth intention, detached to some extent from specific preconceived outcomes, is the key operating principle. There is less or relatively little individual will to power, but a significant will to truth. In Gadamer's words, the questioners are simultaneously called into question:

> [Dialog] is the art of questioning and of seeking truth. . . . To conduct a dialog means to allow oneself to be conducted by the subject matter to which the partners in the dialog are oriented. It requires that one does not try to argue the other person down but that one really considers the weight of the other's opinion. Hence it is an art of testing. But the art of testing is the art of questioning. For we have seen that to question means to lay open, to place in the open. As against the fixity of opinions, questioning makes the object and all its possibilities fluid. A person skilled in the art of questioning is a person who can prevent questions from being suppressed by the dominant opinion. A person who possesses this art will himself search for everything in favor of an opinion. Dialectic consists not in trying to discover the weakness of what is said, but in bringing out its real strength. (Gadamer, 1989a, pp. 366–367)

In this sense, Socratic dialog is more a type of praxis in Aristotle's sense: It is a way of acting in which the method is also important for its own sake. It is not a form of poiesis, where the action's value is independent of its means, as in win-lose forcing and win-win integrating methods, whose criteria are primarily instrumental effectiveness.

Action-science Dialog and Habermas

Argyris, Putnam, and Smith directly link action-science method with the work of Habermas. They explain: "Action science is not alone in advocating that communities of inquiry be enacted in communities of practice. This formulation also seems appropriate to critical theory as articulated by theorists of the Frankfurt School (Habermas, 1971; Geuss, 1981). Habermas speaks of creating conditions that approximate the 'ideal speech situation,' which would allow human beings to come to a rational consensus about how to conduct their affairs. To our knowledge, however, Habermas has not devoted his energies to creating such conditions in the real world" (Argyris, Putnam, and Smith, 1985, p. 35).

At least four key elements in Argyris, Putnam, and Smith's action-science method are related to Habermas' philosophy of critical, "communicative action." These are: intention, dialectic process, the phenomena in conflict, and the validity criterion. First, the intention of the dialog is not so much knowledge for its own sake as critical and imaginative improvement in the status quo. Second, there is a dialectic transformation process that includes empirical, interpretative, and normative moments. Third, the phenomena in conflict can be ideas rather than individuals or groups. Fourth, the key criterion for validity claims is consensus in an open community of practice.

Intention. Habermas adopts the normative position that theory and science can and should offer a perspective for criticism of the status quo. That is, the intention of criticism is less knowledge for its own sake than knowledge in relation to practical problems of human existence. Critical talk is considered a form of political action with a sociopolitical purpose. Similar to Aristotle's concept of a poetics of ethics, Habermas advocates criticism of the status quo from a perspective of what might be.

Dialectic process. In Habermas' theory of communicative action there is an interpenetration and combination of empirical, interpretive, and normative perspectives and moments in a change process. There is an affirmation moment when social institutions, relationships and behaviors are empirically described. There is a negation moment when aspects of social institutions, relationships, and behaviors are interpreted critically. There is a transformation moment when improvements are imagined and consensus is built for transformed institutions, relationships, and behaviors.

Phenomena in conflict. As with Socrates, Habermas maintains the possibility that conflicts in ideas about institutions, relationships, and behaviors can be considered without individuals being personally in conflict. That is, it is possible to reason together about differences in empirical descriptions, interpretative criticism, and normative changes without being in personal conflict with each other. Habermas is very well aware of the severe difficulties in doing so.

Validity criterion. The key validity criterion for Habermas is the consensus formed in a community of open inquiry and practice. He recognizes and values the moment of empirical social description and experimentation. Similarly, he recognizes and values the moment of hermeneutic, even aesthetic, critical interpretation. However, the intention of "communicative action" is improvement and change in the status quo in the moment of action. That is, the focus of the approach is practice and the people acting together in practice. With the benefit of empirical testing, critical interpretation, and open dialog about how to transform the status quo, repeated and evolving consensus building takes place. What one generation considers subjective improvement is the object of the next generation's subjective criticism and further change. Unlike classical Socratic method, this method has less hope that there are eternal universals. This is one of the areas where there may be some divergence between action-science method and communicative action theory. Action science method appears to have much more confidence in the idea and hope of progress than does Habermas.

Action-Inquiry and Hegel's Philosophy of Action

In his writings about action-inquiry method, Torbert links it to action-science theory (Argyris, 1962, 1965, 1970; Argyris and Schon, 1974), developmental psychology (Kohlberg, 1969; Loevinger, 1976, 1978; Kegan, 1982), philosophy (Hegel, 1807, 1977; 1837, 1975; Husserl, 1962, 1965), and spiritual philosophy (Ouspensky, 1949; Maritain, 1954). The focus of the following discussion is limited to the links between action-inquiry method and Hegel's developmental philosophy of action.

Torbert is concerned with both types of action. In contrast with Habermas' emphasis on theory development as a challenge to the status quo of the external sociopolitical world, Torbert is more concerned with action-inquiry as praxis, that is, as method for helping actors change developmentally. This is not to suggest that action-inquiry is concerned only with internal-to-the-actor change, or that action-science is concerned only with theory development as an intervention method in the external sociopolitical world, rather it is an issue of nuance. This point is further discussed in the next section.

Torbert explains that his own work

> was originally inspired by Argyris' distinctions and attempts to build on the foundation of his [Argyris'] work. This . . . body of work [Torbert's] also builds on two other resources—constructive-developmental theory and the tradition of search for an integrative quality of awareness. . . . Developmental theory describes different stages from which and to which managers and organizations transform. . . . Both the Argyris and Schon intervention skills and integrative awareness should be associated with persons at later stages of development. (Torbert, 1989, pp. 88–89)

That is, from Torbert's perspective, action-learning method, when appropriately lived and applied, can help both individual and organizational development, including ethical development.

Torbert's developmental method of action-inquiry dialog is related to Hegel's concept of action as an interpenetration of Aristotle's concepts of poiesis (action that changes the external world) and praxis (action that also changes the actor). Aristotle used the analogy of physical production. In poiesis the end or purpose is in the things made, and "making has as an end other than itself" (1955, N. Ethics, 6, 1140b5).

With praxis, the actor is concerned with changes inside the actor: "good action itself is its end" (1955, N. Ethics, 6, 1140b6). Aristotle ranks praxis as a higher form of action than poiesis.

For Hegel, there is interpenetration and unity (not identity) of both types of action, and it is in this space that developmental "becoming" occurs. In his *Philosophy of Right* (1821) he states that one's ethical development proceeds as one acts in such a way as "to make oneself a member of a moment in civil society by one's own act" (1953, p. 207). The emphasis here is upon action as participation that is both meaningful to one's own "becoming" and, in its external effects, to civil society.

Planty-Bonjour elaborates on this key point as follows:

> Hegel loses sight neither of the subjective principle of action: purpose and intention, nor of the objective result of action: morality in the family, the civil society, and the state. Hegel would not say, as Aristotle has said, that the end of moral action stays inside the agent, as if nothing could be more justified than to ignore the concrete outcomes. But, on the other hand, Hegel refuses to judge the quality of the moral action only by the outcomes. Hegel's doctrine is not the ethic of the consciousness concerned only with the intention of the acting subject. It is not a pragmatic ethics concerned only with external actions. (1983, p. 25)

Instead, Hegel's concept of action is the dynamic and potentially developmental interpenetration of both action as internal experience and action as effect on the external world.

SIMILARITIES AND DIFFERENCES AMONG DIALOG METHODS

Iterative, action-science, and action-inquiry dialog may be compared in several ways—as types of double-loop action-learning; regarding their focus on advocacy relative to inquiry; and in reference to the nuance of praxis relative to poiesis, validity criteria, and their friendly affect.

Double-Loop Action-Learning

All three methods are forms of double-loop action-learning, holding open for question and change both driving values and the instrumental actions for achieving them. For example, in the financial aid case where iterative method was used, the driving values of compassion for family financial burdens, employment security, academic versus administrative resource priority, and financial prudence were held open to question and reformulation. Similarly, instrumental actions such as layoffs, hiring freezes, borrowing, and early retirement were held open to question and adoption.

In the Daniels case, with action-science method, the driving values considered had to do with productivity improvement, technological

leadership, profitability, employment security, and consensus decisionmaking. The instrumental actions considered were radical automation, gradual automation, selling jobs, and employment attrition.

In the Tom's of Maine case, with action-inquiry method, the relevant driving values were about the organization's reason for being and
the nature of its business relationships. Instrumental actions such as
different types of mission statements and methods for discussing the
issues were held open to question and adoption.

In the Challenger case, in the initial iterative dialog, Boisjoly and
others within Morton Thiokol held open the driving values of safety
and customer (NASA) satisfaction. Similarly, instrumental actions
such as delaying the launch, going ahead with the launch as scheduled, and pouring warm water on the O-rings to prevent freezing
were held open.

Focus on Advocacy Relative to Inquiry

Socrates' philosopher-leader inquired and led the dialog, but did not
advocate. Both action-science and action-inquiry combine advocacy
with inquiry. This is a key difference. Socrates inquired about positives and negatives associated with others' positions, and with others
he iteratively generated additional alternatives that tried to affirm the
positives and reduce the negatives associated with previous alternatives. He led the dialog but did not advocate an initial position. This
can be very important, as in the Challenger case, when people only
hear advocacy and do not hear or do not believe the inquiry part
because the advocacy appears so strong.

A similar outcome can occur in a normal hierarchical boss-sub-
ordinate relationship. If a boss advocates and then inquires, subordinates may not want to risk offending him by responding to the inquiry
with a different perspective. In such situations Socratic method can be
more effective in eliciting different or opposing perspectives from
subordinates.

Nuance of Praxis Relative to Poiesis

All three methods recognize and attend to the need for Hegelian
interpenetration and unity of poiesis and praxis. However, there are
nuances among the methods with respect to this issue.

The nuance in iterative Socratic method is toward internal-to-the-
actor change—toward method for its own sake. However, Socrates
was killed by the political authorities in Athens because they were
worried about the disruptive effectiveness of his method on the Athenian sociopolitical world.

Argyris, Putnam, and Smith (1985) link action-science method directly to Habermas' theory of communicative action. Habermas emphasizes theory development as a challenge to the status quo of the external sociopolitical world. Consistent with this orientation, Argyris and Schon call their method action-science. The term science is important because it shares with Habermas the concern for a reformulation of social science theory as a challenge to the status quo.

In contrast, Torbert calls his method action-inquiry rather than action-science. While both methods are concerned with both individual and organizational change and development, the nuance is different. Torbert is somewhat more concerned with action-inquiry as praxis, that is, as method for helping actors change internally and developmentally. As such, this method is tied to an elaborate stage theory of personal and organizational development (Torbert, 1987).

The implicit intentions of these authors are not necessarily related to these methods' effectiveness for either internal or external change and development. While the nuance of action-science method leans toward the external and the nuance of Socratic and action-inquiry methods leans toward the internal, it is possible that these nuances may correspond little or even inversely, to each method's actual relative effectiveness for internal versus external change. To some extent this is an empirical question that has not been tested. It would be very difficult to do such testing.

Validity Criteria

For all three methods validity resides at least partially in the consensus of the dialog participants. With iterative Socratic method, as Gadamer has explained, participation in Socratic dialog is "subordinating oneself to the tutelage, the leadership, the guidance of the subject matter to which the partners in the conversations are oriented" (Gadamer, 1989a, p. 367). Validity lies in where the dialogic process among the partners takes us—in the evolving consensus. This validity is temporary, since in Socratic dialog the conversation is never completely finished.

With action-science method, validity also lies in the dialogic process within the community of practice. However, experimentation which was not part of classical Greek epistemology, is an important part of this method. Here again, the word science is important. The design of experiments and the interpretation of experimental data are included within the action-science process.

As with Socratic method, experimentation is not explicitly part of action-inquiry method, and validity lies in the evolving consensus within the community of practice. However, within the "illustrating"

moment of action-inquiry there is the opportunity for the presentation and consideration of directly observable empirical data that could
include experimental data if such data were available.

Friendly Affect

Unlike iterative Socratic dialog, where friendly affect is explicity visible, action-science and action-inquiry methods are, at least initially,
explicitly objective, "professional," and confronting. For Socrates,
friendly affect was important both for praxis and poiesis. Friendliness
and love were important values for Socrates that needed to be lived
and expressed for personal development as well as understood. He
also recognized, as did the Sophists, that friendly affect tends to reduce fear and defensiveness, which in turn permits greater openness
to the "tutelage of the dialogic process" (Gadamer, 1989, p. 366) and
therefore the external effectiveness of the method. This is particularly
important for those very large parts of the world where public and
work life is built upon a foundation of family and friendship relationships, rather than the northeast United States and northern Europe
where the two are often separated.

Argyris writes about his method as if friendly affect were not part of
action-science relative to objective, professional, and rigorous analysis
and expression. However, among the few times I have personally
observed Argyris, he has also exhibited friendly, caring, and personally
respectful affect. This can be very powerful and can contribute both to
the praxis and poiesis processes of dialog participants, including myself, when I have had opportunities to be present when he lives his
method in this manner.

I have also seen discussion suppressed when less powerful people in
a group misinterpret the rigor of proof required by action-science
method to be in the service of powerful people more interested in
maintaining the status quo than in genuine dialog. If a less powerful
person tries to challenge the status quo, a more powerful person can
resist change through both silence with respect to the status quo and
rigorous challenge of the new, in effect intimidating the challenger.
However, the point of action-science is to challange the status quo.

Torbert (1994) considers the development of friendship relationships both an important motivation for and a developmental outcome
of action-inquiry method. That is, one uses this method in part because one is concerned about the development of friendship and community in work relationships.

The explicit intentions of all these authors are not necessarily related to friendship-relationship outcomes. It is possible that these
methods are similarly or even inversely effective in the development

of affective relationships. This question is to some extent also an empirical one that has not been tested. The issue, again, is less one of either/or than it is of nuance.

SIMILARITIES AND DIFFERENCES AMONG DIALOG METHOD AND THEORY X LEADERSHIP, THEORY Y LEADERSHIP, INDUSTRIAL DEMOCRACY, AND PARTICIPATIVE MANAGEMENT

Dialogic method is related to but different from Theory X leadership, Theory Y leadership, industrial democracy, and participative management methods. In terms of how leaders act (e.g., McGregor, 1960), as opposed to the results of their actions (e.g., Burns, 1978; Bass, 1985), there are at least three types of leadership approaches: Theory X, Theory Y, and dialogic.

Dialog versus Theory X and Theory Y Leadership

Theory X or compelling, coercive leadership begins with the assumption that at least in the specific situation, the Others who are involved dislike doing the right thing (McGregor, 1960). The objective of Theory X leadership is for the I to compel these Others to adopt or obey the "right" orders of the I. Tactics, which typically are adversarial and coercive, include force, rules, threats, and punishments. Some advocates of this approach even suggest that many people generally prefer authoritarian direction.

Theory Y or win-win, integrative leadership begins with a different assumption—that people have an inherent desire to do the right thing. The objective is to integrate the I, the Other, and organizational goals and needs. Tactics are typically integrative, for example exploration of solutions that satisfy both organizational and individual needs (McGregor, 1960). For its time, and relative to a Theory X method, Theory Y was a new conception of leadership in the sense that the leader (1) recognizes that others generally want to do good work, (2) listens to subordinates, (3) cares about their sentiments, and (4) integrates their sentiments in a way that will make them willing to contribute their services to the economic objective of the organization.

Theory Y was not new in the sense that the leader continued to make mostly unilateral decisions. What was new was the focus of the decision on how best to integrate individual, group, and organizational needs. This new conception is viewed as effective "human controls exercised by the administrator. . . . This is the intelligent exercising of control" (Roethlisberger, 1941, pp. 192–193). The emphasis is on consensus-building that focuses on the value-free or value-neutral optimization of organizational objectives, constrained by the need to integrate at some level of satisfaction the needs of individuals and constituencies (Nielsen, 1981). Drucker interpreting Herbert Simon's concept of optimal satisficing, explains:

> A manager . . . needs to think through what the constituencies are that can effectively veto and block . . . decisions, and what their minimum expectations and needs should be. This is bound to induce a certain schizophrenia. When it comes to the performance of the primary task of an institution . . . the rule is to optimize. . . . But in dealing with the constituencies outside and beyond this narrow definition of the primary task, managers have to think politically—in terms of the minimum needed to placate and appease and keep quiet constituent groups that otherwise might use their power of veto. Managers cannot be politicians. They cannot confine themselves to "satisficing" decisions. But they also cannot be concerned only with optimization in the central area of performance of their institution. They have to balance both approaches in one continuous decision making process. (1980, pp. 211–213)

With such approaches to integration there is little dialog and mutual inquiry. There is little concern for any transcendent value beyond the optimization of the organization's objective and what it takes to integrate the "sentiments" of others in the pursuit of it. This type of leader listens to others in order to better carry out his function of integrating the satisfaction of individual, group, and organizational objectives, but there is little or no dialog or concern for values or ethics beyond the organization's objective.

Dialogic method builds upon the Theory Y assumption that people have an inherent desire to do the right thing. A further assumption is made: that it is easier for us both to know and to do the right thing in a supportive social process of mutual, interpersonal searching, that is, where there is dialog about what the right thing is.

Dialog as a form of action method is conversation among leaders and others (peers, subordinates, superiors) about potential changes in means or ends behaviors. Dialogic method is both a way of knowing/learning and a way of acting. Dialog respects, values, and works toward organizational objectives, but if there is a contradiction between what is ethical and what is in the material interest of individuals or the organization, there is at least something of a prior ethics truth intention and not just a value-neutral, constrained optimization of organizational objectives. Dialog tries with others to serve ethical truth to some extent regardless of temporal or material wins or losses. The inclusion of a truth intention beyond mere concern for specific preconceived outcomes is the key operating principle.

Dialog versus Industrial Democracy

Since World War II, laws in much of northern Europe require worker voting rights on boards of directors and works councils (Bass and Shackleton, 1979; Grunwald and Bernthal, 1983). This has not been the case just in Europe. For example, in the United States during World War I, the National War Labor Board required similar "shop committees" in some companies doing business with the War Department (*American Company Shop Committee Plans*, 1919; Wolfe, 1919; Muhs, 1982) as a way to reduce conflicts and work stoppages that might interfere with the war effort.

One such plan that existed at that time in the Blumenthal Company textile plants even had a cabinet of company officers, a senate of foremen and department heads, a house of representatives of elected employees, and a three-judge arbitration court with one arbitrator selected by management, one by employees, and one by both (Leitch, 1919; "Industrial Democracy in a Textile Plant," 1919; Muhs, 1982). Similarly, in the William Filene's Sons Company, employees at one time had the right to overrule management decisions by a two-thirds vote (Wolfe, 1919).

Such a structural, political-legal approach focuses on sharing "voting," or political authority, but can involve little or no dialog. Democratic voting on alternative proposals without, for example, inquiring conversation can be much more adversarial than dialogic. For example, it is the difference between two political candidates debating why one should be elected instead of the other and dialoging after the election about what a nonpartisan response to an international crisis should be. Democracy without real dialog and democracy that is more adversarial and sophistic than dialogic are problems that Plato recognized as key in his *Republic*.

One of the early pioneers of both industrial democracy and participative management, Harrington Emerson, recognized a similar potential distinction between dialogic and adversarial democracy. In 1920 he spoke before the United States Society of Industrial Engineers, which had passed a resolution in favor of industrial democracy and participative management. (This was also a time of "scientific management," when industrial engineers were key advocates of reform toward treating people at least as well as machines in terms of rest, maintenance, feedback, and so on.) He explained, "If . . . I am told that the ideal is a class ideal, that the theory is that a certain vague group called management has had its innings, has now been caught out and that some other vague class is going to the bat, I at once dissent. I do not believe in class antagonism, nor in any device that will add to it. . . . There are noble ideals more worthy" (Emerson, 1920, p. 3; Muhs, 1982). One of the higher ideals that concerned Emerson was dialog and what others can contribute to dialog. "I have always considered the workers as one of the most valuable sources of counsel; they are close to the facts" (1919, p. 16).

Dialog versus Participative Management

The phase "participative management" has been used for quite some time. For example, Woodrow Wilson (1919) referred to "the right of those who work, in whatever rank, to participate in some organic way in every decision which directly affects their welfare or the part they are to play in industry" (p. 212). However, there is quite a lot of variation in what concretely the term has referred to. For the most part, it has not referred to dialog.

For example, in one of the earliest studies of participative management (Lewin, Lippitt, and White, 1939), it meant that the leader encouraged the group in choosing an activity, helped provide choices in production techniques, and allowed the group to divide the work. There was no dialog among leader and workers about what the activity should be, the advantages and disadvantages of alternative production techniques, or how to divide the work.

In the Coch and French study, participation meant that "groups were given an explanation of the change (in manufacturing procedures), then provided with full opportunity to work with management in carrying it out" (1948, p. 328). In this experiment there was no dialog about whether the changes should be made; there was some dialog about how best to implement the decision. If this were a case in ethics leadership, it might be equivalent to the leader making the unilateral decision about what was ethical or not ethical, but having some dialog with subordinates about how best to implement the decision. Such participation is not dialog about either what is ethical or what organizational policy should be on an ethics issue.

Perhaps the earliest scholarly, research-based formulation of participative management as something close to dialog was the work of Rensis Likert (1960, 1967) on what he called "System 4 Participative Leadership." He describes such a leader as one who "always gets ideas and opinions and always tries to make constructive use of them. . . . Subordinates feel completely free to discuss things about the job with their superior. . . . Except in emergencies, goals are usually established by means of group participation. . . . Subordinates are involved fully in all decisions related to their work" (1967, pp. 3–10).

This concept of leadership shares with dialog the following two key points: (1) it builds upon the assumption of Theory Y leadership that people generally want to act ethically in organizational contexts; and (2) it makes the further assumption that open discussion can facilitate improved knowing and acting. However, it is still different from dialog in that ends and means are discussed in terms of how best to achieve the predetermined organizational objective. With System 4 Participative Leadership there is still a driving and somewhat neutral, value-free will-to-organizational instrumentality as compared to dialog as will-to-ethical truth and action. Dialog does not preclude organizational instrumentality; it is a matter of priority.

STRENGTHS AND LIMITATIONS OF DOUBLE-LOOP DIALOG

Strengths

Dialog can sometimes help build or sustain an ethical organizational culture, both with respect to processes for considering ethical issues and ethical outcomes that can serve as precedents. For example, through iterative dialog in the financial aid case, ways were looked for and found for caring both for families with financial problems and employees who needed employment security. And the university set a precedent in deciding not to treat the administrative staff merely as a means to the ends of the academic side of the university. It decided not to discriminate between academic and nonacademic employees with respect to job security. And through the emergency committee, the university included representatives of groups that might be effected by budget changes in the decisionmaking process.

Through action-science dialog in the Daniels case, layoffs were considered an ethics issue both in terms of process and outcome. In both areas action-science dialog helped build an ethical organizational culture. Through dialog within the joint production committee, layoffs and compensation for layoffs were considered in a process involving managers, engineers, and workers. In the outcomes, workers shared in productivity gains that resulted both from technological changes and reductions in force.

Through action-inquiry method in the Tom's of Maine case, both ethical process and outcomes were considered and developed. With respect to outcomes, elements of Buber's ethical philosophy were formally included in the company's mission statement. With respect to process, all the people effected by changes in the mission statement were included in the discussions—directors, managers, engineers, workers, suppliers, distributors, and community members.

Such was not the situation in the Challenger case where there was ethical disaster at almost every level. The Socratic method that produced the recommendation not to launch and the action-inquiry method, which tried to consider with the NASA people the rationale and the data in support of not launching, were blocked by adversarial method. All the astronauts died. At least initially, the reaction to these disasters was not further exploration, but cover-up. The precedents for more inclusive processes, for example including the chief of Astronauts in prelaunch safety meetings and giving higher priority for safety issues, resulted less from dialogic method than adversarial criticism of NASA in the subsequent congressional hearings and media reports.

Dialogic method can sometimes result in belief conversion toward the ethical. In the financial aid case, several committee members changed their beliefs about the appropriateness of requiring administrative personnel to bear the full costs of increases in financial aid for students. Others changed their beliefs about the inevitability and necessity of layoffs during downward moments of economic cycles. In the Challenger case, Boisjoly was convinced that at least within Morton Thiokol there was genuine belief conversion that launching at too-low temperatures with the fragile O-rings would not be ethical. In the Tom's of Maine case, there was belief conversion among the board of directors toward appreciation of Buber's philosophy as well as belief conversion about the practicality of a corporate board considering explicitly philosophical issues. In the Daniels factory case, there was conversion among some engineers and managers toward the belief that workers were able and willing to consider issues beyond their special interests.

Dialog can sometimes as a by-product effectively produce integrative, win-win results. While win-win outcomes are not the intention of dialogic method, win-win outcomes sometimes do result. For example, in the financial aid case, students won more financial aid, employees won in that there were no layoffs, and faculty and middle-level administrators won in that they participated in decisionmaking and helped each other make belief conversions toward the ethical. However, there were losses in the areas of delayed maintenance and cuts in travel expenses, and in a sense losses were incurred by those who might have been hired if there was no hiring freeze.

There were also win-win outcomes in the Daniels case. The factory won in that productivity was improved; employees won in that their incomes increased dramatically to parity with the trades workers; Daniels won in that his successful work with the joint production committee was a factor in his promotion to division manufacturing manager, and committee members won in that they helped each other learn that they could both inquire about and act for the common good and not solely special interest concerns.

Win-win outcomes also occurred in the Tom's of Maine case. Chappell won in that the board adopted elements of Buber's philosophy in the company's mission statement. The board members won in that they appreciated the opportunity to consider how philosophical concerns could be integrated explicitly and practically into business practice. The various constituencies of employees, distributors, community members, and customers won in that the company was going to make very serious efforts to develop relationships with them that were based on respect for their individual, personal concerns.

However, win-win outcomes are not always possible. For example, in the Challenger case there were none.

Dialogic method can signal ethical concern from the I that can result in the Other deciding not to engage in potential conflict with the I by acting unethically. Ethical results can come not from the Other's belief conversion but from his fear of getting into conflict with the I that might result in the Other getting caught, or a messy fight that would be difficult in itself and problematical if others heard about it.

For example, some of the financial aid committee members may have gone along with the decision not to have administrative staff absorb all the costs less out of ethical concern than because they did not want to get into a public dispute. In the Challenger case, it is possible that some people at Morton Thiokol agreed with the recommendation not to launch less because of ethical concerns for safety than because they did not want to be perceived as willing to risk the astronauts' lives.

Limitations

People in organizations can understand what is ethical but act unethically for personal or organizational gain or fear of punishment. One of the main strengths of dialog is that it can enlighten those who are doing the unethical because they do not understand what is ethical. However, people in organizations often do grasp what is ethical, what is unethical, and what is in the gray area. They choose to enact, go along with, or ignore the unethical to avoid punishments or gain rewards. In the Challenger case, where Socratic dialog was used it was very effective in changing the understanding within Morton Thiokol toward the consensus conclusion to recommend against launching. But out of fear of the client's displeasure, the well-understood ethical recommendation was reversed.

In a more common and less dramatic type of case, Errol Marshall, who paid kickbacks from his company to its prime contractor (chapter 2), fully understood that the kickbacks were unethical, but said that the contractor "demanded the kickbacks. . . . It was cut and dried. We would not get the business otherwise" (Pound, 1985, p. 25). Similarly, personnel manager Evelyn Grant observed, "There have been cases where people will do something wrong because they think they have no choice. Their boss tells them to do it and so they do it, knowing it's wrong. They don't realize there are ways around the boss" (Toffler, 1986, p. 159). Such "go along and get along" strategy is not uncommon.

Some organizational environments discourage dialog. This can be true in both consensus building and authoritarian type cultures. Robert E. Wood, former CEO of the giant international retailer Sears, Roebuck has observed, "We stress the advantages of the free enterprise system, we complain about the totalitarian state, but in our individual organizations we have created more or less a totalitarian system in industry, particularly in large industry" (Ewing, 1977, p. 21). Similarly, Charles W. Summers, in a *Harvard Business Review* article, observes, "Corporate executives may argue that . . . they recognize and protect . . . against arbitrary termination through their own internal procedures. The simple fact is that most companies have not recognized and protected that right" (1980, pp. 132, 139).

David Ewing concludes, "It [pressure to obey unethical orders] is probably most dangerous, however, as a low-level infection. When it slowly bleeds the individual conscience dry and metastasizes insidiously, it is most difficult to defend against. There are no spectacular firings or purges in the ranks. There are no epic blunders. Under constant and insistent pressure, employees simply give in and conform. They become good 'organization people'" (1977, pp. 216–217).

Most organizations do not permit people in their work lives nearly the same amount of rights that citizens have in democracies, although the responsibilities of citizenship may still be present (Lindblom, 1977). Of particular importance is the right of free speech, which many organizations do not give managers or other employees. If managers cannot speak freely, it can be very difficult to dialog with other managers and employees about what is ethical and what should be done about unethical behavior.

Similar conditions can exist in participative decisionmaking and consensus-building cultures. For example, according to Yoshino and Lifson "A Japanese leader, rather than being an authority, is more of a communications channel, a mediator, a facilitator, and most of all, a symbol and embodiment of group unity. Consensus building is necessary to decision making, and this requires patience and an ability to use carefully cultivated relationships to get all to agree for the good of the unit" (1986, p. 187).

In the example of Dr. Suguro in chapter 2, the doctor expresses his reasoning and feelings about cooperating with his consensus-building culture:

> At the time nothing could be done. . . . If I were caught in the same way, I might, I might just do the same thing again. . . . We feel that getting on good terms ourselves with the Western Command medical people, with whom Second [section] is so cosy, wouldn't be a bad idea at all. Therefore we feel there's no need to ill-temperedly refuse their friendly proposal and hurt their feelings. . . . Five doctors from Kando's section most likely will be glad to get the chance. . . . For me the pangs of conscience . . . were from childhood equivalent to the fear of disapproval in the eyes of others— fear of the punishment which society could bring to bear. . . . To put it quite bluntly, I am able to remain quite undisturbed in the face of someone else's terrible suffering and death. . . . I am not writing about these experiences as one driven to do so by his conscience . . . all these memories are distasteful to me. But looking upon them as distasteful and suffering because of them are two different matters. Then why do I bother writing? Because I'm strangely ill at ease. I, who fear only the eyes of others and the punishment of society, and whose fears disappear when I am secure from these, am now disturbed. . . . I have no conscience, I suppose. Not just me, though. None of them feel anything at all about what they did here. (Endo, 1972, pp. 118, 157)

Some people's developmental environments do not prepare them for dialogic action. In his *Nicomachean Ethics* (Books 2 and 6) Aristotle explains that not everyone grows up in the type of environments we need in order to develop (1) the abilities required for dialog; and (2) an understanding of the desirability of dialog.

For example, a former United Fruit executive, reflecting on his experiences with the United Fruit Company in helping to overthrow the government of Guatemala, observed that there was nothing in his private or public-life background that prepared him for this ethical challenge. "At the time, I identified so closely with the company and my job that I didn't think about it as a moral or ethical issue" (McCann, 1978, 1984). It seems possible that because nothing in McCann's private and public experiences had encouraged dialog, he did not consider talking with others about the ethical and perhaps even strategic issues of killing hundreds of people and overthrowing a democratically elected, somewhat left-of-center government for the sake of larger or safer banana profits and fear of the Soviet Union's expansion of influence. Could such developmental deprivation make it difficult to dialog with other managers about the ethics of helping to overthrow a government, very large bribes, imprisonments, tortures, and killings?

Many people, perhaps most people, believe that dialog and searching with others for what is ethical is too idealistic and not pragmatic. Many people are used to forcing contests and are also familiar with integrative dealmaking. Dialog in search of what is ethical, that may not satisfy more narrowly construed personal or organizational needs, can appear to many to be too idealistic and not "real world." Such people may be reluctant to engage in dialog. They do not understand that unlike such methods as forcing or integrating, dialog is an ethical end in itself and is sometimes also pragmatically effective.

While some people may be good dialogic leaders in their normal specialized work lives, when it comes to issues with ethical dimensions, they don't try dialog with others or they don't do it very well. Some people avoid discussing ethical, religious, and political issues with others in the work environment.

An example is the case of John Geary (chapter 2), who was a salesman for U.S. Steel when the company decided to enter a new market with an unsafe new product, deep oil-well casings (Ewing, 1983b; *Geary v. U.S. Steel Coroporation*). As a leading salesman for U.S. Steel and as a communications channel between customers and various organization departments, Geary normally was very good at dialoging with customers and other managers in searching for what is best in a normal business sense. A salesman frequently does not have specialized knowledge and needs to dialog in this way. He may then choose to compromise, or feel he needs to because of various organizational pressures. Nonetheless, he needs to search for what is best if only to know how and where to compromise it.

Geary should have been good at dialog regarding an unsafe product. Apparently, however, instead of trying to dialog with customers, engineering, manufacturing, and sales, he only used advocacy reasoning, protesting to several groups of upper-level engineers and managers. He believed the casings had too high a failure rate. He tried to convince the groups that selling the casings was wrong, both because they were unsafe and because failures could damage U.S. Steel's long-term strategy of entering higher technology and profit margin businesses. Even though many of the upper-level managers, engineers, and salesmen understood and believed his facts and his ethical reasoning and were sympathetic to his protests, he said, "the only desire of everyone associated with the project was to satisfy the instructions of Henry Wallace. No one was about to buck this man for fear of his job" (Ewing, 1983b, p. 86). Geary was fired by Henry Wallace, sales vice president, apparently for continuing his advocacy against his orders.

Dialog can expose good people to retaliatory harm. Socrates was killed for teaching people how to question and dialog. Geary was fired when he persisted in trying to discuss the safety issue. Authoritarian systems commonly punish people who engage in dialog, their friends, and even people mentioned in the dialog who know about unethical and illegal activities. It can be safer to remain silent or at least to not mention names of others who might be retaliated against. Sometimes win-lose methods such as secret whistle blowing can be safer and more effective than dialog.

COMPARATIVE STRENGTHS AND LIMITATIONS OF ITERATIVE, ACTION-SCIENCE, AND ACTION-INQUIRY DIALOG METHODS

The methods differ with respect to explicit thoroughness, speed, threat, and cross-cultural applicability. Despite the differences and varying nuances among the methods and their theoretical foundations, they are all forms of combined praxis and poiesis, involving the interpenetration of external effectiveness with appropriate means for the ethical development of the actor. That is both a lot and very good company. If the practical debate was concerned with which dialog methods to use, rather than whether to do nothing, use win-lose method, win-win method, or any form of dialog, we would be in pretty good shape.

Nonetheless, with respect to explicit thoroughness, action-science explicitly uses new experimental data, experiential data, secondary data, reasoning, and multiple alternatives. In this sense it is the most thorough of all the methods. Iterative Socratic dialog considers all these factors except for experimental data. As noted earlier, experimental method was not part of classical Greek method. Action-inquiry does not explicitly include experimentation and multiple alternatives, but is open to including them in the inquiry stage if others want to.

Conversely, action-inquiry is potentially the fastest and most direct method, since it is the most focused on the advocated action. Action-science, since it is the most thorough, consequently takes the most time. Iterative Socratic method, since it systematically considers multiple reformulations of the initial alternative, also takes considerable time. However, since it does not include experimentation, it takes less time than action-science.

Both action-science and action-inquiry methods advocate before they question; iterative Socratic method questions but does not advocate. Explicitly friendly and respectful, it is less threatening than the other two, especially with listeners who are unfamiliar with the method and may hear the advocacy but not the inquiry. This can be particularly important when higher-ranking or more powerful people are trying to elicit participation from subordinates who might be reluctant to contribute different perspectives for fear they might be interpreted as oppositional or disloyal.

Threat is related to cross-cultural applicability. In the northeast United States and northern Europe, people are familiar with very direct advocacy from strangers and people one does not have a friendly personal relationship with, but this is not true in most of the world. Such directness and advocacy is often interpreted as aggression and even assault in many places. Therefore, iterative Socratic method may be more applicable cross-culturally.

CONCLUSION

At a minimum, double-loop dialogic politics can be considered (1) an addition to the inventory of single-loop, win-lose, and win-win methods; (2) an interesting variation and perhaps extension to the entangled stream of leadership, industrial democracy, and participative management methods; (3) sometimes a help in building ethical organizational culture; (4) a way sometimes to effectively produce integrative, win-win results; (5) a way to signal ethical concern from the I that can result in the Other preferring not to engage in conflict with the I by acting unethically; and (6) a process that sometimes results in belief conversion toward the ethical.

There are also important limitations with dialogic method. Since both authoritarian and consensus-building organizational cultures can discourage dialog, it may not be possible to use it even if win-win outcomes are possible. Some people in their organizational lives do not understand how dialogic method can be applied in situations involving ethics dimensions. Some people in organizations, particularly those who have had careers in relatively isolated analytical or technical areas where there was not much opportunity to gain dialog experiences, may not know how to dialog very well in any situation. In such circumstances, dialog can be less effective than forcing or deal-making.

When should we use dialog method, and when should we use the different types of dialog?

When friendly and nonthreatening affect is important, iterative Socratic method is more appropriate than action-science or action-inquiry. This is often the case in cultures where directness is interpreted unfavorably, or whenever the people one is dealing with are not used to the directness and advocacy of action-science and action-inquiry, or when dealing with lower-ranking or less powerful people who might be afraid to contribute different perspectives.

Where experimental data and maximum thoroughness are more important than concerns about threat, then action-science method can be more appropriate. However, it can have an unintended conservative outcome. If the burden of proof required of challengers to the status quo is too high, or at least substantially higher than that required to maintain the status quo, this burden combined with silence on the implicit status quo can suppress real dialog and prevent change.

When speed and focus is more important than the time that more systematic and thorough methods would take, action-inquiry method is more appropriate. However, if systematic and thorough methods are sacrificed because of time constraints, decision time may be shorter, but implementation can take much longer and cost more because of the need to correct hasty decisions.

It is possible to combine elements from the various methods. For example, explicit friendliness could be added to action-science and action-inquiry method; experimentation could be added to iterative Socratic method.

What should we do, as individuals simultaneously concerned with our own needs and careers and with acting ethically on our own and as parts of organizational communities? To some extent it depends upon the circumstances and our own abilities. If we know how to dialog, if there's time for it, if the key people in authority are reasonable, and if an integrative solution is possible, then there's a reasonable chance of success and one should probably try dialogic method. If one does not know how to dialog, there isn't time, the authority figures are unreasonable, there is a culture of strong conformity, and the situation is zero- or negative-sum, then the chances of success with a dialogic approach are lower. Only forcing or deal-making action strategies may remain.

But what about the more common middle range of problems? Here there's no easy formula. The more positive-sum the situation, the more time there is, the more dialogic skills one has, the more reasonable the authority figures and organizational cultures are, the more dialog is recommended, and vice versa.

7

Friendly Disentangling: Triple-Loop Dialog I

We must be still and still moving, into another intensity,
For a further union, a deeper communion
— T. S. Eliot

The present chapter examines how friendly, disentangling dialog can address problems of problematical organization traditions. The friendly, disentangling dialog method of John Woolman is considered, followed by examples. The method is then linked to and interpreted within both behavioral science and philosophy theory. Finally, the strengths and limitations of the method are considered.

FRIENDLY DISENTANGLING: WOOLMAN'S "I AM WE"

John Woolman was a Philadelphia-area cloth merchant-retailer and ethics activist in the colonial era (Woolman, 1774; Whittier, 1871; Emden, 1940; Jones, 1947; Tolles, 1948; Raistraick, 1950; Greenleaf, 1977a, 1977b, 1989). He developed and used friendly, disentangling dialog with merchants and farmers to address the issues of slavery, peacemaking with Indians and the British, farmer-banker relations, trading practices with Indians, and child labor. This method was also explicitly used and taught by Robert Greenleaf while he was a manager, management training director, and corporate vice president at AT&T.

106

There are four key parts to the method:

1. Frame to oneself a "we" fellowship relationship with others and look for the source of current problematic behavior within the biases of an embedded tradition rather than solely in the behaviors and governing values of individuals.
2. Approach those involved in a friendly manner.
3. Ask for help in disentangling a problematic behavior from potential biases within "our" embedded tradition system.
4. Work with those who are agreeable to experiment with alternative behaviors and/or governing values that do not rest on the troublesome biases of the tradition system.

The Woolman method can be considered a type of triple-loop action-learning, which fosters change in the embedded tradition system where the governing values are nested. This is, the social tradition is both criticized and treated as a partner in action-learning. The tradition system is respected but also considered to have potential negative biases that can be reformed and transformed, just as individuals and their governing values can.

The examples come from two centuries and two continents. The first example describes how Robert Greenleaf explicitly used the Woolman method to help AT&T greatly increase its employment of black managers.

The second example shows how John Woolman worked to end slavery in colonial Pennsylvania.

In the third example the method appears to have been used implicitly when Chaudhry Mohammad Hussain, a textile manufacturer in postcolonial Pakistan, worked to transform the Punjab cotton industry. This example shows how the method can be used in different cultural environments, and without specific reference to Woolman's strategies.

Robert Greenleaf and Black Management Development at AT&T   Robert Greenleaf, a graduate of Carleton College, began work at AT&T as a laborer's assistant in a line crew in 1929. In 1964 he retired, after having served as corporate human resources vice president and director of management development and research. Among the management issues he was concerned with was the development of black managers. He explicitly used Woolman's method and taught this method within AT&T. When Greenleaf began work at AT&T there were very few black managers, with the exception of a few telephone operator supervisors. In significant part through his efforts, between 1955 and 1964, before the 1968 Civil Rights Act, AT&T increased the total of black managers from about .5 to about 4.5 percent of total managerial employment. Greenleaf used four-part Woolman method.*

Frame to oneself a "we" fellowship relationship with others, and look for the source of the current problematic behavior within "our" shared tradition system rather than solely in the characters or idiosyncratic views of individuals. Greenleaf reminded himself that he had worked well, for his entire adult working life, with many of the managers who were not hiring blacks for managerial positions. He reminded himself that "we" have shared and overcome many difficulties, and most of us very much like being "phonemen" and being part of the AT&T system and tradition. In the potential heat of dealing with this sensitive issue, he did not want to forget that most of the managers he knew at AT&T were basically good people and that he was much like them. An important part of why blacks were not being hired for managerial positions was that there was an "institutional bias" within the AT&T tradition system that silently and perhaps subconsciously kept people from considering blacks for managerial positions. Many of the managers he knew had entered AT&T when its tradition was already established. While they might be maintaining a biased tradition, they did not create it.

He reminded himself that such tradition-system biases might be at least as important as individual and group prejudices against hiring blacks for managerial positions. The issue was too important to ignore or avoid. He wanted to prepare himself simultaneously to confront an important issue critically and realistically at the tradition-system level in all its complexity, and to approach people he cared about in a cooperative rather than adversarial manner.

Approach those involved in a friendly manner and suggest that there may be some problems in our shared tradition system. Greenleaf personally visited many managers, and he believes that he personally spoke to most managers at one time or another in his management development programs. Before raising the issue of black management development, he would explicitly express a friendly attitude, respect, and appreciation toward the managers. Whenever he could he would review past successful relationships with them. He would explicitly mention the many years he and they had worked well together at AT&T. He would then frame the subject he would like to discuss as considera-

---

*Information about Robert Greenleaf's work came from his articles and book and my personal interviews with him. His numbers concerning black manager employment levels within AT&T are the same as those in the Wharton School Industrial Research Unit study by Northrup and Larson (1979). I met Robert Greenleaf and learned of his work in the Society of Friends, of which we are both members.

tion of potential biases in "our" system with respect to the issue of black management development. He suggested that such biases might be at least as relevant and important as potential individual or group differences with respect to the issue.

Request help in disentangling a specific behavior from a troublesome assumption within the tradition system. Greenleaf asked managers individually and in groups for their help in understanding how the issue of black management development might be entangled with potential biases in "our" tradition system. Many of the managers had been framing the issue in terms of the "unsuitability" of blacks for management roles; Greenleaf challenged this framing. Several observations emerged from the discussions. Some managers observed that since they didn't see any black managers at AT&T, they just didn't think of blacks as candidates for managerial positions. That is, the informal tradition of not having black managers led them to not consider the possibility. Other managers observed that it appeared that not many blacks had the training or experience required for managerial consideration and thought part of the reason for this was that since blacks were not expected to become managers, they were not encouraged to complete such training or gain such experience. Several other managers observed that most blacks did not apply for managerial training or positions and thought this might be related to a fatalistic expectation. That is, there was little point in applying for managerial training or positions because the implicit tradition was not to hire many black managers.

Work with those who are agreeable to experiment with alternative behaviors that do not rest on the troublesome biases of the tradition system. Greenleaf repeatedly asked managers individually and in groups for consensus-building help in developing and interpreting experiments in disentangling reform. One experiment involved recruiting blacks for management training programs. Another experiment involved offering black technical specialists a broader range of experiences that would better prepare them for managerial positions. For the most part, blacks did well in the management training classes and exercises, and in the rotating work assignments that led to managerial positions. There were no top management orders to increase black hiring for managerial positions, no quotas, goals, or timetables, and no management performance reviews tied to black management development. Nonetheless, over a ten-year period black employment in management grew from about .5 to about 4.5 percent. Apparently Greenleaf's use of the Woolman method was at least somewhat effective.

After Greenleaf retired, in the period between 1973 and 1979, AT&T was pressured through the rate-setting powers of the FCC to accept a consent decree with the EEOC whereby affirmative action quotas were agreed upon. At the end of a very acrimonious internal and external seven-year struggle, in 1979 AT&T had increased its employment of black managers to about 9 percent (Northrup and Larsen, 1979). While there were several other factors influencing black managerial employment, in both the dialogic Greenleaf period and in the adversarial consent decree period, the increase in black managerial employment levels was approximately 4.5 percentage points.

John Woolman, Slave Freedom, and Productivity in Colonial Pennsylvania   John Woolman developed and used his four-step method to address several ethics concerns in a thirty-year period during the mid-eighteenth century (Woolman, 1774, 1818; Gummere, 1922). He used the method in conversations with individuals and small groups.

Woolman was a member of the Society of Friends (Quakers), which was at the time the dominant economic and political group in Pennsylvania. Within the Society of Friends he is considered the primary leader in eliminating slavery from the Society and, derivatively, from Pennsylvania (Gummere, 1922; Tolles, 1948; James, 1963). Slavery was peacefully, gradually, and voluntarily eliminated from the Society of Friends in the late eighteenth century; shortly thereafter it became illegal in Pennsylvania. By 1800, of the states south of New England, only Pennsylvania had outlawed slavery. According to Nash and Soderland's *Freedom By Degrees: Emancipation in Pennsylvania and its Aftermath* (1991), Quaker influence was primarily responsible for this action.

According to Greenleaf "Some assume great insitutional burdens, others quietly deal with one person at a time. Such a man was John Woolman, an American Quaker, who lived through the middle years of the eighteenth century. He is known to the world of scholarship for his journal, a literary classic. But in the area of our interest, leadership, he is the man who almost singlehandedly rid the Society of Friends (Quakers) of slaves" (1977a, pp. 29–30). Woolman devoted thirty years to this issue. Many Quakers were wealthy, conservative merchants and farmers who owned slaves; by 1770 no Quakers owned slaves. The Society of Friends was the first religious group in the United States to formally denounce and forbid slavery among its members.

Woolman addressed the slavery issue with farmers and lenders as follows. Before meeting with the slaveowner farmers and merchants, he framed to himself a "we" fellowship relationship with them, and reminded himself that there might be important tradition-system biases causing problems and conflicts, and that these biases could be at least as important as individual differences. He recorded his preparatory thoughts and feelings in his *Journal:* "From small beginnings in errors, great buildings, by degrees, are raised; and from one age to another, are more and more strengthened by the general concurrence of the people: and as men obtain reputation . . . their virtues are mentioned as arguments in favour of general error: and those of less note, to justify themselves, say, such and such good men did the like" (Woolman, 1774, 1818, p. 39). Woolman believed that good people could contribute to unethical behavior in part because they were entangled in what he called "biases" and "oppressive customs." He observed, "The prospect of a road lying open to the same degeneracy, in some parts of this new settled land of America, in respect to our conduct toward the negroes, hath deeply bowed my mind in this journey. . . . Deep-rooted customs, though wrong, are not easily altered" (p. 45). He was as concerned about the people doing the problematic behavior as about the direct victims. He explained, "We feel a Tenderness in our Hearts toward our Fellow Creatures [the slaveowners and traders] entangled in oppressive Customs" (p. 54).

This framing to oneself is not as strange as it may appear. For example, in a perhaps reverse type of preparative framing to oneself, coaches and athletes before competitive games frequently "psych" themselves up by focusing on the "opposition," the "enemy," and the intense, competitive engagement to come. Some coaches even quote negative things "they," the opposition coaches and players, are reputed to have said about "us."

In a friendly and not a cooly analytic, positional, or adversarial manner, Woolman approached the farmers and directed the conversation in terms of potential negative bias entanglements in "our" tradition system. In addressing the slavery issue with a group of farmers who were opening up new farmland, Woolman spoke with them as follows: "Dear friends . . . as you are improving a wilderness, and may be numbered amongst the first planters in one part of a province, I beseech you . . . to wisely consider the force of your examples, and think how much your successors may be thereby affected: it is a help in a country, yea, and a great favour and a blessing, when customs first settled are agreeable to sound wisdom: so when they are otherwise, the effect of them is grievous; and children feel themselves encompassed with difficulties prepared for them by their predecessors" (1774, 1818, p. 59).

Woolman asked slaveowners for their help in disentangling the slavery-related problems from negative biases in "our" tradition system. The slaveowners, from their positions of authority and perceived economic self-interest, had been framing the ethics issue in terms of a laziness problem among the slaves. They spoke of "the untoward slothful disposition of the negroes," and said, "one of our [free white labourers] would do as much in a day as two of their slaves." Woolman challenged this framing through a criticism of the tradition system within which this ethical framing was nested. Emerging from the discussions were the observations that "free men, whose minds were properly on their business, found a satisfaction in improving, cultivating, and providing for their families; but negroes, labouring to support others who claim them as their property, and expecting nothing but slavery during life, had not the like inducement to be industrious" (Woolman, 1774, 1818, pp. 50–51).

Woolman asked for consensus-building help in developing and interpreting an experiment in disentangling reform. A decision emerged from the discussions to try an experiment where a few slaves would be freed and offered sharecropping opportunities. The productivity of these freed farmers was higher than the slaves'. Within twenty years of this experiment (1790), many farmers adopted this ethical and political-economic reform. There followed formal Society of Friends Minutes, and later state laws, against the practice of holding and trading slaves, and by 1800 slavery was eliminated in Pennsylvania (Gummere, 1922; Nash and Soderland, 1991).

Most of the farmers and merchants Woolman approached were wealthier and more powerful than he. However, since they were all members of the Society of Friends, it would have been considered inappropriate for them to refuse to talk with him. As Greenleaf's position as a human resources manager gave him access to line managers to discuss black management development, Woolman's position as a member of the Society of Friends, and in his later years, a "weighty" and well-known member, gave him access to the wealthy and powerful Quaker farmers and merchants. While most of the farmers and merchants responded favorably and gradually to Woolman's efforts, not all of them did. Some even refused to discuss the issue with him. This problem is discussed later in the section on the strengths and limitations of the Woolman method.

Chaudhry Mohammad Hussain and the Punjab Cotton Textile Industry (Amjad, 1988)   In this example the method was used in a culture very different from colonial Pennsylvania or a twentieth-century corporation. We can see the method being used by someone who never heard of Woolman or Greenleaf.*

---

* I learned about Chaudhry Mohammad Hussain while I was working as a professor on a management development project in Pakistan in 1987 and 1988. In one stage of the project, I collected Pakistan case data and later used it in my management development seminars. I interviewed several people who worked with Hussain and knew him well. In addition, Mohammad Amjad, the CEO of the company Hussain founded, gave a lecture and participated in a seminar about him.

Chaudhry Mohammad Hussain never graduated from elementary school. He began his working life at the age of eight as an assistant in a small vegetable stand in Lahore, then part of British India and today part of Pakistan. From these humble beginnings he built one of Pakistan's largest industrial and trading corporations and also served as mayor of Lahore.

For over forty years Hussain invited people to his home for seven-hour dinners on almost every Friday, the day of the Muslim sabbath. The people who came usually included family members, friends, workers in his businesses, managers, suppliers, customers, other owners and competitors, and political and religious leaders. In the 1950s Hussain used this process to address the self-destructive cycle of high-interest loans to cotton farmers, farmer bankruptcies, and lender bankruptcies. He was instrumental in transforming the low-quality Pakistan cotton industry into the prosperous, high-quality industry it remains today.

Hussain would prepare himself for the sabbath dinners. The people he invited were quite varied, including Muslims, Hindus, Sikhs, Christians, managers, workers, politicians, owners, and merchants. He would remind himself that the different types of people coming to his dinners were all part of one Punjab community that predated British colonial India and the current nation-states of India and Pakistan. He would remind himself that the disagreements and conflicts that emerged at the dinners were often caused by problems and biases in shared religious, political, business, and family traditions and systems as much as individual and group differences.

At his dinners he specifically referred to all his guests as friends and members of the Punjab community. It had come to his attention that there were a large number of farmer bankruptcies, that farming interest rates were very high, that his buyers were having difficulty obtaining high-quality cotton for his yarn factories, and there was racial animosity between the mostly Muslim farmers and the mostly Hindu retailer lenders. He suggested at one of his dinners that "our" problems might be linked to some bias in "our" tradition system of cotton growing, farm financing, and yarn manufacturing that might be at least as important as the conflicts and differences among farmers, retailer lenders, and manufacturers.

He asked the people at the dinner for help in understanding how these problems might be entangled with potential biases in "our" tradition system. The following entanglements emerged from the discussions. Most loans to farmers came from local retailers who also sold food, clothing, medicine, seeds, fertilizers, and farm equipment to them. The retailers charged very high interest rates because they had to make up for the losses they incurred from the farmers who could not repay their loans. High-quality cotton was scarce because with the high interest rates and debt servicing the farmers did not believe they could invest the resources required to grow higher-quality cotton. Without adequate crop investment, many crops were so poor that the farmers could not earn enough money to repay their loans and care adequately for their soil, animals, and farm equipment.

After such discussions at the dinners, Hussain asked for help in developing an experiment in disentangling reform. Someone suggested that Hussain, as a yarn manufacturer, might offer interest-free loans to farmers in exchange for first pick of their cotton. One of the farmers at the dinner said that he would be very happy with such an arrangement and he thought many other cotton farmers would be also. People agreed that such an experiment would be worth trying. So Hussain offered interest-free loans to several of his farmer suppliers in exchange for first pick of their cotton, indicating that he was looking for high-quality cotton. The quality of his cotton supplies improved, as well as the prices he received for the yarn he manufactured from them. Over the years at the Friday dinners, the results of the experiment were interpreted and discussed. Hussain emerged as one of the highest-quality and most profitable yarn manufacturers in the Punjab. As more and more farmers and manufacturers learned of the results of the experiment, more manufacturers offered interest-free loans to farmers for first pick of their cotton. The industry was transformed. There were relatively few farm bankruptcies. The retailers sold more and better supplies and equipment to the farmers. The farmers improved the quality of their cotton. The Punjab yarn manufacturers increased their profitability and became known worldwide for producing very high-quality yarn.

Woolman himself had addressed a similar problem of high interest rates and farm bankruptcies. The experimental solution that emerged in the Philadelphia area was somewhat different but equally positive: The farmers' Monthly Meetings (parish-like communities) guaranteed individual loans. With such risk-sharing, bad loans could usually be repaid, the lenders could charge much lower interest rates, and the negative cycle of increasing farm bankruptcies and increasing interest rates was transformed.

WOOLMAN'S METHOD AS TRIPLE-LOOP ACTION-LEARNING

In triple-loop action-learning, the embedded social tradition system is both criticized and treated as a partner in mutual action-learning. (See figure in chapter 2.) Continuing with and extending the Argyris, Putnam, and Smith (1985) single- and double-loop example described in chapter 2, the agent considers changes in actions, governing values, and the embedded social tradition system. More specifically, the agent holds open for learning and change: (1) the effectiveness of the action strategy of not talking about controversial issues; (2) the appropriateness of the governing value of short-term conflict suppression; and, (3) possible biases in the embedded social tradition that may be causing individuals inappropriately to accept this governing value.

The Woolman method of triple-loop action-learning uses friendly criticism and voluntary experiments designed to reform negative biases within the shared tradition system.

STRENGTHS AND LIMITATIONS OF WOOLMAN'S METHOD

The strengths of Woolman's method include the following: (1) it facilitates peaceful change; (2) it reforms organization tradition biases; (3) like double-loop dialog, it can sometimes as a byproduct produce integrative, win-win results; and (4) like double-loop dialog it can facilitate belief conversion toward the ethical and not solely win-win behavior change.

Situations in which the method is less effective include: (1) when the people involved perceive no "we" fellowship relationship or when a conflicting "we" relationship is more important; (2) when there really is not much of a negative bias in the tradition system and the reason for the unethical behavior is primarily or fully individual; (3) when powerful people in authority frame ethics issues in a self-interested manner and ignore alternative frames; and (4) when the method is misinterpreted and stimulates negative "us"-versus-"them" cognitions and behaviors.

Strengths

The method can facilitate peaceful change. Peaceful change is one of the key strengths of the Woolman method. Woolman used it to address one of the most difficult and violent issues of his time, slavery, yet his method facilitated first the peaceful, voluntary elimination of slavery in Pennsylvania, and then the passing of Minutes and laws against it.

The post–World War II partition of Pakistan and India was a very violent event; millions of people were killed in the social upheaval that accompanied the separation of Muslim Pakistan from Hindu India. Yet Hussain achieved mostly peaceful change in the cotton industries of the Punjab, a predominantly Muslim region bordering predominantly Hindu India. Peaceful change in this case was particularly impressive, since many of the retailer lenders were Hindus while almost all of the cotton farmers were Muslims.

While Greenleaf was using the Woolman method, employment of black managers at AT&T increased from about .5 to about 4.5 percent. This change occurred without any enforcements such as top management orders, performance reviews tied to hiring and promotion of black managers, and external court orders or consent decrees. The peaceful changes during Greenleaf's time are in marked contrast to the later intense, external conflicts between AT&T and the EEOC and FCC, internal conflicts among top management under the consent decree quotas, and employee resistance to the preferential hiring and promotion of black managers.

Peaceful Woolman method and politically generated and legally enforced change are not necessarily mutually exclusive. Paul Ricoeur has observed, "The State of law is . . . the actualization of ethical intention in the political sphere" (1991, p. 334). Politics can provide the space for ethics to act; law can be the result of ethics-driven politics. The Woolman method can serve as peaceful preparation for changes that may later be encoded as rules or laws.

What is it about Woolman method that facilitates peaceful change? Several parts contribute: friendly affect, consciousness of a "we" relationship, consciousness that sources of conflict may be caused as much by tradition system-level biases as individual or group differences, consensus-building experimentation, and the user's sincere interest in transcendent and not solely individual welfare.

The method can help reform organization traditions. The focus on potential biases in "our" tradition system is one of the method's key strengths. It is designed to address and improve ethical organization traditions by identifying and correcting such negative biases. This focus is particularly important compared to more individually focused methods such as single- and double-loop action-learning. In the slavery example, the focus was on considering and reforming the slave economy. After indentifying the biases—the inhumanity of slavery, the low productivity of slavery, and the perceived "untoward slothful disposition of the negroes"—and trying the experiment of paid workers and sharecropping, many farmers and merchants voluntarily discontinued the practice of slavery. Later they voluntarily voted to outlaw it. The terrible slavery-supporting bias in the economic tradition system of the Pennsylvania Society of Friends and later the state of Pennsylvania was reformed and transformed.

In the Punjab example also a bias in the system was corrected and the culture was reformed. Negatively escalating behaviors were intercepted and transformed. The high interest rates for farmers were causing problems for the whole system. The farmers had to pay too much for debt servicing; they could not invest enough to produce the high-quality cotton the manufacturers needed; their lack of productivity led to lower effective demand from the retailers; and all these conditions were increasing the stress on already stressful Muslim-Hindu relationships. When the negative bias was reformed, the industry was transformed.

In the AT&T example, the apparently largely systemic and institutional bias within AT&T with respect to the training, hiring, and promotion of black managers was significantly improved. While black managers remained in the minority, the culture changed from one where black managers were practically nonexistent to one where it was not uncommon to find them in all areas of the company. This is to suggest not that the problem was solved, but that a significant improvement appears to have been made with respect to the managerial and leadership role of blacks in the AT&T society.

As a byproduct the method can generate effective, but not perfect, integrative, win-win solutions. The focus of the Woolman method in the cases considered was more on transcendent tradition system-level concerns than on individual criteria. In all these cases, while there were not perfect solutions without any negative effects, integrative, win-win solutions mostly resulted. That is, what emerged appeared to be not so much win-lose outcomes or compromises but solutions that were large enough to encompass and reconcile many, if not necessarily all, diverse extremes.

For example, in Pennsylvania the slaveowners increased their productivity with paid workers and sharecroppers, the slaves gained freedom and employment, and the conscience of society benefitted by eliminating slavery. One group that may not have benefitted economically were the slave traders, who were generally different from the farmer and merchant slaveowners.

In the Punjab the farmers benefitted by not having to pay high interest rates, the yarn manufacturers got more profitable, higher quality supplies, and the retailer lenders increased their sales of goods to more prosperous farmers. The Punjab society became more prosperous and avoided much of the Muslim-Hindu violence that occurred in other regions and industries. Some retailers did lose revenues as the farm lending market was reduced, and some yarn manufacturers who could not make interest-free loans to the farmers and did not have preferential access to the higher quality cotton lost profits and market share.

The method can facilitate belief conversion toward the ethical and not solely win-win behavior change. Belief conversion toward the ethical is a strength of the Woolman method relative to win-win negotiating and enforced regulatory approaches. The Woolman method neither explicitly compels nor rewards. The decision to experiment with a solution to an ethical problem is made after there has been some voluntary agreement that there is a negative bias in the tradition system that needs to be addressed. That is, some belief conversion toward the ethical occurs before behavior change. People may reject what they think is an unworkable or inconvenient solution to the negative bias in the tradition system, but there is nonetheless some belief conversion. While this is a strength relative to win-win negotiating and forcing methods, other methods such as double-loop action-learning also can stimulate belief conversion.

Limitations

The method can be ineffective when the people involved perceive no "we" fellowship relationships or when a conflicting "we" relationship is more important. Insiders may regard the person trying to use Woolman method as an outsider or relative outsider, and can choose not to consider seriously or to resist the changes suggested.

For example, Rufus Jones, George Walton, and Robert Yarnall, representing the American Friends Service Committee, tried to use the Woolman method in helping Jews emigrate from Nazi Germany (Jones, 1947). They visited Gestapo headquarters in 1939, in part in response to the "Day of Broken Glass," November 9, 1938. They addressed Reinhard Heydrich, who was Himmler's immediate subordinate, head of the SS, and in charge of the Dachau concentration camp, through two of his deputies in a foyer outside his office where he could hear the conversation.

Their written and spoken words to him and his two deputies were as follows. They first reminded them that there was a history of friendly relations between the German people and the British and American Friends Service Committees. "We have had close and friendly relations with the German people throughout the entire post-war period" (Jones, 1947, Appendix 3, p. 1). In addition, they indicated that there were some shared points of view. "We have always been concerned over the conditions of the Peace Treaty and in spirit opposed to these conditions" (Jones, 1947, Appendix 3, p. 1). They tried to remind the Nazis that the Quaker relief efforts were built on a foundation of previous service to the German people. "We came to Germany in the time of the blockade; organized and directed the feeding of German children, reaching at the peak no less than a million two hundred thousand children per day. . . . And at the time of 'Anschluss' we were distributing food to a number of Nazi families" (Jones, 1947, Appendix 1, pp. 1–2). They reminded the Nazis that during this period of service no propaganda or conversion efforts had been made. "We have not used any propaganda or aimed to make converts to our views . . . We have come now in the same spirit as in the past and we believe that all Germans who remember the past and who are familiar with out ways and methods and spirit will know that we do not come to judge or criticize or to push ourselves in, but to inquire in the most friendly manner whether there is anything we can do to promote life and human welfare and to relieve suffering" (Jones, 1947, Appendix 3, p. 2).

Matters of relief, quicker emigration, and transient camps were discussed. Heydrich announced through his deputies that everything the Quakers asked for would be granted. For a few weeks Jews from Germany were able to emigrate through the American and British Friends Service Committees. According to Clarence Pickett, then executive director of the American Friends Service Committee, as a result of this visit to the Gestapo "Workers in our Berlin Center found they had a new freedom in making emigration arrangements for Jewish families and in bringing relief. This short reprieve meant the difference between life and death to some families, at least" (Vining, 1958, p. 294). However, in the light of subsequent history, Jones, Walton, and Yarnall had relatively little positive influence in changing Nazi policy or helping German Jews escape.

Clearly, there are circumstances where the effectiveness of the Woolman method is limited. While Jones, Walton, and Yarnall were able to communicate something of a positive "we" relationship, based on the Service Committees' service of feeding German children after World War I, that resulted in some relief and saved some lives, it did not last very long. It was relatively weak compared to the contradictory, distorted, destructive, and even depraved internal sense of "we" within the Nazi society.

The method may be ineffective when there really is not much of a negative bias in the tradition system and the reason for the problematical behavior is primarily or fully individual. The Woolman method may be less appropriate in situations where the ethical problem is primarily individual and personal. Traditions and systems are not always the primary or even an important source of the problematic behavior. As Argyris (1990, p. 60) has observed, some people blame the organization or the system simply as an excuse for avoidance of individual responsibility. While this is often true, the Woolman method sometimes can still help people to understand that there is no tradition system-level bias and the ethical problem is primarily individual. Exploration of the tradition system can make it clear that the source of the problem is one's own behavior, and thus encourage the individual to change voluntarily. Exploration of a tradition system can also reveal that it supports ethical behavior, which can increase pressure on an individual to "get in step" with it.

Powerful people in authority sometimes frame ethics issues in a self-interested manner and ignore alternative frames. Many of the powerful farmers and merchants whom Woolman approached chose, at least initially, to frame the issue in terms of the "untoward slothful disposition of the negroes." This outlook conveniently shifted the burden to the victim. While Woolman was able to overcome this framing with most of those people, some chose to ignore alternative framing and did not change their behavior until they were required to either by the Society of Friends' Minutes or Pennsylvania law.

Similarly, in the AT&T case, several powerful managers chose to frame the problem in terms of the "unsuitability of blacks" for management roles rather than the embedded and systematic channeling of blacks into nonmanagerial training, experiences, roles, and expectations. While Greenleaf was able to overcome this framing with many managers, some only changed their behavior when they were required to by company policies and federal law.

Powerful people can sometimes choose not to pay attention to or talk about an alternative framing that is not in their perceived self-interest. If the user of the method is considered an insider or peer, as was the case in all three examples, such people may feel some pressure to at least listen to him. The Woolman method sometimes can also trigger a positive response among people who articulate a biased, self-interested framing but simultaneously understand that the behavior in question is unethical. Many of the slaveowners Woolman talked with already understood that slavery was unethical, but on the surface accepted the biased framing and were inactive about the issue because they were benefitting from owning slaves. Some became willing to risk losing those benefits when Woolman spoke with them and they realized they were not alone in their reservations about slavery. Similarly, some of the managers Greenleaf spoke with already understood that it was unethical to discriminate against blacks. On the surface, they accepted the "unsuitability of blacks" framing and were inactive about their belief because they feared that other white managers and workers might disapprove of contrary actions. Some became willing to risk such disapproval when Greenleaf spoke with them and they realized they were not alone in their reservations.

However, there are circumstances where no conversational method is effective, including the Woolman method. Powerful people may understand what is unethical but choose to continue it because of their perceived self-interest. Correspondingly, less powerful people may choose to respond negatively because of fear of a powerful person who is supporting the problematic behavior.

The method can be misinterpreted and stimulate negative "us" versus "them" cognitions and behaviors. Raising the salience of a "we" fellowship relationship can have some negative consequences. A person considering the "we" fellowship relationship might respond positively to people within the "we" as insiders but might view people not part of the "we" as outsiders to be defended against or attacked. For example, during the Pennsylvania abolitionist movement, the Punjab cotton industry restructuring, and the post–consent decree period at AT&T, there was some intense adversarial behavior on all sides. There were heightened emotions about "their" evil compared to "our" righteousness. Sometimes the followers of Woolman, Greenleaf, and Hussain exhibited behavior as insensitive and nasty as the behaviors they were criticizing. Peacefully intentioned methods do not always result in peaceful outcomes. Sometimes peaceful methods can even stimulate, at least for a while, more violent and hostile reciprocal interactions. "I am we" can slip into "us versus them."

8

Friendly Upbuilding:
Triple-Loop Dialog II

Life can only be understood backwards, but it must be lived
forwards. . . . Dialectically the position is this: the principle
of association, by strengthening the individual, enervates him.
. . . It is only after an ethical outlook . . . that there is really
joining together.

—Søren Kierkegaard

The struggle of man against power is the struggle of memory
against forgetting.

—Milan Kundera

Destructive external environments can make it difficult to act ethically
inside organizations, and can threaten the foundations of internal
ethical traditions. Nonetheless, we can choose to build such traditions
from within so as to solve ethical problems while also adapting and
protecting the traditions. Ethical traditions are worth protecting, are
useful in solving ethics problems, and need to adapt. A method that
has been effective in achieving this process is upbuilding dialog.

Upbuilding dialog is a problem-solving change process that explicitly builds from within and adapts an ethical internal tradition in the
context of a problematical environment. Upbuilding dialog is a type of
action-learning. Upbuilding dialog combines (1) explicit building
from within an ethical tradition in relation to a problematical environ-

ment as a guide to framing and solving problems; (2) the generation of tradition-informed ethical decisions; and (3) holding the tradition open to criticism, adaptation, and further development. Limitations of the method include situations where a tradition may be questionably ethical or there is inadequate consensus about what the ethical components of the tradition are.

The concept of upbuilding dialog in ethics is Kierkegaardian. Upbuilding is the translation of Kierkegaard's Danish term *opbuggelig* (Steere, 1938). However, it is applied and extended here to problems of organization ethics, which Kierkegaard did not consider specifically.

There are many different types of strong, ethical organization traditions and many different types of problematical environments. The key to the upbuilding dialog method is not the particular organization tradition or problematical environment, but building upon the ethical foundations of an internal tradition to solve problems while also adapting and protecting the tradition within a problematical environment.

CADBURYS: AN ILLUSTRATION

Following are a description of the Cadburys* tradition and the particular problematical environment, a description of the specific tools Adrian Cadbury used to help give the Cadburys tradition a voice in the problem-solving process, and a discussion of the four upbuilding dialog steps taken in this process.

The Cadburys environmental situation and tradition   Cadburys has an almost two-hundred-year tradition of cooperative learning, high productivity, and ethical employee relations that has survived and prospered in spite of very problematical environmental pressures (Gardiner, 1923; Emden, 1939; Child, 1964; Windsor, 1980; Nielsen, 1982, 1996a; Dellheim, 1987; Smith, Child, and Rowlinson, 1990). In contrast to much of the history of British labor relations, there have been very few strikes or other forms of work disruption at Cadburys.

In the early years of the Thatcher administration in England, 1978–1983, management-labor relations at the national level were destructively adversarial. There was an intense adversarial climate between

---

*The literature generally uses the name Cadburys in referring to past events within the company (e.g., Dellheim, 1987; Smith, Child, and Rowlinson, 1990), as does Adrian Cadbury. The company has undergone several minor name changes since the early 1800s.

labor and the Conservative Party government (Krieger, 1987). The labor unions thought Thatcher was trying to break them, and the Conservative Party thought the unions were trying to sabotage its plans to restructure and reinvigorate the economy.

The unions were perceived as being allied with the Labor Party opposition to the Conservative Party government, and management was generally perceived as being allied with that government. There were many organizational-level strikes and work stoppages in Britain. Productivity in many organizations was declining. This difficult environment was compounded by an increasingly difficult competitive situation within the British food sector (Smith, Child, and Rowlinson, 1990).

Adrian Cadbury, the CEO of Cadbury's, anticipated this labor-management problem as early as 1964, when he served as discussion leader in a series of talks on the future of international industrial relations. In the conclusion to the volume that published the talks, he wrote that national-level labor-management negotiations were making it increasingly difficult to maintain cooperative workplace-level relations (A. Cadbury, 1964; Smith, Child, and Rowlinson, 1990).

However, he did not perceive the situation as hopelessly adversarial; he had a different perspective that included the cooperative tradition of Cadburys. "In any kind of institution, what you're after is getting the maximum motivation. To do that you involve people as much as you can and you are as open as you can be. . . . My great-grandfather, who founded the Cadbury business . . . had a belief in achieving, as far as one can, agreement by consensus" (Cadbury, 1983, p. 141).

Such beliefs, reflected in Cadburys' employee relations, had already been articulated by earlier generations of Cadburys managers. Edward Cadbury, a company personnel managing director in 1912, summarized the perspective as follows: "The supreme principle has been the belief that business efficiency and the welfare of the employees are but different sides of the same problem. . . . The test of any scheme of factory organization is the extent to which it creates and fosters the atmosphere and spirit of cooperation and good will, without in any sense lessening the loyalty of the worker to his own class and organizations" (1912, p. xvii).

Similarly, George Cadbury, Jr., the CEO at that time, explained that Cadburys' "labor strategy was to elicit commitment rather than exercise control. The interests of capitalist and laborer complemented each other. Cooperation is the basis of business" (G. Cadbury in Hodgkin, 1918, p. 73). Through most of its history, with a few exceptions, Cadburys has maintained a tradition of employee welfare and peaceful, cooperative, consensus-building employee relations (Gardiner,

1923; Emden, 1939; Child, 1964; Windsor, 1980; Nielsen, 1982; Dellheim, 1987; Smith, Child, and Rowlinson, 1990).*

Nonetheless, Cadburys was not immune to the present adversarial environment, which Adrian Cadbury was concerned might contaminate and cause long-term damage to the Cadburys' cooperative internal tradition. He was also concerned that the problematical environment might make it difficult for Cadburys to address a specific worker displacement issue, as Cadburys was considering a major technological change in its tea packaging facilities.

Cadburys' TyPhoo brand of tea had a large share of the United Kingdom tea market. The tea was packed in two plants, one in Birmingham, whose sole business was this packing, and one in Liverpool, where there were also other operations. Birmingham-Bournville was the historical center of Cadburys' operations, while there were many other Cadburys factories in other product lines.

When the United Kingdom moved to metrication, Cadburys had to address the issue of changing TyPhoo's packaging from quarter-pound packets to 100-gram packets. Cadbury thought it might be necessary to invest in new packing technology that was much faster than the old and required far fewer people to operate. It appeared that one of the tea packing plants might have to close. Technological investment and change had also resulted in employment displacement in several other areas of operations (Smith, Child, and Rowlinson, 1990).

Adrian Cadbury considered the worker displacement issue both an ethics and productivity problem. In referring specifically to business ethics, technological change, and worker displacement, he explains:

> The . . . aspect of ethics in business decisions I want to discuss concerns our responsibility for the level of employment; what can or should companies do about the provision of jobs? . . . The company's prime responsibility to everyone who has a stake in it is to retain its competitive edge, even

---

*Historically, the ideal of cooperative consensus building by management and labor even included management's support for the unionization of their own employees. According to Smith, Child, and Rowlinson "It was within the tradition of Cadburyism that trade unions should be fully recognized. This is evident not only in the writings of the Cadburys, but also historical accounts" (1990, p. 177). George Cadbury, a former CEO of Cadburys, stated, "I think I am voicing the wishes of the Directors when I say, we look ultimately for the whole of the workpeople to be organised . . . we understand and recognize that the workpeople must be organized too" (Rowlinson, 1987, p. 257). Adrian Cadbury shared this perspective. He stated, "We as managers should be at the forefront in organizing shop stewards' training and collecting union dues. Anything which makes for an efficient union with a stable membership must be in our interest" (Smith, Child, and Rowlinson, 1990, p. 194).

if this means a loss of jobs in the short run. Where companies do have a
social responsibility, however, is in how we manage that situation, how we
smooth the path of technological change. Companies are responsible for
the timing of such changes and we are in a position to involve those who will
be affected by the way in which those changes are introduced. (1987, p. 72)

Adrian Cadbury believed in participative management. He states
that this belief "stems directly from the . . . influence of the foun-
ders" (Minkes and Nuttall, 1985, p. 61). "I have absolutely no doubts
about the rightness of it [such management]. I take it seriously, and I
do something about it myself. Your policy will be effective only if you
actually practice it yourself. And we have a climate of opinion in the
company which is supportive of it" (Cadbury, 1983, p. 134).

For Cadbury process is key to organization ethics. The process he
used was upbuilding dialog, that is, explicitly building a solution from
within the tradition and adapting the tradition to the context of a
problematical environment. He gave voice to the tradition as a guide
to the change process, an object for criticism and reform, and an
organizational defense against what he considered destructive aspects
of the external environment.

Cadburys did succeed in solving the specific ethics problem while
maintaining and adapting its historical tradition through the upbuilding dialog process. More specifically, Cadburys (1) built upon its cooperative tradition; (2) compared its historical cooperative tradition to
the current adversarial labor-mangement environment; (3) cooperatively solved a major worker displacement problem; (4) held the cooperative tradition open for criticism and reform; and (5) achieved a
consensus decision with workers to introduce a new packing technology that reduced employment by fifty percent, closed a factory,
smoothed worker displacement, and modified the Cadburys tradition.

Adrian Cadbury's situation and tradition-specific behavior was
Kierkegaardian, though he articulated and understood his approach
in the context-specific language of Cadburys' particular tradition
rather than Kierkegaard's general "upbuilding" approach. Such similarities between particular local traditions and more general philosophical principles are common. For example, Kant's general principle affirming the need to treat people as ends in themselves rather
than merely means to an end is also found in several different types of
cultural and religious traditions.

The upbuilding dialog at Cadburys   The upbuilding dialog followed
four steps; in addition, Cadbury used five different techniques to help
give the Cadburys tradition a voice in the change process. First I will
discuss the five techniques, and then the four dialog steps.

A working party was formed to address the problem, and it was specifically stated that such inclusive problem-solving working parties were part of the Cadburys' tradition. The working party included managers, engineers, and shop stewards from both of the factories involved, who were trade union representatives. Several older employees who had worked for Cadburys most of their lives were also invited to be members of the working party. These older workers understood and valued the Cadburys tradition and had served effectively on previous problem-solving committees. Such participative working parties were common within Cadburys (Gardiner, 1923; Child, 1964; Nielsen, 1982, 1988a, 1988b, 1996a; Cadbury, 1983, 1985, 1987; Dellheim, 1987; Child and Smith, 1987; Smith, Child, and Rowlinson, 1990).

Specific and frequent references to the Cadburys tradition were made at every step in the dialogic process within the working party deliberations. Further, Cadbury made frequent public statements about the Cadburys tradition. And statements about the Cadburys tradition were included in company documents such as the annual chairman's statement, the 1973 "Employee Relations Policy" (the "Pink Paper"), and the 1981 "Security of Employment Agreement." According to Smith, Child, and Rowlinson the "Pink Paper philosophy . . . represented a continuity with the Cadbury ideology of worker involvement and consultation" (1990, p. 354). According to Child and Smith (1987), the 1981 security of employment agreement "institutionalized retraining, transfers and redundancy payments for those displaced by automation and rationalization."

The four upbuilding dialog steps were as follows.

Working party members were approached in a friendly and respectful manner, not in coolly professional, authoritarian, or adversarial ways. Upbuilding from within a tradition of friendliness is central to both Kierkegaard's general approach and the specific Cadburys tradition, which originated in ideas developed within the Society of Friends (Quakers).

According to Smith, Child, and Rowlinson, "Adrian Cadbury has attached the family's traditional belief in community to the possibilities of close corporate identity and personal relationships" (1990, p. 330).

Adrian Cadbury further explains:

Openness of discussion goes back to the firm's origins and to the Quaker view of individual worth and of the ability of everyone concerned to contribute to decisions. That same view led to a willingness to listen to criticism in order to turn it to constructive use. The length of the joint consultative tradition . . . encouraged the open expression of views, whether palatable or not, and this assisted the transformation process. . . . Along the same lines, the trust and confidence which joint consultation had built up over the years played its part in enabling fundamental change to be brought about with less conflict than might otherwise have been expected. . . . This is all part of the paradox that a background of continuity and stability is resistant to change, but it may also facilitate the process of bringing change about. A past investment in good working relationships can up to a point be drawn upon, when far-reaching changes need to be made. (1990, p. xii)

This perspective was also stated in company documents, such as the 1973 employee relations policy, which emphasized the need for "a people oriented informal approach at all levels" (Smith, Child, and Rowlinson, 1990, p. 354).

The conversation was framed as a request for help to address a problem related to an ethical value within "our" tradition that might be threatened by the external environment. The possible change in packing technology was potentially related to the important shared historical values of employment security, operations efficiency, and consensus decisionmaking. Shared historical values within Cadburys were reviewed that were already articulated in organization documents such as the following:

Starting with the assumption that Capital and Labour, Management and Workers, Manufacturers and Distributors, are to be collaborators in the enterprise of serving the community, it is worth while trying to determine the sort of industrial organisation which can pursue this aim most effectively. . . . What opportunities can the workers be given to fit themselves for positions of responsibility? How can the introduction of labour-saving machinery be reconciled with the claims of the displaced worker?" (Cadbury, 1983, p. 136)

Working party members considered how "we" have more and less successfully addressed similar issues in the past within "our" tradition, and considered potential solutions to the current problem. Together they considered specific past cases of employment security and efficiency-motivated technological change. Cases were remembered and discussed where employees had engaged in participative decisionmaking that had at various times resulted in increased employment, better employment conditions, better service to customers and the community, as well as times when technological change resulted in worker displacements and occasional destructive conflicts, such as the rare and brief strike of 1979.

Cadburyism remained a strong ideology in the consciousness of family members, management and workers, who all perpetuated it. It appears to have been both a benchmark for change and a force mediating that change.

As a benchmark it provoked key change agents deliberately to set out their case against the fundamentals of the tradition. . . . At the same time, the company was able to invoke elements of the ideology and remould these in different circumstances—probably because those new circumstances were neither wholly different nor came upon the company too suddenly. The search for precedents for radical changes has been apparent among those family managers who in effect act as official historians for the company. Thus, Sir Adrian Cadbury has attached the family's traditional belief in community to the possibilities . . . created by a process of employment rationalisation and restructuring such as has been pursued in his company. (Smith, Child, and Rowlinson, 1990, p. 330)

A tradition-informed solution was adopted, and the Cadburys tradition was modified. Working party members were asked to help develop and try an action that would be informed by "our" internal tradition and that also might require some modification of it. Potential actions were considered such as delaying metrication, investing in new equipment for both plants, reducing employment at both plants, and closing one plant. The solution the working party, including the trade union and other employee representatives, unanimously recommended was producing the same or greater output with the new machinery and half the number of workers. In addition, if closing a plant was decided on as a permanent action, a package of employment displacement benefits with intraorganization transfers, preferential rehiring, and layoff benefits should be adopted.

Due to severe perceived external, national union pressure and perceived responsibility to local factory workers, the shop stewards did not think that they could participate in a decision about which plant to close, so the working party asked top management to make this decision.

The tradition-informed consensus decision that was asked for and taken required some modification of the Cadburys tradition.

We put two questions to the working party: (1) Does it make sense to put all the tea packing in one place? (2) If it does make sense, which one ought it be? We gave them all the figures on which the decision had to be based. We got unanimous support for the view that we should put all the tea packing in one place, and on the second issue they said, very understandably, you can hardly expect us to make that decision for you. We did, in the end, close the factory in Birmingham. It was a very disagreeable decision and it obviously disrupted the lives of a number of people. (Cadbury, 1983, p. 135)

The final decision of the working party, to pack the tea in one plant with three hundred fewer people, to close one plant, and to provide a package of employment displacement benefits including intraorganization transfers, preferential rehiring, and layoff benefits, was consistent with shared values within the internal tradition. Some employees explored and accepted intraorganization transfers, some left the organization permanently with generous layoff financial packages, and others moved to other Cadburys operations at later times with preferential rehiring as openings from attrition and expansion in other areas developed.

Cadbury stated, "The point I want to make . . . is this: we reached that difficult decision with a degree of understanding which would have been quite impossible if the decision had come down from on high that we're closing the Birmingham factory, we're putting tea packing up in Liverpool. That would have been quite unacceptable. . . . Although the decision inevitably was unacceptable to the people involved, the fact that their own representatives had seen the figures, and had accepted the sense of putting it all together in one place, produced a high degree of understanding about the situation" (Cadbury, 1983, p. 136).

The upbuilding approach was effective in addressing a difficult ethical and economic issue. The Cadbury tradition was also modified: The scope of the participatory decisionmaking tradition within Cadburys was localized and narrowed at the request of the shop stewards. In order to protect participation in other important areas, it was necessary to localize and narrow the range of decisionmaking participation in this area.

What the working party members considered a good aspect of the Cadburys tradition had to bend somewhat in response to the negative external environment, in order to permit productive, ethical, and cooperative internal change and development relationships to continue. As Giuseppe di Lampedusa observed in *The Leopard*, "If we want things to stay as they are, things will have to change" (Lampedusa, 1961; Gilmour, 1988).

KIERKEGAARD'S UPBUILDING PHILOSOPHY

Four elements in Kierkegaard's philosophy of upbuilding ethics correspond to the four steps in upbuilding dialog: friendly, respectful affect; framing the issue as a problematical environment that is threatening ethical action and tradition; a solution process of upbuilding action-learning by individuals from within a tradition; and ethically transformed association (Kierkegaard, 1941, 1944, 1946, 1956, 1962, 1967, 1968; Steere, 1938, 1949, 1957; Lowrie, 1942; Bernstein, 1971).

Friendly, respectful affect. Like Adrian Cadbury, Kierkegaard was concerned with ethical process. For both, an important part of ethical process was friendly, respectful, and even loving expression while in actual or potential conflict with others. Kierkegaard suggested not that we understate our ethical concerns in order to avoid conflict, but that we should speak both fully and in a friendly, respectful manner. He also recognized that this is difficult. Nonetheless, he believed that ethical process, including full and friendly expression, was very important.

He explained his friendly, respectful approach as follows: "a man can, to be sure, have an extremely different, yes, have a precisely opposite opinion from our own, and one can nevertheless deal earnestly with him if one assumes that finally there may be a point of agreement, a unity in some universal human sense, call it what you will. But if he is mad [angry], then one cannot deal with him. One can dispute with a man, dispute to the farthest limit, as long as one assumes, that in the end there is a point in common, an agreement in some universal human sense; in . . . respect" (1956, pp. 183–184).

By extension, Kierkegaard also was opposed to adversarial "us-versus-them" group divisions in ethics, including adversarial management versus labor divisions. He asks the question:

> And what is your attitude toward others? . . . Alas, there is something in the world called clannishness. It is a dangerous thing because all clannishness is divisive. It is divisive when clannishness shuts out the common citizen, and when it shuts out the nobleborn, and when it shuts out the civil servant. It is divisive when it shuts out the king, and when it shuts out the beggar, and when it shuts out the wise man, and when it shuts out the simple soul. For all clannishness is the enemy of universal humanity. But to will only one thing, genuinely to will the Good . . . which things each person without exception is capable of doing, that is what unites. (1956, p. 206)

This friendly aspect of upbuilding dialog is also discussed in the strengths and limitations section later. Depending upon the circumstances, friendliness can be both a strength and a limitation of the method.

Framing the issue as a problematical environment that is threatening ethical action and tradition. Cadbury framed the worker displacement issue as a concern that the adversarial labor-management environment might threaten ethical action within Cadburys and also threaten what he considered Cadburys' ethical tradition. Kierkegaard also explicitly framed an ethics problem in relation to a potentially destructive environment. In the 1840s, when he was writing about his upbuilding approach, Europe was experiencing both progress and very powerful, often destructive changes that accompanied the growth of industrialization and the spread of ideas, often distorted ideas, from the French Revolution. Napoleon's massive revolutionary armies had swept across, up, and down Europe, had left much devastation in their wake, and had only been defeated, at least for a while, some twenty-five years earlier. The growth of mass production and industry was accompanied by rapidly increasing urbanization, industrial conflict, public health problems, and serious breakdowns in local communities.

From the vantage point of the small, relatively peaceful country of Denmark, large parts of Europe appeared to be buffeted by waves of uncontrollable, destructive social forces. Many people thought these external forces were abetted by "crowd" (Kierkegaard's word) mentalities that were unable to discriminate among the positive and negative aspects of ongoing mass social changes.

Kierkegaard compared trying to do ethics, which he considered an essentially local activity, on the basis of "world-historical" trends with trying to find one's way about "Denmark with the help of a small map of Europe, on which Denmark shows no larger than a steel penpoint—aye, it is still more impossible" (Kierkegaard, 1968, p. 277).

He was also concerned about unthinking conformity to mass, popular opinion trends. "More and more individuals, owing to their bloodless indolence, will aspire to be nothing at all—in order to become the public: that abstract whole formed in the most ludicrous way, by all participants becoming a third party, an onlooker" (Kierkegaard, 1962, pp. 64–65).

As Douglas Steere explains, "Instead of heightening his core of [local] responsibility and integrity, man is invited to do what he is already enamored with doing, to join the crowd, the mass, to be dissolved into the organic whole" (1956, pp. 17, 18).

> [J]oining the crowd in its noisemaking, would be folly that would lead only to fresh folly. . . . You see . . . a man counts and says: "One over against a hundred, after all what can come of that?" So he grows cowardly in the face of—number. . . . But a man wins something by this cowardly indulgence. He does not win a bed in a hospital. No, but he wins the amazing thing of becoming the strongest of all, because the crowd is always the strongest. . . . For many fools do not make a wise man, and the crowd is doubtful recommendation for a cause. (Kierkegaard, 1956, pp. 181–183)

A solution process of upbuilding action-learning by individuals from within a tradition. Both Kierkegaard and Cadbury were concerned with doing ethics, not just understanding ethics. Kierkegaard recognized that ethics was an interactive and continuing acting and learning process, that one learns through action, and learning in turn informs action. "The ethical is not merely a knowing; it is also a doing that is related to a knowing, and a doing such that the repetition may in more than one way become more difficult than the first doing" (Kierkegaard, 1968, p. 143).

For Kierkegaard, dialog was key to ethical action.

The speaker is then . . . the listener, if I may say so, is the actor. . . .
The talk asks you, or you ask . . . by means of the talk. . . . See that you
question . . . by means of the talk. Talk . . . contains the possibility of
change. . . . If the circumstances are difficult, the obligation to speak is
doubled. The difficulty is precisely an invitation. . . . if he dared remain
silent and therefore by his silence . . . by his consent, he had . . . contributed to a condition where the circumstances became still more unfavor-
able. . . . The fault was not that he did not manage to get the circumstances changed. The fault was that he was silent because it is the most
prudent to be so. . . . At the dawn of day, give to the young man the
resolution. . . . As the day wanes . . . give to the old man a renewed
remembrance of his first resolution, that the first may be like the last, the
last like the first. (Kierkegaard, 1956, pp. 208–209)

Further, ethical dialog and ethical doing are not abstract activities, but need to be grounded in one's own concrete, local tradition
"The smaller the circumstances in which the ethical is appre-
hended . . . the more clearly it is perceived; while whoever needs
the world-historical accessories in order, as he thinks, the better
to see it, proves thereby precisely that he is ethically immature"
(Kierkegaard, 1968, p. 128).

Kierkegaard's biographer, Walter Lowrie, observed that a factor
that exerted a prodigious influence on Kierkegaard and his work was
that

he had an unusually vivid feeling of solidarity with the family, the clan, the
race. . . . He was not opposed to change as such but contended against
the effort to impose upon Denmark the abstract theories of the French
Revolution, without taking into account the character of this Nordic race,
the history of the nation and the institutions which had grown up in conformity with the genius of the people. The modern development of the Scan-
dinavian nations . . . with institutions peculiar to the people and appropriate to their situation, has amply justified S.K.'s contention. (1942, pp. 30,
90)

More recently, Fleischacker interprets Kierkegaard's upbuilding
approach as follows: "I acquire an adequate sense of my possibilities
for action only when I accept the fact that my place in the world
is given by my emotional and historical circumstances. . . . These
various and conflicting requirements can be met by trusting a particular narrative that gives me my place in the world rather than allowing
me to imagine I have created that place. . . . So the particularity of a
story points toward the universal, while its point at the universal only
demonstrates that the universal can and must be sought in particular
ways" (1994, p. 78).

For both Kierkegaard and Cadbury, local embedded ethical wisdom
does not have to be overwhelmed by waves of crowd phenomena. Just

as such wisdom can be positively and negatively influenced by such waves, so also it can inform them. Such mutual informing proceeds in mutual "talk," listening, and questioning.

In a sense, Kierkegaard's upbuilding approach is an attempt to constructively criticize and balance what he considered the self-fulfilling overemphasis on the power of macro social waves of Hegel and his potentially even more extreme followers—(possibly an anticipation of the Nietzsche-Derrida stream of postmodernism).

Ethically transformed association. For Kierkegaard, upbuilding method holds open the possibility of ethically imagined and transformed association. He refers to a "poetics" of ethics where potentialities, and what ought to be, can be enacted and made incarnate.

Cadbury similarly hoped for and appears to have achieved the renewal and reform of Cadburys' tradition, community, and association of management and employees. As Smith, Child, and Rowlinson observed, "Cadburyism remained a strong ideology in the consciousness of family members, management and workers, who all perpetuated it. It appears to have been both a benchmark for change and a force mediating that change. As a benchmark it provoked key change agents deliberately to set out their case against the fundamentals of the tradition. . . . At the same time, the company was able to invoke elements of the ideology and remould these in different circumstances" (1990, p. 330).

Kierkegaard explains such a change process dialectically. "Nowadays the principle of association . . . is not positive but negative; it is an escape, a distraction and an illusion. Dialectically the position is this: the principle of association, by strengthening the individual, enervates him; it strengthens numerically, but ethically that is a weakening. It is only after . . . an ethical outlook, in the face of the whole world, that there can be any suggestion of really joining together" (1962, p. 79).

That is, if one allows oneself to be absorbed within the macro-level "crowd," for example either the national Conservative or Labor "side," one becomes stronger in that one is allied with a very large group. But such affiliation and loyalty can interfere with ethical responsibility, ability, and freedom at the local and, in our case, organizational level. For Kierkegaard, ethics starts with responsibility and action within a local tradition.

If we allow ourselves to be enemies at the environment level, that can make it difficult to do cooperative, ethical problem-solving at the local level. For Kierkegaard, doing is inseparable from knowing. Such a loss of local ethical responsibility is an "ethical weakening." But if we can upbuild from within our local ethical association and tradition "in the face of the whole world," then ethical problems can be solved and local association can be transformed and deepened.

UPBUILDING DIALOG AS TRIPLE-LOOP ACTION-LEARNING

Kierkegaard stated, "The ethical is not merely a knowing; it is also a doing that is related to a knowing" (1968, p. 143). While Argyris and Schon use the terms acting and learning, Kierkegaard's translators have used the terms doing and knowing. Ways of doing and acting are similar just as ways of knowing and learning are similar. In philosophy the latter are both considered epistemology, and the former are both considered praxis. A different translator might as easily have used the terms acting and learning instead of doing and knowing.

Upbuilding dialog is a specific type of triple-loop action-learning. It has the following similarities to Argyris' and Schon's double-loop method: (1) it holds open initial values, assumptions, frameworks, and positions for mutual inquiry, dialog, and challenge; (2) it seeks disconfirming data with respect to these initial values and frameworks; and (3) it recognizes the value of mistakes in the service of mutual learning.

Upbuilding approach differs from double-loop action-learning in three key respects: (1) it intentionally includes emotive, respectful, friendly affect; (2) it explicitly frames the triple-loop mutual action-learning as a problematical environment that threatens ethical action and ethical tradition; and (3) it explicitly requests upbuilding help from within a tradition rather than pursuing advocacy with inquiry.

STRENGTHS AND LIMITATIONS OF UPBUILDING DIALOG METHOD

The strengths of upbuilding method include the following: (1) it can help an organization to constructively resist negative external pressures while helping its own tradition learn and develop; (2) as with Woolman's method, friendly, respectful affect can facilitate peaceful change; and (3) as with dialog method generally, the process can facilitate ethical action-learning by individuals.

Limitations of upbuilding dialog include the following: (1) it can be too conservative; (2) it is not applicable in situations where a tradition may be questionably ethical or there is inadequate consensus about what its ethical components are; and (3) some negative external environments can be perceived as too powerful to resist.

Strengths

Upbuilding can help an organization to constructively resist negative external pressures while helping its tradition to learn and develop. For example, within the Cadburys tradition, there was the ideal that management and labor shared responsibility for ethical, productive cooperation. The shop stewards continued to share this responsibility even to the extent of sharing decision responsibility for closing a factory. But the tradition also had to learn and change, and not require them to share more responsibility than they could. In order to maintain shared worker responsibility for such a hard decision, the shop stewards had to be relieved of deciding which factory to close.

According to Smith, Child, and Rowlinson referring to Cadburys, "In short, a dominant traditional corporate ideology should not necessarily be seen merely as an obstacle to transformation. For it may encourage a clearer articulation of alternatives the more highly developed it is, and if reshaped or reapplied flexibly, it may provide an important legitimatory bridge for the transition from one organizational policy/structure configuration to another" (1990, p. 330).

As with the Woolman method, friendly, respectful affect can facilitate peaceful change. The Argyris-Schon assumption that people with different initial positions on sensitive and important issues can interact with each other civilly and objectively is a somewhat idealized and inaccurate expectation. When ideas are in serious conflict, people can also be in serious conflict. Upbuilding builds upon Argyris-Schon method by including friendly, respectful affect instead of detached, civil professionalism as a vehicle for facilitating cooperative action-learning. Apparently, the TyPhoo tea packing discussion proceeded without bitterness and acrimony.

If key people trying to use the approach are not trusted or are perceived as insincere, then the attempt to establish friendly, respectful affect might well fail. Use of this approach might be restricted to those situations where at least one of the key players had already established relationships of trust before the current crisis occurred.

As with dialog method generally, upbuilding can facilitate action-learning by individuals. Upbuilding method embraces both Argyris-Schon action-learning and classical Socratic dialog, sharing with them the focus Law ... nc. terms the classical concern "to really ask questions, to suspend a subject matter in its possibilities among various alternatives. . . . subordinating oneself to the tutelage, the leadership, the guidance of the subject matter to which the partners in the conversations are oriented" (1984, p. 23).

For example, in the tea packing case, the Liverpool factory manager, the Birmingham factory manager, the shop stewards, the engineers, and the corporate-level managers all appeared to be mostly nonadversarial and nonlobbying. Instead they looked for a reasonable solution that was "neither mine nor thine." The shop stewards even recommended closing one plant, a very unusual, perhaps unique phenomenon in Britain at the time. The working party members and the organization learned that technological change was necessary, a factory had to be closed, and employee welfare needed to be and could be cared for during the change.

According to Cadbury, "We spent longer than we might otherwise on the preliminary stages of involving people and discussing the steps to be taken and how they would be taken—but spent a very short period in implementing. So we did not extend the span of decision making, we altered the constituent parts. The other way around, we would have made a quick decision at the board level and we would have had one enormous hassle at the implementation level. And I think we would have got off to a far less satisfactory start with the new production layouts" (1983, p. 136).

Limitations

Upbuilding can be too conservative. The method focuses on transformation from within an ethical tradition, but the key problem might be an internal tradition rather than the environment. The external "crowd" could be enlightened, and the internal tradition might not be.

Kierkegaard's approach also may not recognize the possibility of extreme, deconstructive, postmodernist thinking. That is, the approach may not appreciate the possibility that many people might believe that there are such fundamental negative biases in most traditions and that improvement and development within traditions are impractical and absurd (Derrida, 1977, 1981).

The approach is less applicable in situations where a tradition may be questionably ethical or there is inadequate consensus about what its components are. The J. P. Stevens textile manufacturing organization, for example, has been characterized by a history of acrimony, bitterness, and violence between management and labor. Similarly, the method may not be applicable when ethical tradition is overwhelmed in a merger or acquisition by the problematical tradition of the acquiring organization. For example, Buono and Bowditch (1989) document a case where they found that the cooperative, ethical tradition of an acquired bank was overwhelmed and poisoned by an acquiring bank that had a very problematical tradition. Employees of the acquired bank were even forcefully discouraged from discussing ethical issues.

If there is not enough agreement about what the ethical components really are, then there is no foundation for upbuilding. Either too many people or key people might not believe that there are ethical components or agree on what they are. For example Chester Walsh (see chapter 4) blew the whistle outside G.E. on several upper-level managers who were defrauding the Defense Department (Naj, 1992). Mr. William Lytton, general counsel of G.E. Aerospace, suggested he should have used the G.E. internal ethics compliance system at G.E. But Mr. Walsh felt that he had to go outside the organization because he thought it was the tradition within G.E. to look the other way with respect to disobeying the rules when it is convenient for more senior managers and that internal whistle blowers were often punished, not rewarded.

Several similar cases at G.E. could be cited. There appears to be a perception among some employees within G.E., including Walsh and Cimorelli in the two different G.E. ethics cases, that it is part of the tradition within G.E. to obey one's boss's orders, even unethical orders, and that G.E. selectively looks the other way when senior managers behave unethically.

G.E. chairman Welch appeared to recognize the internal contradictions among a very strong bottom-line emphasis, an intimidating, Theory X style of management, and organization ethics. He stated that G.E. "can't afford management styles that suppress and intimidate subordinates. . . . The most difficult type for many of us to deal with. That leader delivers on commitments, makes all the numbers, but doesn't share the values we must have. This is the individual who typically forces performance out of people rather than inspires it: the autocrat, the big shot, the tyrant. Too often all of us have looked the other way because . . . they always deliver—at least in the short term" (Hyatt and Naj, 1992, p. B1).

Some environments can be perceived as too powerful to resist. This was the experience of IBM's top management when they considered changing IBM's no-layoff, full-employment, employee welfare tradition. Buck Rogers, a former vice president of IBM, describes part of the old tradition:

> The First Commitment. . . . Since IBM opened its doors, the company has had a full-employment tradition. This is as true today, with nearly 400,000 employees, as it was when there were only hundreds of people in the company. . . . In nearly fifty years, no person employed on a regular basis has lost as much as one hour of working time because of a layoff. Like all businesses, IBM has had its share of difficult times. It has taken careful

planning and commitment to maintain full employment. . . . For example, during the economically troubled years 1969–72, more than twelve thousand IBM employees moved from plants, labs and headquarters with light workloads to locations where they were needed. More than five thousand employees were retrained for new careers in sales, customer engineering, field administration and programming. Most ended up with comparable or better jobs. (Rogers, 1986, pp. 10–12)

The problematical environment of the 1992–1993 recession within the computer industry and subsequent financial performance pressure from IBM's board of directors was too powerful even for an organization as large and strong as IBM to resist. Chairman John F. Akers said, "The decline has been precipitous and it has happened at a much faster rate than we expected. . . . We have disappointed ourselves and we have disappointed other people. . . . It's my expectation some businesses will not be able to make 'full employment'" (IBM's term for its no-layoff tradition) (Hooper and Miller, 1992, p. 3).

Since then, Akers has been dismissed from his position for moving too slowly in changing IBM's financial performance and tradition. The tradition has been changed not in some IBM businesses but in all. This is more than a reform and adaptation of a tradition as at Cadburys; it is the elimination of a tradition. IBM is now closer to the bottom-line financial orientation of a G.E. than to its old tradition of employee welfare. Hays has observed, "The new chief executive shelved the three 'basic beliefs' that had guided IBM for decades: pursue excellence; provide the best customer service; and, above all, show employees 'respect for the individual.' In their place came eight goals that had worked well for Mr. Gerstner at RJR Nabisco Holding Corp. and American Express Co." (1994, p. 1).

CONCLUSION

Upbuilding dialog helps frame and solve problems related to destructive environments that make it difficult to act ethically inside organizations and that threaten the ethical foundations of internal traditions. Upbuilding dialog treats an internal tradition as both a subjective guide for meeting such environments and as an object for criticism and adaptive reform. The upbuilding method treats "our" tradition system as a subjective participant and potential partner in friendly, mutual action-learning. There are circumstances where the probable effectiveness of this method is limited. It is particularly appropriate in circumstances where there is an internal ethical tradition, there is adequate consensus about what its ethical components are, and the problematical environments are not too difficult to resist.

Some double-loop specialists might prefer to consider triple-loop action-learning more a type of double-loop action-learning than a new type of action-leraning. In double-loop action-learning, the conversation is between and among individuals. Such specialists might perceive that the recognition and valuing of an organization's tradition is just another type of individual perspective, rather than viewing a tradition as a potential partner and ally in mutual action-learning. Even so, one can still examine the relative effectiveness and appropriateness of the method. That is, within a double-loop framework, one can do comparative research that explicitly includes an individual's perspective that an organization's tradition can and should be a partner in mutual action-learning. The action-learning research stream still could expand.

The Woolman and Kierkegaard methods are only two types of triple-loop action-learning. While researchers for a generation have been exploring the various aspects of double-loop method, we have barely scratched the surface of the varieties of triple-loop action-learning.

9

Varieties of Postmodernism: Triple-Loop Dialog III

In the previous two chapters, the problems of biased external environments and biased internal traditions that cause or encourage unethical organization behavior were addressed with disentangling and upbuilding dialog methods. With both these methods the people who engaged in the dialogs more or less believed that they belonged to the same internal tradition. However, in other situations the key participants believe that they are part of very different and even antagonistic traditions.

Exploring the Asian child worker safety case described in chapter 2, this chapter illustrates how a conversation method was effectively used to address such a cross-tradition ethics problem. This method includes, as moments in one continuous process, three different postmodernist approaches—Gadamer reconstruction, Derrida deconstruction, and Rorty neopragmatism. The method also combines effective mutual learning and effective action.

This chapter is developed as follows. First, the case is presented in three parts that roughly correspond to the three different postmodernism approaches; second, the case is interpreted in terms of these three approaches; third, the strengths and limitations of combining the three approaches as moments in a continuous process are discussed.

ASIAN CHILD WORKER SAFETY CASE

The buyer for the American retailer who was concerned about brain and lung injuries to child workers in the Asian acid-washed clothing factory was able to use a conversation method to effectively address the issue, in a context of serious cross-cultural differences.

As stated in chapter 2, individuals from several different cultural traditions were involved. The Indonesian factory manager was a middle-class Muslim from a lower-class family. The American buyer was a middle-class Caucasian Christian. The factory owners were wealthy "overseas" Chinese. In addition, they had to give a piece of their ownership in their company to a wealthy Muslim general as part of the cost of doing business, which also permitted the factory to operate independently of many local employment and other laws. The American retailer was a publicly owned company with relatively large shares held by a mixed group of top managers and institutional investors.

The buyer perceived that there was a cross-cultural ethics problem. In high school and college he had had a little experience discussing ethics issues within the framework of Catholic Scholasticism. As an MBA student he had had some experience discussing ethics issues within a framework of nineteenth-century European utilitarianism and Kantianism. He had also had some introduction to classical Aristotelian virtue theory and Socratic dialog in his MBA program. He knew almost nothing about modern Chinese neo-Confucian ethics, Muslim ethics, local public or private life ethics, or ethics within the country's military framework. He thought that the ways he had previously talked about ethics issues might be inappropriate for what he perceived as a very different cross-cultural setting. He felt that there was no or very little center that all the different groups shared.

Buyer colleagues from his own company and other American and European companies knew about the unhealthy working conditions but didn't try to address the issue. Their common perception was that the working conditions were unfortunate but not particularly unusual and were "none of our business." It was part of the implicit ethics tradition of the buyer's company to address employee working conditions problems within its own U.S. facilities, but to confine conversations with foreign suppliers to product design and quality, reliability of supply, size of shipments, and pricing—not internal human resources conditions or ethics. Local businesspeople told him that poor families in this country had the realistic expectation that not all of their children would survive through adulthood. Even if one child suffered serious injury or death, if another could be helped to receive an education through that child's earnings, the family would be better off. A poor family could not afford to protect or help all its children.

The conversation method the buyer used included three different postmodernist approaches. The method alleviated the problem, at least temporarily, and appears to have some potential as an effective cross-cultural ethics approach. The process illustrated in this case

(Nielsen, 1993d) was dialectic (Bernstein, 1971, 1985), in that something was affirmed, something was negated, and a transformation emerged. These three moments correspond roughly to the three post-modernist approaches—Gadamer reconstruction, Derrida deconstruction, and Rorty neopragmatism. A description of the case follows; the next section discusses these approaches in the context of the case.

In the first moment of the conversation, corresponding to Gadamer (1975, 1989) reconstruction, the American buyer and the local factory manager recognized that it was likely that there was no mutual center amidst everyone's different cultural, social, political, and economic backgrounds and the different types of situational pressures they were experiencing. But they recognized that they had at least a couple of things in common within their different traditions. They began to reconstruct, from the limited commonalities of these traditions, temporary improvement. While the pressures they were under differed greatly, as middle managers they were able to talk about the shared experience of being under a lot of different pressures from the top, from peers, from subordinates, and in their private lives. It was part of both their traditions for middle managers to be empathetic with one another and to help each other when they could. And while they came from very different traditions concerning the economic role of children in families, they shared a vague, unarticulated, but real and common concern for the health and safety of the children. They were each able to reach back within and reconstruct from their own very different traditions a shared place for a beginning, if not a center.

In the second moment of the conversation, which corresponds to Derrida (1981, 1988) deconstruction, they were each able to explore the negative biases in the other's tradition that might have to be addressed or accommodated. The American buyer saw and talked about the negative pressures of the local military corruption, the overseas Chinese owners who appeared to have more concern for profits and financial liquidity than child worker safety, and the local political system that did not permit full citizenship participation for either the Chinese minority or the lower- and middle-class Malaysian majority. The factory manager saw and talked about the negative impacts of the history of his country's exploitation by European and Japanese colonizers and multinational corporations including American multinationals, and the irony of Asian children being injured and dying while producing acid-washed jeans for American and European children. As in the first moment of the conversation, the buyer and the factory manager recognized that there was very likely no ethical center among these entangled factors. Further, these macro tradition system-level factors were not controllable by them or perhaps anyone else.

In the third moment of the conversation, corresponding to Rorty

(1991) neopragmatism, the managers considered together the possibility of designing and implementing a limited experiment that might at least improve the situation temporarily. From their conversations emerged a plan. The factory manager told the Chinese owners that the American buyer was interested in increasing orders from the factory, but there might be a problem because he might need safer working conditions in the plant. An improved ventilation system was agreed upon in exchange for an increase in orders. The experiment worked. The ventilation sytem was installed, the American buyer increased orders, and the incidence of lung and brain disease appeared to be reduced. The experiment was extended to a few other factories within the country. At least for a while, the children's working conditions were improved. When the American retailer was later the victim of a hostile takeover, there was a downsizing and restructuring, and the buyer was laid off and had to leave that company for another. His layoff did not appear to have anything to do with the local Asian situation. Fashions in the United States changed from acid-washed jeans to other types of jeans. The working conditions of the child workers remain very difficult. However, at least for a while, in a few factories there were some improvements with respect to the acid-washing process and child worker health.

VARIETIES OF POSTMODERNISM

Postmodernism in Historical Perspective

The term "postmodernism" identifies a movement in relationship (post) to another movement (modernism). In order to understand what postmodernism is about, it is necessary to consider the earlier movements from which it distinguishes itself.

Historically there have been four distinct periods or waves of thought about human affairs (related to, but different from the evolution of physical sciences). There are several subapproaches within these four, but they will not be considered here, with the exception of the varieties of postmodernism.

All four perspectives can "see" parts, at least temporarily and contingently, of what is true. In any particular situation all these different streams may be relevant and be operating. Sometimes we can choose which emphases and combinations of the streams to work with.

The time periods of the different perspectives are as follows:

1. Classicism (Greek and Roman, about 600 B.C.–500 A.D., and extending to the present)
2. Scholasticism (Medieval, about 700–1500 A.D., and extending to

the present in certain corners of, for example, universities and secondary schools affiliated with religious organizations)
3. Modernism (about 1600 to 1930, and today the dominant perspective outside the relatively few philosophy, literature, law, sociology, and feminist studies departments and journals that focus on postmodernist perspectives)
4. Postmodernism (unfriendly deconstruction, friendly reconstruction, and civil experimental versions, about 1930s–present)

Brief Descriptions of the Different Approaches

In classicism, broadly considered, there is a center. The ideal purpose or end of life is union with embedded, underlying "forms" of harmony and perfection. The means to achieve this purpose are: cocreation with these underlying forms, friendly dialog as a method of simultaneous learning and civic action within communities, and virtuous living.

In scholasticism, broadly considered (there are Christian, Jewish, and Muslim versions) there is also a center. The ideal purpose or end of life is union with "God" and/or the "Spirit" "in all things." The means for achieving this purpose are to use reason and dialog to understand and collaborate with God/the Spirit so as to transform current situations into closer consistency with central, revealed truth. The revealed truth comes from sacred texts such as the Bible, the Koran, the earlier recorded teachings of religious prophets, and earlier case decisions of the religious courts.

In modernism there is also a center. The ideal purpose or end of life is the objective, science-informed discovery and creation of infinite progress. The method for achieving this progress is science-based reasoning in the social sciences and the humanities. Continuing experimentation is key. There is dialog about experiment designs and further experimentation based on the results of past experiments. Liberal social democracy, Marxism, psychoanalysis, Kantianism, utilitarianism, and so forth are included in this movement. There are macro social, cultural, and system-level biases, but there is also a belief that science-informed objectivity can eventually overcome bias.

Within postmodernism there is no universal center. I will consider three branches of postmodernism, which I call, for lack of better terminology, adversarial deconstruction, friendly reconstruction, and civil, experimental neopragmatism. (Some scholars within the deconstruction stream consider the latter two more late modernist than postmodernist.)

In adversarial deconstruction (e.g., Nietzsche, 1878, 1887; Heidegger, 1927; Derrida, 1981, 1988; Foucault, 1972), there is no center or single ideal purpose of life. There is an indirect sense that one should appreciate both one's own and others' separate tradition-based identities and differences. The method of achieving and maintaining difference and diversity is adversarial criticism of negative biases and oppressions in tradition systems. In addition, there is often adversarial criticism or mocking of individuals who speak from the mainstream, majority, or dominant tradition system. Recognizing that power corrupts, the best this approach hopes for is continuing criticism of the new powerful, who succeeded the old powerful, and will in turn be replaced by the newer powerful. On an interpersonal level, Derrida himself appears both friendly and critical (Kearney, 1984). However, since so many others within the deconstructive stream approach deconstruction adversarially, the term adversarial deconstruction is used here.

In friendly reconstruction (e.g., Gadamer, 1989a, 1989b) there is also no single ideal or purpose of life, and there is the same indirect sense that one should appreciate one's own and others' separate tradition-based identities and differences. However, there is a belief and hope that within our fundamental differences there are also tradition-based positive prejudices and commonalities that can be reached back into, reconstructed for contemporary circumstances, worked with, and built upon. At least temporary improvements and progress are possible. Amidst positive and negative biases and randomness and or chaos can be periods of relative improvement and progress. With respect to method, we can choose to work with different combinations of positive and negative biases and commonalities within our different, but not totally mutually exclusive, traditions. There is friendly reconstruction upon shared positive prejudices and friendly criticism and dialog about positive and negative biases in cultures and systems. While continuing, strongly chance-influenced change is the expectation, more than minimal peaceful coexistence is hoped for and is made possible by these actions.

Civil, experimental neopragmatism (e.g., Rorty, 1982, 1991) differs from the other two approaches in both the process and the ending. Neopragmatist postmodernists recognize that both positive and negative biases are operating. However, expectations are limited regarding both the positive bridging of differences and the potential benefits of the critical exposure of negative biases. The focus is on nonjudgemental coexistence and marginal improvement through detached and civil experimentation. The neopragmatist postmodernist perceives that while there may be no such things as objective standards or principles, it is nonetheless possible to experiment with a win-win solution. This approach contrasts with modernist experimentation, where a fundamental belief is that win-win solutions are based on objective science and/or principles that can be mutually learned about and acted upon.

With neopragmatist postmodernism there is minimal discussion of the positive or negative biases that emerge from different traditions. More simply, one asks about and accepts the possibility that people from different traditions have different needs, and negotiates relative, temporary win-win solutions. Experiments are explored for satisfying different needs without the consideration of objective principles.

POSTMODERN, MODERN, SCHOLASTIC, AND CLASSICAL STORIES

In reference to the cross-cultural child worker safety case, the four historical stages of thought can be illustrated in terms of the following three stories.

A Classical Story

The year is about 400 B.C. Our hero is a young Athenian man who is both a beginning "man of the world" and a beginning philosopher. He goes on a journey to visit another Athenian man. (Greek dialogs didn't happen much with non-Greeks.) The purpose of the journey was to buy cloth from a workshop where his family had been buying cloth. The cloth was of good quality, reliable supply, and low price. When he arrived at the workshop he found that all of the workers were children, and some of them seemed very sick. He engaged in civil conversation (perhaps double-loop, iterative Socratic dialog) with the master about what he saw.

In the first part of the conversation he learned that the children were sick because they constantly breathed toxins from the clothmaking and contracted various lung and brain injuries, sometimes even dying. Our hero sensed that the phenomenon of the diseased and dying children represented an unfortunate and unnecessary departure from the forms of harmony and perfection that exist in the universe beyond our immediate perception, understanding, and behavior. It was his belief and experience that through conversation and dialog, we could approach more closely these underlying forms.

If the story has a happy ending, through further Socratic dialog, the buyer and the master agree that it is inharmonious with the underlying forms of the universe for children to suffer and die this way and that ventilation can solve the problem. Ventilation is installed and the situation is brought into closer harmony with the underlying forms. The young man continues to grow and is recognized for his virtue and practical wisdom. He matures into a just and wise philosopher-leader.

Outline of Different Approaches/Perspectives

Philosophical Perspective	Purpose or End of Life (Teleos)	Method of Living (Action-Learning, Praxis-Epistemology)
Classicism	union with the underlying forms of harmony, perfection	Cocreation with the underlying forms; friendly dialog as action-learning
Scholasticism	union with God/the Spirit that is in all things	use of reason and dialog to understand and cocreate; making concrete cases consistent with sacred texts and previous revelation
Modernism	infinite creation of progress; objective progress is possible	social scientific reasoning, experimentation-based dialog
Postmodernism		
Adersarial deconstruction	appreciation of both one's own and others' separate tradition-based identities, reducing the abuse of power by the current dominant group	adversarial, mocking criticism that exposes negative biases in the dominant culture or system
Friendly reconstruction	appreciation of both one's own and others' tradition-based commonalities and differences; some, at least temporary, reforms are possible	friendly upbuilding upon shared commonalities and positive biases; friendly criticism of negative biases in each other's cultures or systems
Experimental neopragmatism	appreciation of both one's own and others' tradition-based commonalities and differences, some, at least temporary, improvements possible	civil, consensus-building experimentation that evolves and can result in at least temporary improvements

The story could also be a tragedy. Through some bad luck or imperfection (e.g., lack of clear or rigorous conversation and dialog), inordinate passion (e.g., pride), or lack of virtue (e.g., lack of practical wisdom or courage), the master could continue and the young man could accept the discordant practice. Later, the young man learns that the master is his long-lost father, and they then learn that his long-lost brother died in the workshop from acid poisoning.

A Scholastic Story

Christians, Jews, and Muslims each have versions of scholasticism. I'll use a Christian traveler. The year is 1300. Our hero is a Florentine priest. The master is also a Christian, but perhaps a Parisian. Our hero visits the workshop and sees that children are dying. In their conversation they frame the specific, concrete case of the dying children in relation to specific passages from Christian texts, such as the Bible or the works of the early Christian church fathers, or specific cases that previous church courts decided and recorded. The purpose of the conversation is together to figure out how to bring the current situation into closer correspondence with what was revealed in these sacred texts and/or previous cases.

If the story has a happy ending, the children are saved because the priest and the master learn through their conversation and study that the situation is contrary to Christian principles and case history. If the story is a tragedy, the master decides to act against the Christian framework and the children suffer. As a consequence the master, because he has chosen to be out of the light of God, experiences a terrible darkness of the soul both in this world and the next.

A Modernist Story

Modernist stories have mainly long-term, macro happy endings, but individual micro tragedies. The year is 1880. There are now several specialist heroes. One is an Oxford-educated English industrial scientist. He goes on a journey from perhaps England to Germany to visit a cloth factory.

Through clear, rigorous deductive reasoning and scientific observation, our scientist hero observes and comes to the conclusion that children are unnecessarily and nonproductively dying in the factory. Through close observation and analysis he diagnoses a cause for this that is directly related to his specialized profession. Through reasoning and experimentation, he has learned that win-win solutions are usually possible and desirable. The foundation for the solution is sound, universal, objective science: long-term productivity and employee welfare are both improved by having safer working conditions.

There are other specialists in this story. Our hero has dinner with a German social scientist. The German macro-oriented social scientist points out to the micro-oriented English industrial scientist that both German and English societies are neither as fair or as productive as they could be because they both have upper industrial classes that are exploiting lower working classes.

After dinner, they go to a cafe and bump into a German psychoanalyst, who suggests that the factory manager is probably a psychological victim of a repressive society and family, causing him in turn to act oppressively and dysfunctionally with his employees.

Several likely long-term happy endings can emerge after much short-term suffering. In one, the scientist and the factory manager enact a win-win solution through reasoning, observation, and action-science dialog. Working conditions are improved, employees are happier, and profitability increases. This solution gradually spreads to the industry, other industries, and other countries.

In another happy ending, through heroic and progressive social science-based thinking and social engineering, union organizers, worker party leaders, workers, and progressive intellectuals join together to transform backward, nonscientific German society to create good working and living conditions in a classless society. The movement gradually spreads to more primitive societies and the world is transformed.

In another happy ending, the factory manager undergoes psychoanalysis. In dialog with the therapist he begins to understand that he is a victim of abuse by repressive parents, the factory owners, and society. He gradually learns that he is perpetuating this repression in his relations with his wife, children, and workers. Through therapeutic dialog he is liberated and transformed into a more progressive and liberated person, husband, father, friend, and manager. The cycle of repression is broken. His transformation touches others, and an upward, progressive spiral begins and continues.

Postmodernist Stories

Postmodernist critics see powerful biases in cultures and societies that act as prejudices. Some (e.g., Gadamer) recognize that there can be positive and not just negative prejudices. We have adversarial critics (e.g., Nietzsche, Heidegger, Derrida), friendly critics (Gadamer), and civil experimental critics (e.g., Rorty, perhaps also Habermas).

Our stories change again. The textures, layers, differences, and perspectives within the stories multiply. Communication, dialog, and mediation across multiple perspectives, differences, and groups are very difficult, and for some postmodernists ultimately impossible. Both happy endings and tragedies are possible, but they are temporary and are not necessarily movements in any one better or worse direction.

The time is present. The setting is global, cross-traditional, and cross-cultural. This time, the key actor-interventionist (there are no heroes or tragedies in postmodernism) is a professor-critic who believes that, at least within human relations, there are multiple truths operating simultaneously. People with different perspectives and from different traditions see different aspects of a story such that, in effect, there are several stories operating, not one objective story. Our professor does not perceive universals, objectivity, infinite progress, or universal centers. Postmodernists perceive that there are enormous amounts of chance, biases, and chaos that both shape history and oppress individuals and groups. Many believe that the concept of progress is meaningless and/or there is no hope for progress with respect to the elimination of cultural biases that oppress. ("The poor will always be with us"?) Many believe that the most we can hope for is fluctuating plurality and tolerance of peacefully coexisting differences. In postmodernist stories there are no final endings. There are continuing changes and adaptations, but not necessarily any positive evolutions.

While there are some commonalities among postmodernists, there are also important differences. These differences can be illustrated in terms of variations in our child worker health case.

A Reconstruction Story

In a postmodernist reconstruction story, a happy ending would be for the American buyer and the Asian factory manager to be able to solve the child worker health problem on the basis of commonalities they share within their different but bridged traditions. More specifically, comparisons would not be made about whose tradition is more oppressive, whose tradition is more the cause of the problem, or who has suffered more. Through dialog that focuses on the child worker health issue in relation to positive commonalities within traditions, a joint solution would emerge. Within the context of their commonalities, both parties would offer something. In this case, capital investment in ventilation systems by the Asian company was exchanged for increased buying by the American company. This solution was facilitated by the shared sense of a common experience of the pressures of being middle managers and a shared concern for children. The actors reconstructed from within their separate traditions a way to improve, at least temporarily, the children's lives.

In an unhappy ending, the positive prejudices would not be enough to overcome the negative ones. Nonetheless, through dialog and cooperation they would keep trying to look for more commonalities, more positive prejudices, and more bridges that might eventually overcome the prevailing negative biases.

A Deconstruction Story

If a postmodernist deconstruction story has at least a temporary happy ending, both the process and the ending are different from that of postmodernist reconstruction. Instead of focusing on commonalities and positive prejudices within traditions amidst the differences, the chaos, and the conflicts, the focus is on negative prejudices. Adversarial postmodernist critic-interventionists relentlessly criticize and expose the negative prejudices operating in the situation.

In this story, corruption within the Asian country would be exposed. The exploitation of child workers by an American multinational would be exposed. Powerful Asian executives and generals would be exposed. Powerful American executives would be exposed. The powerful people and organizations, in response to embarrassment and negative criticism, would act. Either the Asian production company and/or the American retailing company would correct the child worker health problem, while blaming the other.

In an unhappy ending, the negative prejudices would be exposed, but would be so powerfully negative that they prevail. For example, newspaper and magazine articles would be censored. Critics would be denied access to the media, arrested, tortured, disappeared, and killed. Or the power abusers, once exposed, would still be so powerful that they would not have to modify their behavior. The problem is not solved. Nonetheless, relentless criticism and exposure continues overtly or covertly amidst the oppression.

A Neopragmatist Story

If postmodernist neopragmatism has at least a temporary happy ending, both the process and the ending differ from postmodernist reconstruction and deconstruction. Neopragmatist postmodernists recognize both positive and negative biases, but expect little benefit from attempts to bridge differences positively or to critically expose negative biases. Instead, the focus is on nonjudgemental coexistence and marginal improvement through experimentation with relative and temporary win-win solutions.

In such a story, the American buyer might simply offer to try an experiment where increased purchases were exchanged for improved ventilation without any discussion of commonalities, positive biases, or negative biases. Each side would evaluate the experiment with respect to how well the experiment satisfies their tradition-specific needs, without reference to cross-cultural bridges, cross-cultural negative biases, or objective principles. In an unhappy ending, experiments do not succeed in satisfying the different sets of needs, working conditions for the children worsen, but we continue to develop and try new experiments. Relatively peaceful coexistence within the experimental process continues.

STRENGTHS AND LIMITATIONS OF THE THREE POSTMODERNIST APPROACHES AS MOMENTS IN AN INTEGRATED PROCESS

Strengths

Postmodernist reconstruction can provide a combined emotional and cognitive bridge for mutual problem-solving amidst important cross-cultural differences.   As illustrated in the example, the American buyer and the Asian factory manager were able to bridge their important differences in nationality, religion, race, and culture. From within their own traditions they found commonalities of concern for children and the pressures of being middle managers. Their different traditions had very different conceptions about the socioeconomic role of children and the different types of pressures middle managers shared. Nonetheless, the commonalities provided an emotional and cognitive bridge from which they together could address the issue. They were able to find some basis for working together and not solely concentrate on their very real differences.

This bridging appears to have been very important in this case. The American buyer did not think that his superiors would be interested in the child worker health issue. He was reluctant to discuss it with the factory manager without having first established a basis for mutual confidentiality. Otherwise, he feared that word might get back to his American superiors that he was negotiating an issue other than price, supply, and reliability. The factory manager was similarly reluctant to discuss the issue with a foreigner in the absence of some bridging, for fear of word getting back to the general and the owners, who had clearly indicated their exclusive interest in financial gain with no concern for health and safety issues.

Postmodernist deconstruction can relieve actors of individual blame and free them to act constructively. The macro tradition system-level pressures were real and powerful. It was serious that the overseas Chinese owners had to have a general as a partner. It was important to the general to obtain his financial objectives. Middle-class Muslims moving up from the lower classes did not have a lot of political space in this country. He could lose his job and career. The poverty of the large lower-class families was very real, and the money the children earned was very important to them.

The multinational company the buyer worked for was very serious about its goals of low price, high quality, and reliability. This company managed by the numbers; other buyers had been fired and laid off for not making the numbers. He had not worked for the company for very long. His bosses had revealed no interest in working conditions of foreign suppliers.

Neither the factory manager nor the buyer had personally caused the child workers to become sick and to die. Openly discussing the macro pressures enabled the two to be empathetic with the children and each other without becoming entangled in personal blame and defensiveness.

Postmodernist neopragmatism can facilitate relatively low-risk, incremental, experimental improvements. It was easier and more practical for the two to develop and implement an incremental solution than to correct the macro tradition-system biases. Developing experimental actions further permitted them to take limited risks. Since they were only dealing with experiments, they were not committing themselves to anything for too long. If there were unforeseen negative consequences, the experiment could be reversed or not expanded. And it was easier to talk about experiments than long-term, fixed solutions, because there was less chance of being trapped by the direction a conversation might take.

Postmodernist reconstruction, deconstruction, and neopragmatism are not necessarily mutually exclusive and can be mutually reinforcing. In the child worker safety case it was possible to discuss commonalities, build bridges, discuss macro tradition-system biases, and develop and test experiments. None of these excluded the others; the various moments were in fact mutually reinforcing. Reconstructing positive biases from within different traditions helped build bridges. The bridges made it easier to openly discuss the negative biases in each other's tradition systems. Understanding these biases helped create a degree of freedom for individuals to act singly and jointly. There was thus more freedom and less risk in trying experiments to create incremental improvements.

Limitations

The bridging power of positive biases may not be enough to counteract the separating power of negative biases. While the power of the commonalities of mutual concern for children and shared pressures of being middle managers were important in addressing the child worker issue, these reconstructions might not have been strong enough to address other issues. For example, it is unlikely that they would have been sufficient to challenge the military's extortion of ownership from the overseas Chinese. The military has a very strong interest in maintaining an economic share of Chinese businesses, and the Chinese have a very strong desire not to revive memories of the military's past persecutions of Chinese for what it perceived as Chinese-inspired plots against it. The American buyer had no desire to directly test his company's implicit policy of ignoring the poor child working conditions of its third-world suppliers. He perceived the cost advantages to his company as greatly outweighing their social concern for child workers.

Deconstruction can be escalatingly destructive. It was and is dangerous in this Asian country to directly challenge powerful forces. Relentless, adversarial criticism of the negative biases that oppress the weak can be escalatingly dangerous. Protesters and their relatives have been arrested, tortured, and killed. Violence has spread very quickly.

On a micro scale, people often react defensively to adversarial criticism and attack the source of the perceived accusation. As Argyris and Schon have observed, "When individuals display integrity in the . . . sense [that they] speak up and stick to their principles . . . individuals who are targets . . . respond to the originators through confrontation. . . . [T]his is not tolerable to the originators . . . and so, schismogenetically, the more, the more" (1988, p. 205).

Successful experiments that satisfy mutual needs may not be possible. Win-win experimental outcomes are not always possible. For example, if the demand for acid-washed jeans had not been increasing at the time, it might not have been possible to exchange capital investment in ventilation for increased purchases of acid-washed jeans.

If any one of the moments is inoperative, the process may not be effective. The process can break down at any one stage. For example, if a win-win experimental solution was not possible, then both reconstructive bridging and deconstructive criticism might have also been ineffective. Similarly, even if an experimental win-win solution was practically possible, and the parties were able to do deconstructive criticism, in the absence of some reconstructive bridging, they might be so angry or afraid that they would be unwilling to try an experiment.

CONCLUSION

The cross-cultural child worker safety case illustrated how postmodernist method (1) can include elements of both learning and action, (2) can include different types of postmodernist approaches as moments in one action-learning process, and (3) can be effective in addressing a cross-cultural ethics problem. The case also illustrates how the different streams of postmodernism are not necessarily mutually exclusive and can be complementary and mutually reinforcing.

Whether the strengths of postmodernist approaches outweigh the limitations depends largely on the situation and on our willingness and ability as actors to utilize these approaches. As this chapter has shown, postmodernism is multifaceted, not monolithic, and can be positively ethical rather than nihilistic or aethical. There are important potential synergies between postmodernism and practical ethics action-learning method. There may be an exciting challenge in further considering how to balance and integrate various postmodernist approaches with a view to more effective ethics action-learning.

While the focus of this chapter has been on the action-learning potential of postmodernist approaches, this is not to suggest that classicism, scholasticism, and modernism are not also important. Postmodernism recognizes that there are many layers and dimensions operating simultaneously, many stories being acted and written simultaneously. The different stories have potentially different pieces of multiple truths.

10

Internal Due-Process Systems: Ethics Processing Machines

The previous chapters considered various methods for individuals within organizations to act and learn with each other, with traditions systems, and with environments. Internal due-process systems are somewhat different, and may best be described as ethics processing machines.

Once an individual activates a due-process system, the machine takes over, as in a legal process. The individual can sometimes intervene or participate, but must to some extent stand back while the machine processes and produces an outcome.

These systems, not necessarily designed solely to address ethics issues, do process them. The systems have different types of objectives such as (1) correcting and punishing policy violations, (2) fairly processing cases, and (3) continuing individual and organizational learning and development. Some systems combine objectives, while others emphasize one at the expense of another. For example, some are more concerned with punishing policy violations than with learning about potential improvements in policies or potential biases in organization tradition systems.

As with the methods discussed in the previous chapters, there are single-, double-, and triple-loop types of due-process systems. The two major forms of single-loop systems are investigation-punishment and grievance arbitration systems, both of which mainly investigate, punish, and control deviations from current ethics policies. There may be more or less opportunity to defend oneself against untrue charges, but there is little opportunity for feedback, discussion or challenge.

The two major forms of double- and triple-loop systems are mediator-counselor and employee board systems, which permit discussion, criticism, and reform.

There are also combinations of these four types. Some organizations also have different types of system operating in their different parts. And some organizations use different types of system for different types of issues.

Examples of Systems

As an introduction, brief examples follow of the four types of systems, all dealing with work-related drinking and driving.

A commercial bank, which had an investigation-punishment system, had a policy against employees drinking alcohol and driving on company business. A loan officer anonymously reported to the human resources director that another loan officer was regularly drinking alcohol at lunch and dinner and then driving other employees and clients in his company car. An investigation was conducted. It was determined by the investigator from the human resources department that the charge was true. The finding was reported to the loan officer's boss, the vice president, and he told the loan officer that he could either resign or be fired for violating company policy. No discussion was permitted. The loan officer resigned. The investigation, resignation, and spread of news about the resignation all occurred within a week.

A natural-gas public utility company had a policy that forbade operations employees to drink any alcohol during their working hours, including lunch hours. Most of these employees were members of a labor union and had a grievance arbitration system as part of their union contract. An employee anonymously reported to a supervisor that an employee was drinking beer with shots of whiskey almost every day while having lunch and then driving company trucks. The supervisor investigated and found that the charge was true. When the employee returned to work the supervisor told him to come to his office. The supervisor reminded him that he had warned him several times about not drinking at lunch and told him that he was being fired.

The employee went to his local union business agent to file a grievance on his behalf. The business agent and the supervisor met to discuss the firing; the supervisor did not change his decision. The business agent then went to the area operations manager, who supported the supervisor. The union local president then met with the company's human resources vice president, who also supported the supervisor. The case then went to an outside arbitrator from the American Arbitration Association. The arbitrator ruled that the employee had to be reinstated with back pay because there was not enough evidence that the company's progressive discipline policy had been followed. The human resources vice president told the area operations manager and the supervisor that it was important that in the future they document in writing any violations of the company's drinking policy and give written warnings and suspensions to violators before firing them.

A large financial services company, which had a mediator-counselor system, had a policy against driving and drinking alcohol. It was reported to the human resources manager of the company's municipal pension sales unit that one of the salesmen was drinking alcohol excessively with customers and then driving his car with both customer and employee passengers. The manager passed on the information to his manager in the corporate human resources office. This manager passed on the information to the human resources vice president, who told him to assign an employee relations counselor to mediate the problem. The counselor talked with the accused salesman, and he admitted that he sometimes drank with customers, but that it was part of his job to entertain customers at lunches, dinners, and sporting events.

The counselor then arranged a meeting with the unit's sales manager and a corporate human resources manager. In addition to the individual case, the issue of salespeople drinking with customers was discussed. It was agreed that the company's policy of no drinking while on company business was being generally ignored and was also impractical for the salespeople. There was an apparent conflict between the values of safety and customer satisfaction. The mediator, the sales manager, and the human resources manager came to the conclusion that the policy should be modified to permit alcohol consumption in certain circumstances, including customer entertainment, but that a nondrinking driver had to be designated in all such instances. The company's policy was later modified to permit alcohol consumption in any circumstances as long as arrangements were made in advance for nondrinking drivers.

A high-technology company, with an employee board system, also had a policy against drinking and driving while on company business. After a party for employees in one of the company's laboratories, there was an automobile accident in which a passenger and a driver, both employees, received minor injuries. The driver was arrested for driving under the influence of alcohol. He was fired for violating the company's policy. The case was brought before the employee board.

The board discussed whether the driver violated the company's policy, whether he should be fired for doing so, and whether the company policies needed to be modified. The question was also asked whether the company's culture encouraged dangerous alcohol consumption. The employee committee decided that the employee was guilty of violating the company's policy and should be suspended without pay for one month but not fired. The employee was warned that a repeat offense would result in dismissal and directed to participate in an employee assistance substance abuse program. The company's policy was modified to require arrangements for nondrinking drivers at all company social events where alcohol was served. In addition, the employee board formed a subcommittee to study and make recommendations about whether the company's culture needed to be modified with respect to the encouragement of alcohol abuse.

The investigation-punishment system produced the fastest result, the resignation of the employee, but he had very little opportunity to defend himself; discussion was not permitted. In the grievance arbitration example, the employee had ample opportunity for fair defense at the supervisor, unit management, corporate, and arbitration levels. However, what the organization learned from this case was how to not lose the next arbitration case, not anything about the ethics problem itself. In the mediator-counselor case, the potential conflicts between the values of safety and customer satisfaction were examined and the company's policy was modified. In the employee board case, not only were potential conflicts between the values of employee morale and safety examined and the company policy modified, the culture of the organization was criticized.

Adversarial versus Developmental Frameworks

There are two largely unintegrated and, in a sense, competing frameworks for thinking about and building organization ethics due-process systems: the legalistic, adversarial, labor relations-based grievance arbitration framework, and the behavioral science- and philosophy-based developmental action-learning framework. The former emphasizes guilt-innocence judgment, punishment, and control. The latter emphasizes individual and organizational learning and development. Conversation and action-learning in the former involves single-loop, win-lose advocacy and defense. Conversation and action-learning in the latter involve dialog and potential ethical development.

The different methods have different strengths and limitations. Investigation-punishment systems tend to facilitate quick correction of policy violations, but sometimes are lacking both fair process and organizational learning. Grievance arbitration systems tend to facilitate fair process but are often very narrow, time-consuming, and intimidating. Mediator-counselor systems tend to facilitate learning and development, but not quick correction of violations. Participatory board systems effectively combine dialog, mediation, investigation, and adjudication elements but can be very time-consuming.

How can we build ethics due-process systems that facilitate ethical organizational learning and development, that are fair, and effectively make timely correction of unethical behavior? This is not a totally new problem in human resources management and organizational development. There have been similar problems with respect to contradictions within employee evaluation versus development systems. For example, evaluations that reward and punish also increase defensiveness and can hinder employee development if need for development is interpreted as inadequate performance. Not all contradictions can be eliminated and not all contradictions are necessarily bad.

In this chapter, each type of due-process system is first described. Second, examples illustrating how they work are considered. (While the cases are all real, the identity of the organizations are mostly not disclosed because of their confidentiality and privacy requirements.)

Third, the strengths and limitations of the various systems are discussed. Fourth, a conclusion is offered concerning the components of an ideal system.

INVESTIGATION-PUNISHMENT SYSTEMS

Examples of organizations with strong elements of investigation-punishment systems include G.E., Bank of Boston, and General Telephone and Electronics. A typical investigation-punishment system includes the following four steps:

1. An employee makes a complaint to a higher level of management.
2. A top-down investigation is conducted.
3. The findings are discussed with senior management, and a decision is made.
4. The findings and punishment are announced to the offender with some discussion.

The following race discrimination, airline safety, and sexual harassment cases illustrate the process.

Race discrimination   An employee makes a complaint to a higher level of management. A black, male consultant who worked for a management and engineering consulting company was fired for inadequate performance. He lodged a verbal complaint with his unit manager, who passed it on to the managing director. The managing director contacted the human resources vice president.

A top-down investigation is conducted. The human resources vice president told a senior human resources manager to conduct an investigation. The employee's supervisor and colleagues, and clients he had worked for, were interviewed. The nearly unanimous conclusion was that he was performing inadequately. His supervisor had earlier told him that his performance was inadequate and given him a three-month period to get back on track. According to the human resources vice president, "We had reviewed the individual's performance on a formal basis and came to the conclusion that the person was not performing adequately. At that point, we pointed out to the individual what he had to do to get back on track. We gave him a three-month trial period to do that. At the end of the three month period, we decided to terminate the individual. We gave the employee a two-month salary continuance to give him enough time to find another job. We offered him outplacement counseling which he refused."

The findings are discussed with senior management, and a decision is made. A meeting was held of the CEO, the human resources vice president, the managing director, and the unit manager. They decided to support the termination. It was also decided, after consultation with the company's employment attorney, that since the employee was a minority, since the attorney perceived the state commission against discrimination to be heavily biased in favor of minorities, and since the company wanted to avoid legal costs and negative publicity, every effort should be made to settle with him. It was also decided that a large settlement would be less expensive than a legal fight with the state commission and/or the employee's attorney.

The findings and punishment are announced to the offender with some discussion. The managing director and the human resources director met with the employee and announced that the results of the investigation supported the decision to terminate, but that the company would be willing to offer additional salary continuance and outplacement counselling. He accepted the salary continuance but refused the outplacement counselling, and filed a discrimination and unjust discharge complaint with the state commission. The commission investigator indicated to the company that the commission would most likely find in favor of the employee. His attorney indicated that they would pursue the case in court if necessary. The company offered a settlement. After some negotiating, the employee accepted a settlement of seventy-five thousand dollars, an additional three-month salary continuance for a total of five months, and an agreement by the company to say nothing negative about him to any future potential employer.

Airline safetyAn employee makes a complaint to a higher level of management. A maintenance employee of an airline told a lower-level human resources professional that his supervisor was cutting corners on preflight safety inspections. The human resources professional referred him to a senior human resources manager. He repeated his story and indicated to this manager that he did not want his identity to be revealed. The manager explained to him that it was both organization policy and required by law to investigate reports of preflight safety violations and that the organization would do so, assuring him that he would be protected from retaliation and his identity kept confidential.

An investigation is conducted. The senior human resources manager ordered two human resources professionals to conduct an investigation, and they interviewed all the people in the department in question. The interviewees were told that they were required to answer the interviewer's questions, that the airline periodically conducted such interviews, and that their responses would be kept confidential. Their verbal responses were written down by the interviewers. They analyzed and discussed the responses and concluded that the maintenance manager was in fact cutting corners on preflight safety procedures.

The findings are discussed with senior management, and a decision is made. The investigators brought their findings and conclusion to the senior human resources manager, who brought them to the human resources vice president. He arranged a meeting with the senior human resources manager and the maintenance manager's boss. The findings and conclusions were presented to the boss, and the human resources vice president asked him what he thought an appropriate punishment would be. The three managers discussed potential punishments, and concluded that they would suspend the manager and offer to work with him to improve safety procedures, but that if he did not accept the findings and/or could not manage the safety procedures he would be fired.

The findings and punishment are announced to the offender with some discussion. A meeting was arranged of the senior human resources manager, the maintenance manager, and the maintenance manager's boss. The maintenance manager was informed that an investigation had been concluded and he had been found guilty of violating the airline's safety procedures. If he was willing to change his behavior management would work with him, but in the meantime he was being suspended for a month without pay. If he did not think he could accept the findings and conform to the airline's requirements he would be fired immediately. He accepted the findings.

Sexual harassment *An employee makes a complaint to a higher level of management.* A female secretary at a university complained to a lower-

level female human resources professional that she felt that she was
being sexually harassed by a professor in her department. She said
that she did not want to make a formal complaint but just wanted to
talk with someone about the problem. The human resources professional referred her to a higher-level human resources manager. She
repeated her story and indicated to this manager that she did not want
to make a formal complaint but wanted to talk about the problem. He
explained to her that while he would be happy to talk with her about
the problem, it was both organization policy and required by law to
investigate reports of sexual harassment. He assured her that she
would be protected from retaliation and her identity kept confidential
as much as possible.

A top-down investigation was conducted. The human resources manager contacted the dean of the school the department was located in
and informed him of the problem, reminding him that an investigation had to be conducted. The dean interviewed the department's
chairperson, each faculty member in the department, and several
graduate and undergraduate students. The human resources manager interviewed the department secretary and the secretaries of departments in the same physical location. He also contacted two former
secretaries of the department, one who worked in another area of the
university and another who had left the university.

*The findings are discussed with senior management, and a decision is
made.* The human resources director, the dean, the provost, and the
president of the university discussed the findings. The conclusion was
that the professor was guilty of sexual harassment. A decision was
made to investigate whether the university had the legal right to re-
voke his tenure and fire him. The university counsel advised the human resources director that the university could do so, but might have
to prove in court that he was being fired for just cause. In order to do
so at least one of the victims would have to testify against him. While
several women had indicated they had been victims of his sexual harassment, none were willing to testify in court against him. The university counsel advised the human resources director that without
a victim or witness willing to testify and be available for cross-
examination, the university might lose if the professor sued it for
unjust discharge and/or defamation of character. The president of the
university, after consultation with the dean, the provost, the human
resources manager, and the university counsel, decided to offer the
professor the choice of being suspended without pay for one year or
being fired.

*The findings and punishment are announced to the offender with some
discussion.* The dean and the human resources director held a meeting
with the department chairman and the professor. The professor was

told that an investigation had been conducted and he had been found guilty of sexually harassing several female employees, as well as several students. He denied that he was guilty of any sexual harassment. He was offered the choice of being fired immediately or suspension without pay for one year and then reinstatement. He accepted the suspension.

GRIEVANCE ARBITRATION SYSTEMS

Grievance arbitration systems are typical where there are employees represented by labor unions or public sector employees. For example, heavily unionized sectors such as the automobile industry and public schools have grievance and arbitration systems for unionized employees. Federal government employees also have access to grievance arbitration systems. Public broadcasting companies have grievance arbitration systems for their unionized employees that are essentially the same as the systems used by commercial broadcasting stations. Some industries, such as the United States securities and brokerage industry, require use of industry grievance arbitration systems for all employees. A typical grievance arbitration system includes the following five steps:

1. An employee files a complaint with an employee representative.
2. The employee representative and the employee present their objection to the employee's supervisor.
3. If the grievance is not resolved, a middle-level employee representative presents the objection to an upper-level manager.
4. If the grievance is still not resolved, a middle-level employee representative and a top-level employee representative consider the issue with a top-level manager, typically a vice president of industrial relations or of human resources.
5. If the grievance is not resolved at the upper level, the case goes to a jointly chosen outside arbitrator who makes a decision within the policy framework of the organization.

The following drug abuse, stealing, and sexual harassment cases illustrate the process.

Drug abuse *An employee files a complaint with an employee representative.* A maintenance crew supervisor of a natural-gas public utility observed that an employee was acting strangely on the job. When he asked another worker what was wrong, he was told that the employee had just bought and consumed some drugs. This supervisor had once been a worker and a member of the labor union, and the employees would talk to him about a wide variety of issues on an informal basis. He and the employee witness agreed that it was dangerous to both the public and the other employees to have someone working while under the influence of illegal drugs. The supervisor terminated the offending employee for violating the company's drug and alcohol policy. The employee filed a grievance with his local union's shop steward.

The employee representative and the employee present their objection to the employee's supervisor. The shop steward objected to the supervisor that it was unclear whether the employee had consumed illegal substances and that even if he had the penalty of termination was too severe. The supervisor responded that it was well known that consumption of illegal drugs on the job was against the company's policy and that the employee posed a danger to fellow workers and the public, and indicated that he would not change his decision.

If the grievance is not resolved, a middle-level employee representative presents the objection to an upper-level manager. The union shop steward and the union business agent repeated the objection to the operations manager of the area where the employee worked. This upper-level manager told them that he stood behind his supervisor.

If the grievance is still not resolved, a middle-level employee representative and a top-level employee representative consider the issue with a top-level manager, typically a vice president of industrial relations or of human resources. The union shop steward and business agent and the president of the local union presented their objections to the company's vice president of human resources, who was also responsible for administering the contract with the union. This vice president indicated to them that the matter was very serious. While he was sympathetic to the plight of the employee losing his job in such a bad economy, he had a responsibility to the public and the other workers not to tolerate drug abuse on the job.

If the grievance is not resolved at the upper level, the case goes to a jointly chosen outside arbitrator who makes a decision within the policy framework of the organization. Pursuant to the labor union contract, the dispute was sent to outside arbitration. For termination arbitrations, the contract called for a tripartite arbitration panel whereby the company named an arbitrator, the union named an arbitrator, and those two individuals selected a third arbitrator. All three arbitrators were on the American Arbitration Association's panel of labor relations arbitrators. The company wanted the employee witness to testify about the drug purchase and consumption at the arbitration hearing. However, the employee, also a member of the labor union, refused to testify. The arbitrators took the position that inasmuch as the witness would not testify and could not be cross-examined by the union, his original discussion with the supervisor would not be allowed as evidence. They ruled that there was insufficient evidence that the employee was using drugs on the job, and that he must be reinstated with back pay. After the hearing the shop steward told the supervisor off the record that the union would not have objected to a lesser form of discipline such as suspension and/or drug rehabilitation, particularly since this was a long-time employee with an otherwise good record.

Stealing *An employee files a complaint with an employee representative.* A supervisor caught an electric power company employee putting company cable into his van. This employee had previously been suspended for stealing from the company. The supervisor told the employee to meet him in his office in an hour, and called the factory manager and explained the situation, indicating that he wanted to fire the employee. The factory manager agreed, but told him to wait a few minutes while he checked with human resources. The manager called the human resources director, explained the situation, and indicated that he agreed with the supervisor's decision to fire the employee. The director agreed. When the employee came to the supervisor's office, the supervisor told him that he was being fired for repeated stealing from the company. The employee filed a grievance with the union shop steward.

The employee representative and the employee present their objection to the employee's supervisor. The shop steward and the employee apologized to the supervisor for taking the cable, indicated that it was a small amount of cable, and promised that it would never happen again. They asked for a suspension instead of termination. The supervisor refused.

If the grievance is not resolved, a middle-level employee representative presents the objection to an upper-level manager. The shop steward and the business agent met with the factory manager, indicated that only a small amount of cable had been taken, and asked for a suspension instead. The factory manager refused to change the termination decision.

If the grievance is still not resolved, a middle-level employee representative and a top-level employee representative consider the issue with a top-level manager, typically a vice president of industrial relations or of human resources. The shop steward, the business agent, and the local union vice president repeated to the director of labor relations what they had told the factory manager. The director refused to change the decision.

If the grievance is not resolved at the upper level, the case goes to a jointly chosen outside arbitrator who makes a decision within the policy framework of the organization. The union vice president and the director of labor relations agreed on an arbitrator who had decided several cases in the factory. The supervisor testified that he had witnessed the employee

putting the cable in his van. The labor relations director testified that
the employee had previously been suspended for stealing. The local
union vice president argued that it was a small amount of cable and
the termination penalty was too severe. The arbitrator found that the
company's "application of the policies, rules, and procedures was not
arbitrary," upholding both the guilt of the employee and the termination penalty.

Sexual harassment *An employee files a complaint.* Helen L. Walters, a
secretary at a California brokerage firm, filed a grievance saying that
her boss had called her a "hooker," a "bitch," and a "street walker"
(Jacobs, 1994, p. 1). She also accused him of waving a whip in front of
her, leaving condoms on her desk, and using such language as "Hey
bitch, come over here . . . drag your ass." Witnesses corroborated
that he had once said in front of a group of employees that they
"should take her upstairs" and investigate whether her breasts had
been enlarged (Jacobs, 1994, p. 1). Her boss admitted to the condoms,
the whip, and using the epithets, but not the remark about investigating whether her breasts had been enlarged. He said the language was
common to the industry, the whip was for humor, and the condoms
reflected his concern for safe sex when employees went to conven-
tions.

When Walters had accepted employment at the brokerage house,
she had signed an employment agreement that included a provision
to use the industry's grievance arbitration system instead of going
to court with any employment grievance. At the time the company had
no sexual-harassment complaint procedure. She testified that she
had resigned from the company because of the sexual harassment
and later had tried to go to court. However, the California court had
found that since she had signed the employment agreement, she had
to use the industry's grievance arbitration process.

The case goes to arbitration. The grievance was referred to a three-
person arbitration panel appointed by the New York Stock Exchange.
Unlike the two previous cases in labor union environments, cases in
this industry can go directly to arbitration without the intermediary
steps of going through higher levels of management. There is also no
employee association to represent the employees. Employees typically
represent themselves or hire lawyers to represent them before the
industry's arbitration panel. Normally, arbitrators are full-time employees in brokerage and securities firms in the industry who are
chosen by the New York Stock Exchange to serve on a case-by-case
basis. They receive very little training either in employment law or
arbitration method.

While Walters had not gone to higher-level management, the company's former personnel manager did testify that her department had received numerous complaints about the abusive behavior of this particular manager. She also testified that she had informed two senior managers about it, but they did not think it was "that big a deal" (Jacobs, 1994, p. 6).

Witnesses corroborated much of Walters story. Her boss did admit to the condoms, the whip, and the epithets, but not the remark about investigating whether she had enlarged breasts. The arbitrators decided that the brokerage company was not guilty of any wrongdoing, but should pay the cost of the arbitration. According to Jacobs (1994), the arbitrators based their decision partly on their belief that it was common practice in the industry to use such language and they did not know that common industry practice was not an adequate legal defense.

There is little chance of successfully appealing arbitration decisions. According to Jacobs, "Ms. Walters, like most others who lose their arbitration cases, won't appeal. Under federal law designed to favor arbitration and reduce court dockets, there is virtually no hope of a court's overturning an arbitration decision unless fraud is involved. The fact that an arbitrator didn't know the law, or misunderstood or misapplied the law, isn't enough" (1994, p. A6). This particular industry's grievance arbitration system is unusual in that arbitrators are not jointly chosen, they are not outside arbitrators, and they have relatively little training in employment law, rules of evidence, or arbitration method.

MEDIATOR-COUNSELOR SYSTEMS

Examples of organizations with strong elements of mediator-counselor systems include the John Hancock Mutual Life Insurance Company, the National Broadcasting Company, and Mitre Corporation. A typical mediator-counselor system includes the following four steps:

1. An employee contacts a counselor to discuss a problem confidentially.
2. With the employee's permission, and promising as much confidentiality as possible, the counselor clarifies the facts and discusses the issue with those involved.
3. The relevant policy and other implications of the case are discussed as confidentially as possible with employee relations staff and upper management.
4. The counselor advises, mediates, and persuades, but has no authority to make judgments or decisions.

The following product safety, age discrimination, and sexual harassment cases illustrate the counselor-mediator process.

Product safety *An employee contacts a counselor to discuss a problem confidentially.* An employee of a high-technology defense contractor contacted a counselor to discuss a situation where his supervisor appeared to be reintroducing into the testing process parts that had failed an earlier test. The employee was concerned because he thought the failed parts could lead to failure of the final product and potential injuries and deaths.

With the employee's permission and promising as much confidentiality as possible, the counselor clarifies the facts and discusses the issue with those involved. The counselor discussed the issue with other employees and the supervisor. Other employees had observed similar reintroductions of failed parts and thought the supervisor was fraudulently passing parts, but they didn't want to get involved. The counselor asked the supervisor about the issue. The supervisor explained to the counselor that the product was in a "proof-of-design" phase of product development. Some of the components were being produced solely for the purposes of testing and the government did not require the parts to pass every test. He further explained that he was also looking at how well the parts performed on later tests when they failed earlier tests and that was why the parts were being reintroduced.

The relevant policy and other implications of the case are discussed as confidentially as possible with employee relations staff and upper management. The counselor discussed the problem with other managers. One manager indicated that what the supervisor was doing did not necessarily violate company or government policies, as long as the government knew about and had given permission to this form of testing. He also explained that in a previous case at the company an employee had secretly blown the whistle to the government about a similar procedure, and the company had ended up paying a large fine for not consulting with the government about this type of testing. Another manager pointed out that there appeared to be a communication problem between the supervisor and the testers; they did not know why he was reintroducing the components after failed tests.

The counselor advises, mediates, and persuades, but has no authority to make judgments or decisions. The counselor again discussed the matter with the supervisor. He did not know that he was supposed to check with the government client before he changed the testing procedure. He thought he was just being creative. He also had no idea that several employees suspected him of fraudulent testing. He agreed to in the future consult with both the government and his subordinate testers about any changes in the procedures. The counselor also discussed the problem with the director of training. There was nothing in the training program about this issue, so the training director changed it to include instruction on the need to consult with both clients and testers before reintroducing failed parts during the "proof-of-design" phase of product development. The company director of research and development also changed company policy to formally require such consultation. The counselor followed up several days, weeks, and months later and found that there was no further problem in this area.

Age discrimination   *An employee contacts a counselor to discuss a problem confidentially.* A department was reorganized in a food marketing company because the external business conditions were changing. A newer, younger employee was promoted to a managerial position, leaping over another long-term employee. The employee who was leapt over became very agitated and verbally abused the person who was promoted, and then went to see a human resources counselor and told him that she thought she had been passed over because of age discrimination—that the manager who had made the decision simply wanted to work with a younger woman.

With the employee's permission, and promising as much confidentiality as possible, the counselor clarifies the facts and discusses the issue with those involved. The counselor found that the requirements for the managerial job were different from the skills the grievant had. In addition, the business had changed quite a bit since when she had first started working in the company, and she had not kept up with the changes.

The relevant policy and other implications of the case are discussed as confidentially as possible with employee relations staff and upper management. The counselor discussed the issue both with the grievant's manager and the human resources director. The discussion revealed that such problems were not uncommon in the company. After their initial training, employees received no subsequent training. The training of the new employees was more advanced than that of those who had been with the company longer. While this was true for both older and younger employees, most of the new employees who received the more advanced training were also younger.

The counselor advises, mediates, and persuades, but has no authority to make judgments or decisions. The counselor advised the manager that he had made an appropriate promotion decision. The counselor explained to the grievant how the skills required for the new position really were different from the skills she possessed. In the course of the discussion with the human resources director it was decided to change the training program to offer continuing and advanced training to all employees and not just new employees. The grievant employee was invited to attend several of these training sessions, accepted the training, and was later promoted in a different area. The counselor followed up with the manager several times to make sure that he was notifying employees who had been with the company many years about the ongoing training programs and permitting them to participate.

Sexual harassment (Ewing, 1989)   *An employee contacts a counselor to discuss a problem confidentially.* A secretary at a television network was assigned to a new boss. The boss used terms such as "sweetie" and "dear" in addressing her. The counselor was notified about the situation.

With the employee's permission, and promising as much confidentiality as possible, the counselor clarifies the facts and discusses the issue with those involved. The counselor asked the boss whether he had used these terms in addressing the secretary. He admitted that he had, but said he didn't mean anything by it; it was just his style.

The relevant policy and other implications of the case are discussed as confidentially as possible with employee relations staff and upper management. The counselor discussed the issue with the boss's manager. They agreed that while this was not a case of severe sexual harassment, the use of such language fell within the company's policies against the use of sexist terms. They also recognized that there were managers at the network who did not understand that use of sexist language, while not necessarily sexual harassment, was nonetheless inappropriate. Part of the problem was too narrow a conception of a manager's job description. Several managers were concentrating so much on bottom-line output criteria that they were not thinking about their personal impact on their subordinates and their subordinates' productivity. They concluded that this dimension needed to be included in the training programs for managers.

The counselor advises, mediates, and persuades, but has no authority to make judgments or decisions. The counselor explained to the secretary's boss that his personal behavior was having a negative effect on her. He further explained that while he might not have meant anything by the terms "sweetie" and "dear," they were nonetheless sexist. The manager agreed to stop using such terminology. The counselor followed up and found that he had done so.

EMPLOYEE BOARD SYSTEMS

Examples of organizations with strong elements of employee board systems include Northrop Corporation, Federal Express, and Donnelly Corporation. A typical employee board system includes the following four steps.

1. An employee files a complaint with an employee representative.
2. The employee representative and/or the employee discuss the grievance with the employee's supervisor.
3. If the grievance is not resolved, the employee representative presents it to an upper-level manager.
4. If the grievance is still not resolved, the employee board decides the case within the organization's policy framework and can make recommendations about policy changes.

In some contrast to investigation-punishment, grievance arbitration, and counselor-mediator systems, there is an extraordinary amount of variation among different organizations' employee board systems. In most such systems, all employee relations issues are eligible for consideration by the employee board, including performance reviews and terminations. However, in at least one division of the G.E. system the rules state, "Panel decisions shall be limited to interpretation of company rules and policies. No panel shall have the authority to change company policy, pay rates, or job evaluations" (Ewing, 1989, p. 248). Since more termination decisions are based on job evaluations, and the system does not permit change of job evaluations, this substantially narrows the role of the panel.

Some organizations provide for both internal and external board arbitration. For example, both the Northrop and the old Polaroid systems provide for appeal to a jointly chosen outside arbitrator if the employee is not satisfied with the employee board's decision.

There is also a lot of variation among organizations in how the members of employee boards are selected (Ewing, 1989). At Control Data members are selected randomly, at Donnelly they are elected, at Honeywell they are appointed by management. There are also combinations: some organizations appoint some members and select others randomly; others appoint some and elect others.

Another important difference is in whether managers are eligible for due-process protection through their organization's employee board. At a few organizations, such as Donnelly and Polaroid, managers are not eligible; at Control Data, Honeywell, Federal Express, and Northrop, they are.

The following cases of unjust discharge, required overtime and family leave, and retaliation for ethical questioning illustrate the process.

Unjust discharge   *An employee files a complaint with an employee representative.* At a large corporation, an executive vice-president's subordinate applied for and attained the position of executive vice president of a different division. After four years, he and his former boss both applied for the position of president of his former division, and he was promoted to the new position of president over his former boss. The new president asked his former boss to resign because of inadequate performance. All his previous performance evaluations from his previous president had been excellent; the executive refused to leave, and the new president fired him. He contacted an employee representative.

The employee representative and/or the employee discuss the grievance with the employee's supervisor. The employee representative tried to discuss the case with the new division president. He refused to reverse his decision but indicated he would not mind if the executive was transferred to another division.

If the grievance is not resolved, the employee representative presents it to an upper-level manager. The employee representative presented the case to the CEO of the corporation, who told him that he believed in the employee board system and would stand by the board's decision even if it went against the new division president.

If the grievance is still not resolved, the employee board decides the case within the organization's policy framework and can make recommendations about policy changes. The case was brought to the employee board for discussion and decision. The employee board found that it was not against the corporate policy of the company to fire executives without just cause; there was a just-cause termination policy for employees but not for executives. However, some top executives did have personal employment contracts that included just-cause termination, but the grievant did not have one. The board found evidence to support his inadequate performance evaluation and termination. The board decided that he should be reinstated. After he was reinstated, he shortly thereafter agreed to be transferred to a different division with a salary increase. The board also recommended that the just-cause termination policy be extended to managers and executives; it was extended to all full-time employees and managers.

Required overtime and family leave   An employee files a complaint with an employee representative. An accounting manager had a sick mother. After work each day he would rush home to take care of her after a day nurse had left. One day the accounting manager's boss saw him leaving the office at 5 P.M., and told him that he could not leave because he was needed for some important work. He explained to his boss that he had a sick mother and would have to leave the office at 5 P.M. for quite some time. The next day the boss told him he would have to make other arrangements for taking care of his mother. He explained that he was already paying for a day nurse and could not afford to pay for more nursing care. His boss told him that he was sorry about his family problem, but that he was needed after 5 P.M. That day he again left the office at 5 P.M.; the next day his boss fired him. He filed a complaint with an employee representative.

The employee representative and/or the employee discuss the grievance with the employee's supervisor. When the employee representative discussed the grievance with the boss, he explained that this was a very busy time of year and the department needed an accounting manager after 5 P.M. If he could not do the job, it was necessary to fire him and find someone else.

If the grievance is not resolved, the employee representative presents the grievance to an upper-level manager. The employee representative presented the case to the comptroller of the division. The comptroller expressed his sympathy for the accounting manager, but maintained that it was necessary to have accounting managers work past 5 P.M., and said he supported the termination decision.

If the grievance is still not resolved, the employee board decides the case within the organization's policy framework and can make recommendations about policy changes. The case was brought before the employee board. The board recognized that accounting managers were often needed to work beyond 5 P.M., and that it was within the policy of the organization to require them, and their accountants, to work overtime. However, the board decided that the penalty of discharge was too severe; instead of being fired, the accounting manager should be demoted. They also recommended that the company institute an unpaid family leave policy whereby employees could take a leave of absence from their jobs for as long as three months to take care of severe family health problems. The company adopted the policy recommendation.

Retaliation for ethical questioning   *An employee files a complaint with an employee representative.* At a meeting of loan officers within the Latin American division of a large commercial bank, a loan officer indicated that he suspected the law firm of one of the bank's Latin American joint ventures of paying bribes to government tax inspectors. He indicated that he had heard from loan officers of competing banks, as well as members of his wife's family, who were natives and citizens of that country, that this was the case and was common practice in the country. The country manager indicated that he would check into it. Nothing was ever reported about the issue. Several months later, when the country manager was promoted to president of the Latin American division, he called the loan officer into his office. He said that he had received several negative evaluations of the loan officer's work and wanted him to resign. The loan officer protested that all his previous performance reviews were very high and he had received several performance bonuses. He then brought the matter to the attention of an employee representative and told him he thought his resignation was being requested not for poor performance, but because he had raised the issue of the bribes.

The employee representative and/or the employee discuss the grievance with the employee's supervisor. The employee representative discussed the matter with the loan officer's immediate supervisor, who said he thought the loan officer was not culturally suited to the Latin American environment, but that he would not object to transferring him to a different division. The loan officer indicated that he preferred to stay in his present job, his wife was from this Latin American country and her family still lived there.

If the grievance is not resolved, the employee representative presents the grievance to an upper-level manager. The employee representative presented the grievance to the new division president, who said he saw no reason not to support the recommendation of the loan officer's boss.

If the grievance is still not resolved, the employee board decides the case within the organization's policy framework and can make recommendations about policy changes. The board decided that there was insufficient evidence to justify the loan officer's termination. It also suggested to upper management that the issue of the bribes should be investigated. The bank found that it was common practice for Latin American banks to make payments to government tax inspectors. For example, if a company's tax bill was legally ten million dollars, the tax inspector told the company that it could either pay fifteen million dollars in taxes, fight the tax assessment in court, or pay five million dollars in taxes with a personal payment of one hundred thousand dollars to the tax inspector. The bank is currently studying the issue, and has found that at least one American bank does not make the payments. That bank refused to pay the bribe the tax inspectors requested, and for a while was regularly inspected, which was time-consuming and expensive. In addition, the bank thought that it was having to pay higher taxes than competing banks. However, the tax inspectors have stopped asking for bribes and stopped putting the bank through unusual inspections.

THE STRENGTHS AND LIMITATIONS OF THE DIFFERENT SYSTEMS

The strengths and limitations of the different systems will be compared according to the following criteria:

1. Accessibility to a wide range of individuals and groups
2. The speed and cost of implementation
3. Concern for short-run behavior control and/or longer-term ethical learning
4. Concern for procedural fairness

Accessibility to a Wide Range of Individuals and Groups

Grievance arbitration systems are usually used by grievants who are members of labor unions or are employees in the public sector. However, in a few industries, such as the financial brokerage and trading industry, all employees are required to use the grievance arbitration system instead of the court system. This situation can be a problem when the arbitrators are selected solely by top management. As illustrated in the brokerage house sexual harassment case, universal access to a biased internal system that denies access to a less biased external system can be problematical.

For the most part, investigation-punishment systems are open to all employees of an organization who might want to initiate an investigation. At least in principle, no employees are off-limits to investigation. In practice, I have not been able to find many cases where an organization's CEO was the object of investigation by an investigation-punishment system.

Mediator-counselor systems are also generally open to all employees with concerns, and at least in principle, all employees also are potentially objects for mediation and counseling. In the cases described, people from the secretarial to top management level were both subjects and objects of mediation and counseling.

Most employee board systems, such as the ones at Control Data, Honeywell, Federal Express, and Northrop, are open to the concerns of all employees, including managers (Ewing, 1989). A few, such as Donnelly and Polaroid, currently exclude managers from using their employee board systems. The Northrop system, which began in 1946, the same year as Polaroid's, was changed to include managers, and there is some interest at Polaroid in a similar change.

The Speed and Cost of Implementation

The fastest and least expensive to operate are investigation-punishment systems. In both the race discrimination and safety cases, the investigation and decision was made within two weeks. The sexual harassment case took a few weeks longer because one of the people conducting the interviews was scheduling the interviews around a very busy schedule. There can be very time-consuming exceptions if the person punished goes outside the organization to the court system and the courts agree to consider the case. In some states the minimum waiting time for an employment law case to begin trial is thirty-six months. That was partly why the consulting company decided to settle out of court, even when its lawyers said it would most likely win the case in court.

Perhaps the most time-consuming and expensive are grievance arbitration systems. They are very formal. There tends to be a lot of preparation at each stage of the process, particularly at the final arbitrations, which are in effect trials. The adversarial nature of the system also tends to be self-fulfilling. That is, when relationships are framed as management versus labor, there is a tendency to be very sensitive to behaviors that might set precedents. Sometimes people file grievances not so much because of the particular case but because they are afraid that if they settle, a negative precedent might be set. For example, in the drug abuse case, the union took the case all the way through arbitration not so much because the union leaders believed that the employee was innocent of drug abuse on the job or that such drug abuse was not a serious problem, but because they were concerned about possible precedents concerning termination decisions. As the shop steward indicated to the supervisor, the union would have agreed to a lesser punishment and/or a rehabilitation. However, since the punishment of termination was so severe, they would not allow their union members to testify against the offending employee.

Even in the very clear-cut case of the employee who was caught stealing several times and then terminated, since termination is such an important decision, the union took the case through all the steps of the grievance system and to arbitration. All the grievance arbitration cases considered took several months, with both sides hiring lawyers and paying large legal fees. While such a system is very expensive for the labor unions and the organizations, the individual employee has very little to lose by going through it. Employees are in an adversarial relationship to begin with. If they do not like how a supervisor is treating them, it does not cost them very much as individuals to pursue the case.

The mediator-counselor system is relatively inexpensive to operate, but can be time-consuming. Since there is essentially only one person involved in pursuing a case, the system is not very expensive. However, the mediator-counselor typically has a very wide arena in which to operate, and can explore violations of policy, modifications of policy, and tradition-system biases. That can take some time.

Employee boards can take even longer than mediator-counselor systems. The typical employee board system can also take a lot of time to explore violations of policy, modifications of policy, and tradition-system biases. In addition, there are many more people officially considering a case and its implications, and the time required expands with the number of people involved. There are important exceptions. One G.E. division employee board (Ewing, 1989) is not permitted to consider modifications of policies or performance evaluations. Compared to other organzations' employee board systems, this system is far narrower, thus takes less time to operate.

Concern for Short-run Behavior Control and/or Ethical Learning

Investigation-punishment systems are essentially single-loop feedback systems, in that their focus is controlling deviations from organization policies. For example, in the race discrimination case, if the investigation had supported the employee's charge that there was race discrimination, the human resources vice president said, the termination decision would have been reversed immediately. Since the finding was inadequate performance and not race discrimination, the employee with the inadequate performance was out of the organization the same day the decision was announced to him.

However, this employee, whose performance was almost unanimously considered inadequate by colleagues, superiors, and clients, was in effect passed on to another organization with a bonus of seventy-five thousand dollars and five months' salary continuance. There was very little learning about how to improve performance or race relations within the organization. In addition, there was negative learning that increased racial tensions: Several employees were upset at what they viewed as the preferential treatment of minorities. They considered the settlement an inappropriate reward for inadequate performance that a non-black employee would not have received.

The organization learned more about the importance of formal documentation in dealing with minority employees. The consultant's manager was supported by the organization in part because he had such good documentation concerning specific negative behaviors, corroboration of those negative behaviors, written warnings, written programs for improvement, and written records of inadequate improvements. This manager was praised for the quality of his documentation.

At one level the short-run solution, in terms of discovering whether there was discrimination against the individual employee, appeared to work well. However, there was not much ethical learning going on about how to improve relations among the races. Cynicism also increased about the fairness of the state commission against discrimination. However, cynicism about ethical race relations and the fairness of the legal process increased.

In the airline safety case, the ground crew supervisor changed his behavior and followed inspection procedures much more closely. However, the human resources manager said that this employee thinks he was being pressured by upper-level management to cut costs and time spent on inspections, and that he was punished less because the organization considered his behavior unethical than because someone blew the whistle on him and upper-level management was trying to protect itself by punishing him.

In the university sexual harassment case, in spite of the extensive evidence against him, the accused believes that he was punished less for inappropriate behavior than because of what he considers "politically correct" people out to get him. Apparently, he has changed his behavior less because he thinks it is ethically appropriate to do so than because he thinks that political power has shifted in the university. While it is very important that the sexually harassing behavior has stopped, there appears to be limited ethical belief change. It is not clear whether his behavior would change in the longer run if it was less well-monitored. Nonetheless, it is much better than no behavior change.

Similarly, grievance arbitration systems are typically single-loop feedback systems, focusing also on short-run behavior control. The organization has policies, and the labor union contract agrees that for the duration of the contract those policies must be obeyed. In addition, most union contracts indicate that what is not in the contract is in the area of management rights. The contract typically spells out progressive discipline procedures, such as a verbal warning, a written warning, a suspension, and then a termination. If a manager is deviating from a policy, an employee can grieve that deviation. If the employee is deviating from a policy, the manager can discipline the employee within the discipline parameters of the contract. However, grievance arbitration systems are typically prohibited from considering longer-run, double-loop issues such as the modification of policies or triple-loop biases within traditions or systems. If the term of the contract is three years, the focus of the grievance arbitration is inappropriate deviation from policy within that time frame.

For example, in the drug abuse case, both management and the labor union learned more about how to win and not lose drug-abuse arbitration cases. However, very little discussion or learning was going on about potential policy changes with respect to what type of employee assistance and/or testing system the organization might develop to prevent drug abuse. Similarly, very little learning was going on about why drug abuse is inappropriate behavior, particularly on the job. Very little learning was going on about how management and labor might cooperate better in addressing the drug abuse issue, which is a problem affecting the employees using the drugs, the employees who are endangered by their drug use, the company, and the public affected by the company's behavior.

Similarly, in the brokerage company sexual harassment case, there may have been some short-term behavior control in that managers were careful about not having to go through an arbitration hearing again. However, there was apparently very little learning about why sexual harassment is inappropriate, or how the organization could eliminate the bias in its tradition that permits sexual harassment. In fact, the reverse may have been true. The bias in the industry of such behavior being common was successfully used as a defense against conviction for sexual harassment, in spite of the fact that the arbitrator's decision was in violation of the 1991 Civil Rights Act. For the sake of the cost effectiveness of the securities industry's arbitration system, which saves the court system from having to handle such cases, misinterpretation of the law was permitted with no requirement to reform this peculiar, industry-specific grievance arbitration system.

Unlike grievance arbitration and investigation-punishment systems, the mediator-counselor and employee board systems are generally given wide latitude to explore both short-run deviations from policies as well as longer-run changes in policies and in embedded tradition systems. Both the systems can be single-, double-, and triple-loop feedback systems. In the age discrimination case, the mediator-counselor addressed both the immediate issue of whether the older woman should have received the promotion as well as the longer-run issue of a bias in the training system against older employees. Similarly, in the case of product safety at the defense contractor company, in addition to the immediate issue of whether the supervisor should reintroduce failed parts in the testing process, the longer-run issues were addressed of policies on how engineering managers should communicate with testing engineers and clients in the product development and testing process.

In the executive vice president termination case, the employee board addressed both the immediate issue of whether a policy was violated and whether the executive should be terminated and the longer-run policy change providing just-cause termination protection for all employees including executives. Similarly, in the required overtime case, the board addressed both the immediate issue of whether a policy was violated and the accountant should be fired and the longer-run issues of whether the company should require overtime in such circumstances and whether it should adopt a family leave policy. In the case of the retaliation for raising ethical issues, not only was the policy violation question examined and the transfer decision reversed, the employee board initiated an inquiry into whether the bank was paying bribes through its law firms and what could be done about such behavior in cultures where it was common practice to cooperate with the extortions of tax inspectors. And in the drinking and driving case considered in the introduction, the employee board not only addressed the immediate policy violation and termination issue, but also initiated a change in the organization's policy and raised the question of whether the organization's culture was encouraging alcohol abuse.

Concern for Procedural Fairness

There is a great deal of procedural fairness in grievance arbitration systems with respect to four important factors: (1) employee representation, (2) rules of evidence, (3) outsider arbitrators, (4) joint choice of arbitrators. The employee has trained, experienced representation at every stage. This can be very important. Under direct personal pressure it is not unusual to lose one's composure and ability to think clearly. A representative is less subject to such pressures. A grievant also typically has very few grievance experiences. A representative normally has had both training and many experiences in grievance procedures that can help him give good support to the employee and the employee's perspective.

Particularly at the arbitration stage, many of the rules of evidence of a normal court system apply. This can be very important. For example, a not uncommon abuse of power, or retaliation against employees who raise ethical issues, is subsequent poor performance evaluation followed by demotion and/or firing. With rules of evidence it is necessary to substantiate such a negative evaluation, and the employee has the right to cross-examine and to challenge the validity or appropriate context of the evidence given.

The arbitrators are normally outside arbitrators who have more independence than inside arbitrators. This also can be very important. If the arbitrator is part of the normal organizational hierarchy, then his job security, promotion, and salary increments can be determined by higher management in relation to his decisions. This is a conflict of interest. It is normally in the interest of employees to please upper levels of management in order to keep their jobs, be promoted, and receive salary increases. A decision of an inside arbitrator might not please higher management. Such conflicts of interest can lead to conscious or unconscious biases in internal arbitrators' decisions. The outside arbitration of most grievance arbitration systems reduces this problem. However, as in the securities industry case, some systems use inside arbitrators.

Arbitrators are usually chosen by both sides. This also reduces the potential conscious and unconscious bias of arbitrators. If both sides have to agree on the arbitrator, extreme biases are likely to be eliminated. However, there is a subtle bias of some arbitrators to stay more or less fifty-fifty in their management-labor decisions. If they have too many decisions on one side, the other side might not choose them and they might lose income. On close decisions some arbitrators make decisions more on the basis of what decision will help balance their record than on the merits of the individual case.

About half of all employee relations grievance arbitration decisions are in favor of the grievant. Many of these are for procedural reasons, but many are also for substantive reasons. That is, after an organization conducts an investigation and orders a punishment, arbitrators often decide, based on information the accused provides in the hearing, that he is innocent or the punishment is unreasonable.

At the other extreme are investigation-punishment systems where the accused has very little opportunity or support for self-defense. Typically, the employee has no representation, few if any rules of evidence are applied, and there are no outside or inside arbitrators. Sometimes the accused does not even know that an investigation is going on until it is over and a decision has been reached. There is very little opportunity for the accused to gather or present any information about innocence, mitigating circumstances, or the appropriateness of the punishment.

Investigation-punishment systems can also be unfair to the accuser because of biased top-down framing. Top-down investigation-punishment systems do not provide much opportunity for discussion about potential biases in frameworks or potential modifications in policies. For example, for many years organizations had difficulty both ethically and legally in correcting sexual harassment. The issue was being framed as a discriminatory rewards-promotion issue, and within this framework it was difficult to address the problem, because an investigation often determined that the accuser received salary raises and promotions, so there was therefore no discrimination. However, one could receive above-average salary increments and promotions and still be sexually harassed. When the issue was reframed in terms of "unequal conditions of work," then it could be addressed, and it is in fact explicitly addressed in an "unequal conditions of work" framework in the 1991 Civil Rights Act.

Investigation-punishment systems can also suppress issues when the penalties are too severe. For example, the human resources vice president of a Boston-area high-technology company responded to complaints about sexual harassment by instituting a very tough investigation-punishment system that required either the accused or the accuser to leave the company after a decision. If the accused was found guilty, he had to leave the company; if he was found innocent, his accuser had to leave. When the policy was introduced the number of sexual harassment cases dropped, but it was not clear whether they dropped because the harassment decreased or because people were afraid to use the system since if they could not prove harassment, they would lose their job.

In between grievance arbitration and investigation-punishment systems with respect to procedural fairness are employee board and mediation-counselor systems. With respect to the factors of employee representation, rules of evidence, outside arbitrators, and joint choice of arbitrators, mediator-counselor systems typically only provide employee representation. While mediator-counselor systems are generally open to nonunion employees, including managers, and permit a wide range of inquiry, including inquiry into changes in policies, they do not generally permit outside arbitration. Also, since they are relatively informal, rules of evidence are not a prominent consideration. Much of the fairness of the mediator-counselor systems depends upon the wisdom, perseverance, and courage of the mediator or counselor. There can be a great deal of variability among mediators and counselors and consequently a great deal of variability among systems in procedural fairness.

As with grievance arbitration systems, employee board systems generally provide representatives to employees pursuing grievances. However, employee boards are generally more flexiable with respect to rules of evidence. To some extent this is necessary since employee board systems not only consider policy violations but potential changes in policies and in embedded traditions systems. In addition, not all employee boards permit outside arbitration and joint choice of outside arbitrators. Some, such as the one at Northrop, do permit such arbitration in addition to their other strengths, such as being open to managers' grievances and being able to consider changes in policies and tradition-system biases.

CONCLUSION

There is a great deal of variability among internal due-process systems. While they can be very helpful in developing ethical organization behavior, the fact that an organization has one does not necessarily mean very much. Some systems and combinations of systems are much better than others.

Overall, the method with the best combination of features is the employee board with outside arbitration system such as the one at Northrop. Most employee board systems are open to all employees, and can handle short-run violations (single-loop action-learning), make inquiries concerning potential policy changes (double-loop action-learning), and address potential biases in organization tradition systems (triple-loop action-learning). With representatives for grievants, access to outside arbitrators, and joint choice of such arbitrators, there is also a great deal of procedural fairness. The only disadvantage of this type of system is that it is relatively expensive. However, as in many other areas, high quality can be worth the cost.

Unfortunately, employee board systems with outside arbitration are relatively rare in both the private and public sector. Even employee board systems without outside arbitration are less common than investigation-punishment, grievance arbitration, and mediator-counselor systems. The primary reason for this appears to be not cost, but top managements' reluctance to share power with middle- and lower-level employees. In addition, many top managements are more interested in top-down, short-run control of policy deviations than in holding open for inquiry with others the appropriateness of policies or potential biases in their tradition system. That is, single-loop action-learning is just as prevalent in organization ethics as in other areas of management and organization behavior (Argyris, 1990).

Perhaps the worst, and the most common, are investigation-punishment systems, whose primary focus is single-loop behavior control. Their strengths are wide access, low cost, and quick implementation, but they generally only consider violations of top-down policies. There is little to no opportunity to consider changes in policies or biases. In addition, while they are very fast, there is little or no procedural protection for the accused.

The key strength of grievance arbitration systems is procedural fairness to the grievant, much better than with investigation-punishment systems, within the constrained framework of existing organization policies. However, generally only unionized and public sector employees have access to such systems, and they are adversarial, within-the-box, single-loop processes. Issues are framed simply in terms of whether management or labor wins or loses the case. And, these systems as well only permit consideration of violations of policies, not double-loop consideration of changes in policies or triple-loop consideration of potential biases in tradition systems.

While there is good procedural protection, those protections are for a narrow range of unionized and public sector employees for a narrow range of questions about policy violations. Rigid formality also makes the procedures quite time-consuming and expensive. Nonetheless, those who find themselves within the range are very appreciative of the strong protections that real grievance arbitration systems offer.

In contrast to this formality and narrowness, mediator-counselor systems are informal and potentially wide-ranging. Many mediators and counselors are able to address improvement in or challenges to policies and biases. All employees have access, and since the system is informal and flexible, it can also be relatively low-cost and fast.

The biggest limitations have to do with such systems' power, procedural fairness, and idiosyncratic dependence on the character of individual mediators or counselors. Effectiveness depends largely on the individual wisdom and courage of the mediators or counselors. By definition, they do not have the authority to decide. They discuss, mediate, persuade, and advise. To the extent that they do this well and are supported by upper management, they can be very effective. However, if the source of the problem is in upper-level management, much depends upon the character and courage of the individual mediator or counselor rather than system characteristics. And among the procedural fairness factors of grievant representation, rules of evidence, outside arbitrators, and joint choice of arbitrators, mediator-counselor systems typically only provide grievant representation.

In summary, grievance arbitration systems apply to a narrow range of issues and a narrow range of unionized and public sector employees. Mediation-counselor systems are very flexible and informal, but depend more on the individual characteristics of the mediators or counselors than on specific system strengths. The worst system, investigation-punishment, is the most common. The best system, employee board with outside arbitration, is the least common.

11

Single-, Double-, and Triple-Loop Politics: Overcoming Obstacles to Ethical Organization Behavior

The present chapter circles back and examines how well the different methods discussed in chapters 4–10 can address the obstacles considered in chapter 2. The appropriateness and practicality of the politics of triple-loop dialog, double-loop dialog, win-win deal-making, win-lose forcing, and internal due-process systems are considered in relation to the obstacles at the levels of the individual, tradition, and the environment.

THE POLITICS OF TRIPLE-LOOP DIALOG

Why should we engage in dialog with each other and our traditions? Different people have different experiences, talents, perspectives, knowledge, and insights. Through individual-to-individual, double-loop dialog we can help each other learn about what is ethically appropriate. Similarly, different traditions have stored within them different experiences, perspectives, knowledge, and insights. Traditions have memory. Just as we as individuals can help each other learn about what is ethically appropriate through double-loop dialog, triple-loop dialog that includes our different traditions can help us remember and learn about what is ethically appropriate.

Furthermore, sometimes biases embedded within our traditions support unethical behavior. Sometimes these biases are entangled with oppressive power relationships. Questioning such biases can also help us learn more about what is more and less ethical.

With both double- and triple-loop dialog we are also helping each other and our traditions learn, change, and develop. While there is often conflict within dialog, dialog facilitates peaceful conflict. We are talking with and helping each other learn. The emphasis is on mutual learning and caring rather than force and violence.

And as Arendt as observed, in addition to helping us learn from each other and our traditions, dialog also helps us build the political space, solidarity, tolerance, and mutual courage necessary for effective, peaceful, and ethical action, change, and transformation. Dialog can help us peacefully build and sustain ethical organizational culture.

How well can the politics of triple-loop dialog address and overcome the obstacles to ethical organization behavior?

Cross-tradition Biases

As the cross-cultural child worker safety case illustrated, triple-loop dialog can be effective when there are important cross-tradition differences and biases. The deconstructive moment made explicit the biases of the different traditions that were supporting the unethical behavior in different ways, without blaming the individuals. The traditions and their biases preceded the individuals. In the reconstructive moment, the individuals were able to establish a common ground for addressing the problem. In the experimental moment, a solution was found.

The solution was an experiment and did not require a commitment in advance that people from different traditions might have been reluctant to agree to. When there are so many differences, it is hard to trust one another and agree; experimentation reduced the risks of misplaced trust. While the method was triple-loop dialog, the outcome was win-win. It might not have been possible to solve the cross-tradition ethics problem if a win-win outcome had not been possible.

Outside Problems with Destructive Environments

As the Cadburys case illustrated, through upbuilding dialog Cadburys was able to resist the destructive British labor relations environment. Management and labor were able to build upon the cooperative and ethical tradition of Cadburys to address and solve the ethics and technological change issues. The cooperative tradition of Cadburys was so strong that the shop stewards were even able to recommend a loss for labor in the sense that they recommended that a factory be closed, a very unusual step for a labor union to take at that time in that environment.

However, the upbuilding dialog did consider and include win-win outcomes, for example the displacement benefits for workers. If management had been unwilling to provide these, the triple-loop dialog might have broken down. And for organizations too new to have an ethical tradition to build upon, or for older organizations without an ethical tradition, upbuilding method would probably not be practical.

Not all destructive environments can be resisted through dialog. As the Nazi environment illustrated, an environment can deteriorate so badly that dialog is not permitted. If the punishments are severe enough, many and perhaps most of us can be intimidated away from doing dialog. When that happens, triple-loop dialog that tries to address the destructiveness of the environment is not very practically effective. While there were some notable and even heroic instances where dialogic method saved some lives and win-win method saved some lives, it was not until the massive application of the win-lose war effort of the Allies that the destructive Nazi environment was changed.

Less violent and brutal, but nonetheless similarly, the Italian "Partitocracy" environment of systematic government extortion could not be resisted through dialog. The environment steadily worsened from the late 1940s until the early 1990s. Not until the use of the win-lose methods of whistle-blowing and massive prosecutions was the situation apparently reformed. There was much triple-loop dialog among magistrates, whistle-blowers, reform politicians, business people who did not want to pay the bribes, and ordinary citizens about the nature, effects, and causes of the destructive environment. This type of dialog helped develop solidarity and courage for the later application of win-lose method. Such triple-loop dialog may even have been a necessary step in the change process. However, it was not sufficient without the later application of the win-lose actions.

Inside Problems with Shared Tradition Biases

As the AT&T discrimination and Pakistan cotton industry cases illustrate, Woolman's disentangling dialog method can identify, disentangle, and reform biases in shared traditions. Through disentangling dialog, employment and promotion opportunities were opened up for women and minorities with AT&T long before the Civil Rights Act of 1968. Similarly, problems in the Punjab between the retailers and farmers, the Muslims and Hindus, and the farmers and the yarn manufacturers were disentangled and solved.

However, if Greenleaf and Hussain had not established their places with the AT&T and Punjab communities over a long time period, they might not have been able to build upon the foundations of fellowship and personal trust to address the ethics issues and to critically discuss the AT&T and Punjab traditions. It is unlikely that this method could be used effectively by people considered to be outsiders.

A different situation appears to exist in the case of G.E. As with AT&T and in the Punjab, there were and are internal biases within the G.E. tradition. These biases appear to consist of top-down authoritarianism combined with a history, perceived at least by the employees quoted, that when it is convenient for upper-level management, unethical behavior is tolerated and on occasion even encouraged by top-level management, as in the price-fixing, market allocation, and contract situations. In addition, as David Ewing observed about at least one G.E. division's internal due-process system, "Panel decisions shall be limited to interpretation of company rules and policies. No panel shall have the authority to change company policy, pay rates, or job evaluations" (1989, p. 248). Particularly with job evaluations, which often form the basis or justification for termination decisions, within such a system there appears to be relatively little protection from punishment for raising sensitive issues such as ethics issues. Arendt was particularly concerned about this type of authoritarian environment because it limits and can eliminate the political space necessary for dialog and critical questioning. Under such circumstances, dialog may not be possible or effective.

Eichmann

In just such authoritarian tradition systems Arendt found the Eichmann archetype who didn't think about the ethical. In such authoritarian environments it is generally much safer to not think about the ethics of one's bosses, to keep one's head down, and to go along. Nonetheless, it is just such people that triple-loop dialog methods can work with.

The focus of triple-loop dialog is to consider the biases in tradition systems. While the Eichmann archetype may still cooperate with the unethical behavior, if we persist in trying to discuss tradition-system biases, the Eichmann becomes no longer the Eichmann. The potential negative biases are now part of his cognitive schema (Nielsen and Bartunek, 1996).

For example, at his interrogation and trial, Eichmann was confronted with the biases of the Nazi system and his role in it, and was able to understand his narrow, in-the-box thoughtlessness. With that understanding he was transformed into the Socrates' Jailer archetype. He said he probably would have cooperated anyway out of fear of the ruthless authority of the Nazi policymakers. Fear can replace thoughtlessness. Triple-loop dialog appears to have been totally ineffective in helping Eichmann understand that he should have somehow acted against the abuses of the Nazi system.

However, in another example, the Ford Pinto case, the former re-call manager does appear to have changed for the better as a partial, at least, result of triple-loop dialog. He said, "Why didn't I see the gravity of the problem and its ethical overtones? Before I went to Ford I would have argued strongly that Ford had an ethical obligation to recall. After I left Ford I now argue and teach that Ford had an ethical obligation to recall. But while I was there, I perceived no strong obli-gation to recall and I remember no strong ethical overtones to the case whatsoever" (Gioia, 1992, p. 386).

At the time, no one talked with him about potential negative biases in the Ford tradition that might have been related to the recall issue. As a result of both personal reflection and triple-loop discussion with colleagues, he was able to see the tradition-system biases within Ford. He explains:

> Most models of ethical decision making in organizations implicitly assume that people recognize and think about a moral or ethical dilemma when they are confronted with one. I call this seemingly fundamental assumption into question. The unexplored ethical issue for me is the arguably prevalent case where organizational representatives are not aware that they are deal-ing with a problem that might have ethical overtones. If the case involves a familiar class of problems or issues, it is likely to be handled via exist-ing cognitive structures or scripts—scripts that typically include no ethical component in their cognitive content. . . . Scripts are built out of situa-tions that are normal, not those that are abnormal, ill-structured, or un-usual [which often can characterize ethical domains]. The ambiguities asso-ciated with most ethical dilemmas imply that such situations demand a "custom" decision, which means that the inclusion of an ethical dimension as a component of an evolving script is not easy to accomplish. (Gioia, 1992, p. 388)

Phaedo

The Phaedo archetype is an ideal candidate for the politics of either triple- or double-loop dialog. The Phaedo is intelligent and cares about the ethical, and with some dialogic help can understand what ethically appropriate behavior is. For example, with some help dis-cussing environments of oppressive police states that systematically use torture and the ethical responsibility of doctors, the forensic doc-tor appears to have changed his understanding of the ethics of tor-ture. This is not to suggest that he will now report forensic evidence of torture, but at least he appears to be questioning the ethics of covering it up.

Similarly, with the help of triple-loop dialog about systematic cor-ruption within his country's state banks and government, the lending officer changed his opinion about the ethics of making unsound preferential loans to friends and relatives; he also changed his subsequent behavior based on this new understanding.

Socrates' Jailer

Socrates' Jailer understands what is ethical but cooperates with and implements unethical behavior because of fear of punishment. He even understands that fear is not an adequate excuse for such cooperation. Occasionally, triple-loop dialog can help with this archetype. However, the dialog does not focus on what is ethical, but on whether it is true that one will be punished for not cooperating.

For example, the dialog can be directed at considering the strengths of the organization's tradition system, such as a strong employee board internal due-process system or union grievance and arbitration mechanism that might protect employees from retaliation. Or the triple-loop dialog can be directed toward an investigation of aspects of the external environment that might protect the employee, such as strong state unjust-discharge laws or regulatory agency protections.

While triple-loop dialog can sometimes be effective with this type, one should not expect a high probability of success. The triple-loop dialog may reveal that there is relatively little protection for him, and he has good reason to be afraid. Or when there are reasonable protections, he may still prefer not to take a chance.

Triple-loop dialog can also reveal biases in the organization's tradition or environment such that those who implement the unethical behavior are more likely to get caught and punished for it than those making the policy decisions. It is true in many traditions and systems that those closest and easiest to trace unethical or illegal behavior to are far from the policymakers who ordered it. Such an understanding and countervailing fear of getting caught can cause the Socrates' Jailer to resist cooperating and implementing unethical behavior. This approach has been successful with some lower-level managers in the hazardous waste area. When in dialog about the problems and the system, they were surprised that they might be personally criminally liable for behavior that higher-level managers ordered and they implemented (personal interview, Environmental Protection Agency investigators, 1988).

Dr. Suguro

Somewhat similarly, the Dr. Suguro archetype cooperates with and implements unethical behavior not because he does not understand that the behavior is unethical or that it is unethical to cooperate, but because he believes it is impractical to resist. If he does not implement the behavior, someone else will. Not cooperating won't change anything.

Triple-loop dialog can occasionally also help with this archetype. However, the probability for success is not high. The dialog can be directed at exploring whether it is true that others will automatically cooperate. As in the Socrates' Jailer situation, ethical strengths of the organization's tradition system, such as a strong employee board internal-due process system, could, through dialog about the system and the unethical behavior, hold that behavior up to scrutiny that would prevent it.

Similarly, dialog about external ethical strengths in the environment, such as a strong, free domestic or international press and/or honest regulatory agencies, can help this type understand that it is not automatically true that one is powerless to do anything about the unethical behavior. However, the opposite can also be revealed. The participants in the dialog may learn that it is true that someone else will implement the unethical behavior, and that there is relatively little help toward ethical behavior in either the organization's tradition or the external environment. In such a case, the Dr. Suguro is further confirmed in the belief that it is not practical to resist.

Faust

The Faust understands that it is unethical to trade unethical means for good ends, but he wants the good ends and is willing to use the means to get them. In the story of Faust, after he experiences dissatisfaction with achieving good ends through unethical means, he regrets the trade and ceases to make such trades (Mann, 1948).

Sometimes triple-loop dialog can help with this archetype. For example, in conversations with him one could explore whether there are any stories of others who have made such trades either in the organization or the external environment and who have regretted them. Sometimes it is possible for such people to learn from the difficult experiences of others rather than having to experience the same things themselves. For those sympathetic to literary analogies, the story of Faust can even be brought into the conversation.

Traditions are composed partly of stories. With triple-loop dialog one can introduce such stories into the conversation for examination and interpretation. For example, the story of the overreaction of Roche and the Swiss government in the jailing of Stanley Adams for his testimony to the European Economic Community was an embarrassment to both the company and the government. Similarly, the story of Procter and Gamble's overreaction to news leaks and its examination of all telephone calls from Cincinnati to the *Wall Street*

Journal was an embarrassment to both Procter and Gamble, the Cincinnati prosecutor's office, and the Cincinnati telephone company. These stories are retold within the companies and government offices. They can have some moderating influence on Faust-type behavior when people learn that past trades have not always turned out as well as the Faust wanted.

Richard III

The Richard III understands and does the unethical for material gain. The top managers of the Pasteur Institute and the National Health system knew that people would be contaminated and die from AIDS. The top managers of Bard knew that when the catheter tips broke off in people's arteries and when the balloon failed to close in a balloon angioplasty there would be severe problems. The G.E. executives knew that price fixing and market allocation were illegal and unethical.

The politics of triple- and double-loop dialog are generally not effective with this archetype when the dialog is focused on what is or is not ethical. Occasionally a triple-loop dialog that explored aspects of an organization's tradition system or the external environment might reveal that there was a reasonable probability the Richard III would get caught and be punished for the intentional unethical behavior. However, if the dialog revealed that the Richard III was unlikely to get caught or that if he did the unethical behavior in a more clever way he would not get caught, triple-loop dialog is unlikely to stop him.

THE POLITICS OF DOUBLE-LOOP DIALOG

The double-loop dialog methods considered in chapter 6 included iterative Socratic dialog, action-science dialog, and action-inquiry dialog. As illustrated in the cases, double-loop dialog method can be very effective in helping us learn from each other about the ethical. In addition, double-loop dialog can sometimes help us build and/or sustain ethical organizational culture, both with respect to processes for considering ethical issues and ethical outcomes that can serve as precedents. Furthermore, double-loop dialogic method can sometimes result in belief conversions toward the ethical and not simply behavior change in response to fear of punishment or hope for rewards.

However, there are very important limitations to double-loop dialog, as with triple-loop dialog. The problem may not be one of understanding. People in organizations can already understand what is ethical but nonetheless act unethically for personal or organizational gain or for fear of punishment. Also, some organization cultures discourage dialog; there may be very little opportunity for it. And dialog can be dangerous; initiating it can expose good people to retaliation just because they raised an ethical issue. How well can the politics of double-loop dialog address and overcome the obstacles to ethical organization behavior?

PROBLEMATICAL ENVIRONMENTS

Double-loop dialog methods focus on the frameworks, beliefs, and positions of individuals, not problematical environments. By definition, this method does not frame issues as inside problems with biases in a shared tradition, outside problems with a destructive environment that threatens to overwhelm internal ethical behavior, or cross-tradition problems with biases in different traditions.

That is, Socratic dialog iteratively considers the strengths and limitations of alternative positions and/or solutions. Action-science and action-inquiry methods frame the discussion around the positions advocated by individuals. The reasons those individuals might use to support their positions, and the reasons others might question those positions, can include aspects of problematical environments; but the focus of the action-learning remains the individual positions and alternatives rather than the inquiry about problematical environments.

For example, in the university financial aid budgeting case where Socratic method was used, several alternatives were iteratively developed and considered. The discussions never focused on potential biases within the university's tradition, differences between, for example, the faculty and staff traditions, or criticism of a potentially destructive government funding environment.

Similarly, in the Cadburys case where action-science method was used, Daniels' solution was advocated, illustrated with directly observable data, and publicly tested. The question of potential biases within the Somerdale tradition was never addressed, and the potential cross-tradition biases among the manufacturing, engineering, and marketing departments, workers, older employees, and recent employees were never discussed. Daniels did use as one of the reasons in support of his solution the deteriorating external competitive position of the company, but this difficult environment was not considered in relation to the company's tradition.

In the Tom's of Maine case, action-inquiry was effective in considering, criticizing, and then adopting the personal ethical vision of the CEO. The discussion was framed, in a sense, as competition between this vision and standard business practice. What were not addressed in the discussion were potential biases with the Tom's tradition or potential cross-tradition biases among the older environmentally motivated employees and the newer more professionally oriented employees. Potential biases in the external environment that might not be favorable to the Tom's tradition were considered, but in relation to the position the CEO was advocating. This narrowed the inquiry somewhat relative to a more open-ended discussion of biases.

In these cases the double-loop methods were effective in solving the somewhat narrowly framed ethics problems. They were not considered in relation to the wider frames of internal tradition biases, cross-tradition biases, or the potential effects of an environment on the organization's ethical tradition. Sometimes this procedure is appropriate and it is not necessary to broaden the inquiry, or there may not be time to do so.

In the university case, the cross-tradition biases and tensions between academic and staff traditions remained unaddressed. In the Cadburys case, while Daniels was able to solve the ethics problem within his unit, his solution was not transferable to the organization as a whole until the triple-loop tradition biases of the outdated works council and the potentially destructive external environment of management-labor conflict were addressed. In the Tom's case, the tradition issues are still framed for the most part as for or against the founder's vision rather than such potential biases as cross-tradition differences between the different types of professional employees. For example, an internal tradition bias that the organization has had difficulty addressing is the power of the CEO's presence, which sometimes overwhelms discussion of issues that the CEO is personally not involved with.

Problematical Individual Archetypes

As already mentioned, the Phaedo archetype is an ideal candidate for the politics of either triple- or double-loop dialog, because he is intelligent and cares about the ethical, and with some dialogic help can understand what ethically appropriate behavior is.

What the Richard III, Socrates' Jailer, Faust, and Dr. Suguro types have in common is that they already understand what is ethical. Triple-loop dialog, if it reveals that the unethical behavior would either not succeed, be resisted, or punished, can sometimes also be effective. However, double-loop dialog, which focuses on individual perspectives, positions, and insights about what is ethical, is not likely to be effective with these archetypes, since they already understand what is ethical. Double-loop dialog is particularly appropriate with ethically concerned individuals when the triple-loop tradition or environment is not a major problem.

SINGLE-LOOP WIN-WIN POLITICS

The single-loop win-win methods considered in chapter 5 include mutual gain negotiating, peaceful minimal coexistence, and persuasion. As illustrated in the cases, win-win method can be very effective in both solving the ethics problem and in building organizational cooperation. An important simultaneous strength and limitation of this method is that it can be effective without belief conversion among individuals who hold different driving values. People can agree to the ethical because of some other gain they are being offered, and this process can be particularly useful in cross-cultural situations where there are different or even contradictory values. On the other hand, win-win politics may not even consider or foster very much ethical organizational learning or culture development, since people do the ethical for rewards, not because it is ethical. How well can win-win politics address the obstacles to ethical organization behavior?

Cross-tradition Biases

Win-win method is potentially very strong with solving ethics problems involving cross-tradition biases, because it can bypass this obstacle. For example, in the Polaroid case, Polaroid was able to locate in the Latin American country without the required bribe. Within the Polaroid tradition, paying bribes to government officials is not acceptable behavior. However, within that country's government, especially its ministry of industry, such extortions were not uncommon.

The problem was solved without having to address the cross-cultural differences. Polaroid located outside the capital district, and the government official and his political party received credit for creating jobs in an economically distressed area. However, the extortion bias remained.

Was triple-loop dialog necessary in the child worker safety case, or should win-win politics have been used? The outcome was win-win, but the method was triple-loop dialog. Win-win method might also have solved the problem—or might not. The deconstructive and reconstructive moments both revealed the system-level complexities of the problem, which were beyond the control of the middle-level managers, and established the common ground and trust they needed to risk even addressing the issue, when it was clear that both of their distant American and Chinese bosses were not interested in the problem. Without such personal trust and understanding of how the biases in the system were causing the problem, it might not have been possible for the two individual managers to address and solve the problem.

Outside Problems with Destructive Environments

Win-win politics can be at least somewhat effective in the midst of destructive environments. In the midst of the very destructive Nazi environment, Schindler was able to save thirteen hundred Jewish prisoner-workers and their families, but it is unlikely that this method would have been effective if used on a large enough scale for the higher Nazi authorities to notice and worry about it.

Similarly, in the Latin American banking industry case, in an environment of political extortion and corruption win-win method was somewhat effective. The chairman of the board wanted the board members to buy a building from himself at an inflated price, which violated that country's banking law, but was also common practice in part of the industry. The one board member persuaded them to purchase the property based on objective outside assessment so as not to be held criminally liable, thus the chairman was able to sell the property at a high price and the board members did not violate the law. There appears to have been less change in concern for the ethical than concern about getting caught; and the chairman did not appear to reform. Deals can be win-win, illegal, and unethical. Similarly, in the G.E. and Roche price fixing and market allocation cases, the deals were win-win for the companies but also violated American and European antitrust laws.

The Middle East win-win, minimal peaceful coexistence deals also appear to be an improvement relative to the even more destructive war situations. While neither of these situations might be called positive, reducing negatives and reducing mutual destructiveness is, in a sense, a win-win improvement. However, there appears to be relatively little belief conversion; the mutual antagonisms, hatreds, and struggle for land in the disputed territories continue.

Inside Problems with Shared Tradition Biases

Win-win method can help solve ethical problems entangled with shared internal tradition biases. For example, in the research company case, the strong bottom-line profitability and high response rate values of the company were entangled with what had become the standard practice of lying to respondents. What had started as a practice of occasionally cutting corners under pressure had become standard practice and part of the organization tradition. Win-win method was able to change this behavior without addressing the ethics issue. The call-back method produced just about the same results as the lying method. However, since the ethics issue was never addressed, there remains the same potential for similarly unethical behavior if the call-back method should falter in producing comparable response rates.

Similarly, in the sexual harassment case at the California brokerage firm, win-win method appears to have been at least somewhat effective in changing at least a behavioral, if not a belief, bias in the firm's internal tradition (Jacobs, 1994).

The executive vice president admitted that he had left a condom on Helen Walters' desk, had used the terms "streetwalker" and "hooker" in addressing her in "banter," and had held a whip in front of her. In his defense he said that this "atmosphere" was "just the way it is" in trading rooms. It was just a way to "vent the stress" (Jacobs, 1994, pp. 1, 6). He said he was sorry if anyone was offended.

A witness who testified for his defense said that she too was offended by the atmosphere but had "learned to block it out" or leave the room. Another woman witness testifying for his defense said, "Indelicate behavior and indelicate language is really intrinsic to that environment."

The industry arbitrators acquitted him in significant part because the locker room atmosphere, the negative bias, was characteristic of trading rooms. He was later promoted to CEO of the firm.

Subsequent to the arbitration, there appears to have been something of a win-win solution. The organization shortly thereafter instituted a formal procedure for handling sexual harassment complaints. In addition, the locker room atmosphere appears to have reformed and the executive's "bantering" language improved. The negative bias in the trading room tradition with respect to sexually harassing language and behavior appears to have reformed significantly. However, this solution was not completely win-win. Helen Walters left the firm with no compensation for her suffering.

Phaedo

With the Phadedo there is generally no need to engage in win-win politics instead of dialogic politics, because he is reasonably intelligent and cares about the ethical, and through dialog can learn about what is more and less ethical. However, one might use win-win politics with him if there was no opportunity or not enough time to have a dialog.

This is not an uncommon problem. Sometimes it is easier and faster to trade than to have a dialog. Sometimes the issue is pressing and there is only enough time for deal-making. In other situations there can be political space for deal-making, but not dialog.

Eichmann

Win-win politics often work well with the Eichmann, who wants to be efficient; if a deal can be constructed that helps his efficiency, it is attractive to him. If the deal also furthers the ethical, as long as it does not detract from his efficiency, it is acceptable.

For example, in the Elkhorn case, the financial managers from the New York corporate headquarters didn't want to hear about environmental and community life issues. Nonetheless, when the factory manager was able to construct a cost-cutting plan that met the financial criteria, the deal was acceptable. However, the key limitation of win-win politics with an Eichmann is that if a win-win deal can't be constructed that meets the efficiency criteria, the ethical loses.

Richard III

Win-win politics can sometimes also work with the Richard III archetype, who is primarily concerned with personal gain. While "evil be thou my good" is characteristic of this archetype, if one can construct a deal such that "ethical be thou my good," he is not opposed. The Richard III is for the unethical not for its own sake, but simply to the extent that he can gain from it. If he can gain from the ethical, that is okay too.

However, since the Richard III is essentially unethical, one has to be very careful in making deals with such a person. If it is to his gain to break an agreement or not live up to the terms of an agreement, he does what is in his interest. At a minimum, precautions such as performance bonds and other forms of security and verification need to be built into any agreements with this type of person.

For example, on a grand scale Hitler and Stalin made a win-win alliance with each other that for a while worked for both their benefits. However, it was not too long before they both broke their agreements. Similarly, Stalin broke many of the postwar agreements that Churchill and Roosevelt made with him, when it was convenient to do so.

On a more modest but not insubstantial scale, the Japanese trucking company Tokyo Sagawa Kyubin made large payoffs to Japanese politicians to help it get new routes and new areas in the heavily regulated parcel delivery industry (Sterngold, 1992). The company also made what it thought was a win-win deal with the Japanese Mafia. With the help of Japanese gangsters, at least one hundred thirty members of the Japanese parliament received payments of about thirty million dollars.

In exchange for the help of the gangsters, the company was giving them a chance to participate in legitimate business and get out of organized crime. The company also made win-win deals with them whereby it made low-interest loans to them for their expansion into legitimate business, in exchange for their help. The executives thought they had a win-win deal with the politicians and the gangsters. The politicians did help the company get the routes and areas it wanted. However, the gangsters did not pay back any of the loans, which totalled about one billion dollars. Several executives from the company were eventually arrested and are serving jail terms.

Socrates' Jailer

A characteristic of the Socrates' Jailer is a type of win-win deal. The Jailer, who knows it is unethical to do so, implements the unethical behavior in order to avoid punishment. The unethical policymaker wins in the sense that the Jailer implements the policy. The Jailer wins in the sense that he is not punished. Win-win deal-making can also be used with the Jailer for the ethical and to stop the unethical.

For example, in the Watergate prosecutions, it was common practice for the special prosecutor to offer lower-level implementers of unethical and illegal policies a win-win deal (Woodward and Bernstein, 1975). If they would testify against their policymaking bosses, they would either be punished less severely or not at all. As a result, they told the truth instead of lying and covering up the break-ins, invasion of privacy, obstruction of justice, violation of campaign finance laws, and nonenforcement of antitrust laws. Similarly, in the Italian "Partitocracy," the heads of the Socialist and Christian Democratic parties and well over five hundred CEOs were indicted and convicted through similar win-win deals with lower-level policy implementers.

Faust

The Faust makes what he believes are win-win deals, trading his soul to the devil for what he thinks are good ends. He trades what he believes are unethical means for ethical ends. From the Faust's perspective, he wins in the sense that he gets the worthwhile ends he wants. After experiencing the poisonous fruits of the win-win deal, he learns that what he thought was a win-win deal is really a win-lose deal, because worthwhile ends achieved through unethical means are poisoned.

Sometimes the Faust can be turned around by another type of win-win deal. For example, John Dean, the former White House counsel to President Nixon, describes his Faustlike experience as follows:

The excitement had my mind spinning. . . . I decided, as I had always known I would, that it was too great a chance to be turned down. . . . For a thousand days I would serve as counsel to the President. I soon learned that to make my way upward, into a position of confidence and influence, I had to travel downward through factional power plays, corruption and finally outright crimes. Although I would be rewarded for diligence, true advancement would come from doing those things which build a common bond of trust—or guilt—between me and my superiors. In the Nixon White House, these upward and downward paths diverged, yet joined, like prongs of a tuning fork pitched to a note of expediency. Slowly, steadily, I would climb toward the moral abyss of the President's inner circle until I finally fell into it, thinking I had made it to the top just as I began to realize I had actually touched bottom. (1976, pp. 30–31)

A win-win deal helped turn John Dean around; he made what he considered a win-win deal with the prosecutors and with himself in the Watergate scandals. He would testify against President Nixon. In exchange, he would receive both a reduced sentence and what he considered an opportunity for redemption. He explains, "I was the guy who had given his heart, body, and mind. . . . I had risen so high and fallen so low. If I were believed, I might put myself back together, I would have something to start with. If I were not, if I were rolled over by the power and deceit I had seen in politics, things could get even worse. I would begin to crack up, maybe go crazy" (1976, pp. 303–4).

Dr. Suguro

The Dr. Suguro implements behavior he knows is unethical because he believes that if he does not do it, someone else will. Sometimes win-win deals can be worked out to turn such behavior around. For example, in Bangladesh, two contractors that were making products for Levi Strauss were using child laborers in their factories. For the contractors, everyone in Bangladesh was doing it. It was not practical to be the only contractors not using child workers.

Levi Strauss was able to work out a win-win deal with the contractors and the families of the children. The contractors agreed to pay the children their wages while they went to school instead of working in the factories. After they graduated, at age fourteen, they would be hired by the contractors. Levi Strauss paid the bill for their books, tuition, and uniforms. Walter Hass, the chairman and CEO of Levi Strauss, believes this deal is also a win for Levi Strauss. He explains, "In today's world, a TV expose on working conditions can undo years of effort to build brand loyalty. Why squander your investment when, with commitment, reputational problems can be prevented" (Mitchell and Oneal, 1994, p. 52).

THE SINGLE-LOOP POLITICS OF WIN-LOSE FORCING

The single-loop politics of win-lose forcing may be the most common approach for doing ethics in organizations. In many organizations top managers unilaterally write ethics rules and then use punishments to force compliance. As discussed in chapter 4, the mirror image of the top-down Ethics General is the bottom-up Ethics Guerilla. Both try to force others to do what they believe is ethical or stop doing what they believe is unethical.

The key strength of a politics of forcing is its short-run behavioral effectiveness. This can be very important, particularly in emergency situations. Another key strength of forcing methods such as secret whistle-blowing or secret threats to blow the whistle is that they can be relatively safe for the users. This can be very important as there is an enormous amount of evidence that organizations do retaliate against employees who raise ethical issues that might hinder the attainment of organization objectives or the objectives of powerful people within organizations. A further strength of forcing method is that it focuses on behavior—and lack of understanding is often not the problem.

However, there are also important problems with a politics of forcing. A key problem is the method's destructiveness. The foundational reason for being of organization is that we can do more through voluntary cooperation than we can do separately and atomistically; the politics of forcing can hurt such voluntary cooperation.

Another very important limitation of the politics of single-loop forcing, as of single-loop win-win politics, is that single-loop method does not give us the opportunity to learn with others about what is more and less ethical. Single-loop forcing can teach narrow, routinized, un-thinking compliance more than individual or organizational ethical learning. When this happens, as the power changes, behavior changes. Might makes right. Also, if we want other "wrong" people, who might be more powerful now or in the future than we are, to exercise self-restraint with respect to the use of force, then we may need to exercise self-restraint ourselves, even if we are "right."

How well can the politics of single-loop forcing address and overcome the obstacles to ethical organization behavior?

Cross-tradition Biases

It is difficult for the politics of win-lose forcing to overcome the complexity of cross-tradition biases, particularly when the cross-tradition biases are in two different countries. Win-win and dialog methods are often more effective in such situations.

For example, in the Asian child worker safety case, while the middle managers could have used whistle blowing in the United States and Europe to expose the situation, they would not have been able to use such force as effectively in the Asian country.

Blowing the whistle to the press in the United States might have embarrassed the American retailer into trying to do something about the child workers being hurt by the acid washing process. Potential bad publicity and bad public image appears to have been a motivation for Levi Strauss addressing a similar problem in Bangladesh. In the United States there is more or less a free press, but this is not the case in most of the world. Since the Asian company was partly owned by a general, it is unlikely that the government would have permitted media criticism. It is not so easy to use force in the service of the ethical in foreign countries to overcome the mutual complexities of cross-tradition biases. Using force for the unethical is more common.

However, there are some cases where forcing method can work in a cross-tradition context in reforming biases in two different traditions simultaneously. For example, the Civil Rights Act of 1991 makes it illegal for United States companies to discriminate against women, including international discrimination. When there is an organization tradition against giving women opportunities to work internationally, blowing the whistle to the EEOC can force a company to change its behavior both in the United States and in a foreign country such as Japan or Saudi Arabia where it is common to discriminate against women with respect to managerial opportunities. For example, some Japanese clubs have made accommodations for American women and call them "honorary men."

Outside Problems with Destructive Environments

It is similarly difficult, but not impossible, for organizations to use forcing methods to solve ethical problems caused by destructive external environments. In a confrontational contest of force, destructive environmental forces usually are stronger than individual organizations who are trying to improve the ethical. For example, the U.S. Foreign Corrupt Practices Act is designed to force U.S. companies not to engage in corrupt practices internationally. However, the act is largely ineffective in environments where government extortion is systematic and pervasive. Organizations that believed that they had to pay bribes before the act simply have their local distributors, law firms, or partners pay them instead.

However, there have been some successes. For example, in several Mediterranean and Latin American countries it is common for tax inspectors to offer both domestic and foreign firms a tax deal that goes something like this: If the tax bill is five million dollars, the company only has to pay three million dollars if it also gives the tax inspector one hundred thousand dollars. If the company refuses, then the tax inspector assesses the company's bill at six million dollars. A few companies have refused to pay the extortion. For a few years the tax inspectors took them to court to force them to pay the higher taxes. However, the companies persisted in fighting in court. Eventually, the tax inspectors found that it was more trouble than it was worth to keep taking them to court to pay the higher than legally required tax bills. However, none of the companies feel secure enough in this success to be willing to allow themselves or the countries involved to be named.

Similarly, William Schwartzkopf had some success in changing an unethical and traditional industry practice with a win-lose method. It was common in the large-scale electrical contracting industry to rig bids. Schwartzkopf, as general counsel of Commonwealth Electric, secretly blew the whistle to the Justice Department. Several companies and managers were convicted and the companies have paid over twenty million dollars in fines. Apparently, the traditional practice of bid rigging in the industry has stopped.

Browning-Ferris Industries, Inc. has had some success using win-lose forcing methods to break into and reform the corrupt New York City commercial trash-hauling business where market allocation, price fixing, and organized crime are important factors (Bailey, 1993). With the invitation and protection of federal and city government officials, the company has entered the market and is gaining market share—not without great difficulty, however.

For example, executives of the company have been the targets of intimidation tactics. One executive had a dog's severed head dumped on the doorstep of his family's home. Trash collectors who would not participate in price fixing have been murdered. The company has had to send armed guards on its trucks. Nonetheless, with the help of prosecutions by the city and federal government as well as extensive police protection, the company is increasing its market share honestly without participating in price fixing or market allocation.

Inside Problems with Shared Tradition Biases

The single-loop politics of win-lose forcing can be very effective in addressing internal organization problems with shared tradition biases. It is also a very common approach. For example, many organizations found that in traditional male occupations there was often something of a locker room atmosphere that women felt was an unfair and even hostile condition of work, both offensive and a hindrance to their work performance. A common top-down, win-lose solution to this type of bias problem was used by a Boston public utility. With the support of the CEO, the human resources director sent a compliance order to all the supervisors and employees in the repair and maintenance areas. The order included punishment warnings of suspensions and dismissals; it prohibited, for example, the use of offensive language, offensive jokes, offensive photographs, offensive T-shirts, and so forth. Subsequently, a few employees were suspended and one was fired. After that, the locker room atmosphere improved.

Bottom-up, win-lose tactics can be similarly effective in addressing shared tradition biases. For example, in the Boston insurance company case related in chapter 4, it was part of the company's sales tradition to misrepresent the cost of whole life insurance relative to term life insurance. This type of misrepresentation had been going on for at least thirty-five years. There was no one in the office who remembered when it was not done. It was not until one salesman sent the anonymous note to the sales vice president threatening to send incriminating evidence to the Boston *Globe* and the Massachusetts insurance commissioner that the bias was corrected, at least for a while.

Similarly, whistle-blowing helped stop what had become a common practice of workers in a factory that manufactured heart valves— falsely certifying that repair work was done when it was not done (Carley, 1991). Over five hundred defective heart valves were placed in patients' hearts. As of 1993, thirty-two of them have broken and at least twenty people have died. There appear to have been biases in the organization's production system that involved pressures to meet production goals and workers who did not understand what they were supposed to do. Part of the problem was that the company hired several Mexican and Vietnamese immigrants whose English was not good enough to understand the repair instructions. Apparently, it was very difficult to reweld cracks in the valves. Instead workers polished the cracks so that they could not be seen and falsified the records to indicate that the parts were repaired.

Richard III

The politics of win-lose forcing may be the only type of politics that really works with the Richard III. Since he already knows what is ethical and unethical and chooses the unethical for personal unethical gain, there is little point to either double or triple-loop dialog with him. Sometimes he responds positively to win-win politics, but when it is in his interest to do so he breaks the win-win deal. He cannot be trusted to live up to win-win agreements unless there are strong win-lose sanctions attached to violations. However, the politics of win-lose forcing, directly applies or indirectly applied through win-lose due-process systems, can be effective.

It was win-lose whistle blowing, backed up with prosecution, that stopped the French National Health Service and the Pasteur Institute from distributing AIDS-contaminated blood that the top officials knew was contaminated. It was win-lose whistle blowing backed up by threat of impeachment and conviction that stopped President Nixon from continuing to break laws with respect to obstruction of justice, privacy, campaign finance, and antitrust enforcement. It was win-lose whistle blowing, backed up by the threat of criminal prosecution, that stopped Bard Company from continuing to market heart catheters they knew were defective. It was Federal antitrust prosecution that stopped G.E. from engaging in price fixing and market allocation.

Ultimately, it was win-lose method that stopped Nero, Richard III, Napoleon, Mussolini, Hitler, Mengele, and the many postwar central European and third world dictators. While the Richard III archetype is relatively rare, he can be enormously powerful, intelligent, coura-geous, relentless, and destructive. Sometimes, there is no effective method other than single-loop, single-minded, win-lose forcing for stopping a Richard III. On the other hand, sometimes there are no effective politics for stopping this type, as was the case with Alexander, Tiberius, Genghis Khan, Elizabeth I, Cromwell, Franco, Stalin, and the many country and organization dictators that prosper and survive to their more or less natural deaths. Success for the ethical is far from inevitable.

Eichmann

The Eichmann responds more to top-down than bottom-up win-lose method. He is interested primarily in efficiently implementing policies received from above and does not think about the ethical dimensions of those policies. He responds relatively easily to changes in orders, because it does not matter to him whether the orders are ethical or unethical, as long as they are coming from authority. If upper man-agement chooses to order the ethical, that is fine with him.

However, from his perspective, bottom-up pressure is illegitimate even if it is for the ethical. For example, according to John McCor-mick, the former head of the Forest Service's whistle-blower program, "The Forest Service simply does not tolerate freedom of dissent; 'whistle-blower' is a four-letter word. The agency has become comfort-able with lying to the public, ignoring long-festering problems and servicing the timber industry as Government agents of environmental destruction rather than environmental protection. . . . As long as

the whistle-blower system at the Forest Service absorbs employee concerns rather than acting on them responsibly, the pattern of lawless-
ness will continue" (McCormick, 1992, p. 37).

Apparently, whistle-blowers bring to the attention of middle- and
lower-level managers many instances of unethical and illegal behavior.
Nonetheless, the middle- and lower-level managers do not pay any
attention to the whistle blowing unless directed to do so by upper-level
management. The middle- and lower-level managers continue to implement the illegal and unethical orders until told to do otherwise by
upper-level managers.

Socrates' Jailer

Win-lose method works quite well with the Socrates' Jailer archetype,
who implements the unethical because of fear of punishment. If he
fears that he will be punished for implementing the unethical, then he
will help with the ethical. This is a familiar technique used by investigators and prosecutors in getting lower-level employees to cooperate
with investigations against their organizations and upper-level managers.

For example, the EPA has found that some middle managers help
cover up hazardous waste dumping by their organizations because
they are afraid that if they cooperate with the EPA, their bosses may
punish them. EPA investigators sometimes threaten middle-level
managers with personal criminal prosecution and a likely jail term if
they do not cooperate with the EPA. The EPA investigators have
found that sometimes when middle managers are more afraid of the
EPA than their companies, they help the EPA locate hazardous waste
locations (EPA, 1988).

Italian prosecutors go even further. Lower-level employees and
managers who at first refused to cooperate with the "Partitocracy"
investigators for fear of being punished by high-level executives and
politicians were put in jail by the Italian magistrates. Literally hundreds of these lower- and middle-level managers were not released
from jail until they agreed to give the magistrates and investigators the
information they needed.

Phaedo

As with win-win politics, with the Phaedo there is generally no need to
engage in win-lose politics instead of dialogic politics. With some dialogic help the Phaedo can understand what is ethical and unethical
and based on that better understanding will help with the ethical. It is
generally not necessary to use force with him. Exceptions might be if

there was no opportunity or not enough time to have a dialog with him.

For example, in the case of the country where the government practices torture, the head of the psychiatric department of the country's highest forensic agency, with the help of the international doctors, was able to question the ethics of not reporting evidence of torture. However, while he was considering the ethical question, and before he had the opportunity to discuss the issue with the international doctors, the torturing and killing of political prisoners continued. Win-lose whistle blowing to the international press might have helped the situation.

Similarly, the university president, with the help of outside criticism of the practice of not having open bidding for contracts performed by board members, was able to rethink and conclude that an open bid process was more appropriate. However, if someone had blown the whistle about the practice years earlier, the closed bidding process for companies the trustees were affiliated with might have been critically examined and stopped much sooner.

Faust

Win-lose politics can also be effective with the Faust. Win-lose politics can increase the costs of obtaining ethical ends through unethical means; if the costs are high enough, the unethical trade may be unattractive, and the Faust may consider the costs too high relative to the benefits.

For example, if someone had anonymously threatened to blow the whistle about the Cincinnati telephone company helping Procter and Gamble obtain the phone records of people from Cincinnati who were making telephone calls to the *Wall Street Journal,* the phone company might not have tried to help Procter and Gamble in this way.

Similarly, in the G.E. Bill Wiggins case, Wiggins falsified workers' time cards in an effort to protect jobs and keep his plant open. If someone had anonymously threatened to blow the whistle about this practice, he probably would not have used this unethical method. The costs of his being exposed for falsifying time cards probably would have outweighed the potential benefits to him of keeping the plant open.

Dr. Suguro

The Dr. Suguro implements what he believes is unethical because he thinks that if he doesn't do it, someone else will. That calculation can be changed by win-lose method. If the win-lose method can prevent others from also implementing the unethical behavior, then it is not true that someone else will automatically do the unethical.

For example, David Buckley, a representative of small appliance manufacturers, says he paid kickbacks to Jim Locker, a J. C. Penney company buyer who had won several awards from J. C. Penney as their "Buyer of the Year." He says he paid the kickbacks because "If I had not paid him and he pulled the line as he had threatened, I'd have gone out of business." He would have just bought the small appliances from someone else who would pay the kickbacks. He also said that he did not blow the whistle on Locker to J. C. Penney because it would have been "my word against the Buyer of the Year, the shining star" (Gerlin, 1995).

However, other manufacturers' representatives did blow the whistle anonymously to J. C. Penney. J. C. Penney, with the help of federal authorities, did investigate and prosecute Locker, who then confessed to demanding and taking kickbacks. Buckley's estimate that someone else would automatically pay the kickbacks if he didn't was wrong and was stopped by win-lose method.

THE POLITICS OF INTERNAL DUE-PROCESS SYSTEMS

As illustrated and discussed in chapter 10, there are at least four different types of internal due-process systems: investigation-punishment, grievance arbitration, mediator-counselor, and employee board. The investigation-punishment and grievance arbitration systems are forms of single-loop politics in the sense that they for the most part investigate, punish, and control deviations from current ethics policies. Mediator-counselor and employee board systems can be both double- and triple-loop. The mediator-counselor and employee board systems more and less, depending upon the organization, permit discussion, criticism and reform of ethical policies and potential policy biases in organization tradition systems.

For the most part, internal due-process systems have the same strengths and limitations as other forms of single-, double-, and triple-loop politics in dealing with the individual and internal tradition-system obstacles to ethical organization behavior.

While there is hope for and optimism about the potential development of wide-ranging, effective, and fair due-process systems, we are far from that reality. While there is much reason for optimism with respect to the potential growth of employee board with arbitration systems, the reality is that such systems are rare. Effective ethics machines are neither common nor on any near horizon. Therefore, for most people in most organizations, the range of political alternatives continues to lie with individuals acting and learning with each other in the limited political space available to us. The individual-based single-, double-, and triple-loop methods remain foundational.

12
Conclusion:
Proteus as Organization Citizen

He goes amid the seals to check their number,
and when he sees them all, and counts them all,
he lies down like a shepherd with his flock. . . .
        —for he can take the forms
of all the beasts, and water, and blinding fire.
                    —*The Odyssey*

Homer's Proteus lived and changed shapes in the constantly changing and floating world of the sea. He made choices and changed shapes: The shapes reflected the choices. This metaphor is related to Aristotle's concepts of poiesis (action that effectively changes the external world) and praxis (action that interdependently changes the external world and the actor).

What praxis, what politics of ethics in organizational life should we choose? Our choices depend interdependently upon ourselves, the amount and type of civic space within our organizational communities, and our environments. Our choices shape ourselves and our organizations.

The key strength to a politics of forcing is its short-run effectiveness, which can be particularly important in emergency situations but can also be destructive, particularly of creative cooperation. The foundational reason for being of organization is that we can do more through creative cooperation that we can do atomistically. Therefore, it is important to maintain and encourage creative coop-

212

eration and not simply force- and fear-based obedience and compliance.

Win-win politics retains much of the effectiveness of forcing while encouraging productive cooperation. This can be very important, especially in situations where there are long-term relationships, a long series of transactions, and when we can accomplish more by cooperating together than we can do individually.

However, an important limitation of win-win politics is that there can be little mutual ethical learning and development among individuals or belief conversion toward the ethical. That is, people can change behaviors because of rewards, but they may not change opinions, values, or developmental stages. If the specific and explicit rewards for ethical behavior stop, the ethical behavior may stop. If the rewards shift to rewarding unethical behavior, if win-win incentives were the primary reason for the ethical behavior, then behavior may follow the rewards instead of what is ethical.

Furthermore, the individual initiating win-win politics and offering rewards for a behavior may have incomplete or wrong information about what is ethical, or because of incomplete or distorted information, may be drawing inappropriate conclusions about what is ethical. In consequence, the behavior he is offering rewards and initiating deals for may be inappropriate.

A key benefit of having different types of individuals with different types of skills, experiences, and specialization in an organization is that there is a potential for different pieces of information, truth, and insight to come together in solving an ethical problem and/or making a decision. Several minds and bodies of experiences can be better than one. Through dialog, we can learn from each other, learn from the dialogic process, and help each other and our organizations develop ethically.

Such dialog-informed mutual ethical learning and development can inform behavior, including win-win behavior. In addition, when we act because we believe it is appropriate ethically and not solely for the purpose of obtaining win-win rewards, ethical behavior can last beyond and independently of win-win rewards.

However, individuals sometimes are less the cause of ethical problems than are the biased traditions, systems, and environments that the individuals work within. There are situations where biased aspects of a tradition or system are more the cause of ethical problems than independent individual choices. Biased systems and traditions can implicitly and explicitly shape choices such that ethical outcomes are very difficult or unlikely.

As discussed in chapters 7 and 8, the problems of biased external environments and internal traditions causing or encouraging unethi-

cal behavior can be addressed with disentangling and upbuilding dialog methods. However, an implicit assumption of both of these triple-
loop methods is that the people who engaged in the dialogs more or
less believed that they belonged to the same internal tradition. This is
not always the case. There are other situations where the key participants in the ethics situation believe that they are part of very different
and even antagonistic traditions. When this is the case, the postmodernist approaches of reconstruction, deconstruction, and experimental neopragmatism can fruitfully be included in the triple-loop dialog.

As illustrated in chapter 9, combining the reconstructive, deconstructive, and neopragmatist postmodernist approaches as three moments in one process had the following strengths: (1) the reconstructive moment provided a combined emotional and cognitive bridge for
mutual problem-solving amidst important cross-cultural differences;
(2) the deconstructive moment somewhat relieved actors of personal
blame for the current situation and helped them act less defensively
and more constructively together; and (3) the experimental neopragmatist moment facilitated relatively low-risk potential improvements.

Depending upon the situation and the individuals involved, there
can be important corresponding limitations with this postmodern approach: (1) the cross-cultural dimensions that lend themselves to reconstructive bridging can be much less powerful than the cross-
cultural dimensions that encourage separating, negative prejudices;
(2) in the absences of adequate reconstructive bridging, the deconstructive moment can be escalatingly destructive; and (3) incremental,
mutual needs-satisfying neopragmatist experiments are not always
physically possible.

With all the different types of environmental and individual obstacles to ethical organization behavior, and with all the different
strengths and limitations of single-, double-, and triple-loop politics,
what shapes should our Proteus as organization citizen take? What
choices should we make as organization citizens? What should we do
simultaneously as individuals concerned with own individual needs
and careers, as individuals concerned with the ethical, and as parts of
organizational communities?

Different philosophers, in different ways, from the time of Socrates,
Plato and Aristotle, as well as the time of the Hebraic Talmud, have
recommended the politics of dialog and reasoning with others, when
practical.

The ethical problem may be very complex and lie as much or more
with biases in traditions and environments as it does with individuals.
There may be little point in focusing on individual differences or
individual faults if the more fundamental cause of the problem is in
the organization's tradition or environment. Therefore, we should

first consider using triple-loop politics to discuss with others whether this possibility exists and, if so, whether it is practical to make reforms at this level.

Instead, if it then appears that the problem lies more with individual differences or faults than with traditions and environments, or if it is not practical to make reforms at the tradition and environment levels, then we can proceed with double-loop, individual-to-individual politics. We may be in a better position to engage in such double-loop dialog after we first explore triple-loop dialog. The experience of working together and helping each other explore potential tradition and environment biases that are not the fault of the individuals present may help build bridges among individuals that can serve as a foundation for the trust that can be helpful in double-loop dialog that focuses more on individual differences.

However, both triple- and double-loop politics depend upon a reasonable quality of protected civic space within our organizational communities. Its absence can be a fundamental obstacle to practical dialog. As discussed in chapter 2, Arendt addressed this problem. She found that it was necessary to understand important principles of organizational authoritarianism in relation to the narrow, routinized, in-the-box, cognitive schemata of an ethically thoughtless Eichmann. She concluded both that thinking must be an independent, out-of-the-box, habitual activity, and that it is essential to act civically with others, that is, as a citizen of an organization.

Arendt's concerns were to be both with oneself, to which the activity of independent thinking corresponds, and to be together with others, from which flows dialog and action. She made a crucial distinction between a "good person" and a "good citizen," between an isolated, individual moral stance and an ethical political action with others. This distinction is key, because in order for action and learning to be effective in organizational contexts, it frequently has to come from people acting and learning together.

Arendt explains that this acting and learning with others is crucial for several reasons. One reason revolves around the idea of a public space. That is, people need to be able to have a space to interact with others in order to discuss and persuade each other on important issues. People need to act and learn with others so as not to be atomized and isolated from the organizational communities they are trying to serve.

Otherwise there is a strong tendency to be concerned only with narrow private security and private interests. This tendency not only makes people ineffective as citizens but also makes them more susceptible to explicit and implicit coercion, narrow in-the-box thinking, unethical ideologies, and unethical archetype behaviors. The act of working and learning with others helps establish a place in the organization, a political space that makes opinions significant and action effective.

Arendt also understood that organizational civil liberties could be important as encouragement and protection for responsible organizational citizenship. She explains, "All other differences between the institutions of democratic and totalitarian countries can be shown to be secondary and side issues. This is not a conflict between socialism and capitalism, or state-capitalism and free enterprise, or a class-ridden and classless society. It is a conflict between . . . civil liberties and the . . . abolition of civil liberties" (Young-Bruehl, 1982, p. 206).

This is a fundamental problem in many organizations—few or no protected civil liberties. As discussed in chapter 10, wide-ranging, effective, and procedurely fair internal due-process systems such as employee board systems with outside arbitration are rare. Often, there is very little or no protected civic space. When there is no or little protected civic space available, this can make it very difficult to dialog, act, and learn civically with others.

The different methods of dialog have more in common than what separates them. If our problem was which dialog method to use, we would be in pretty good shape. This is not the case. In large part because of the lack of protected civic space, dialog of any form is unusual. Often the more difficult practical question than which dialog method to use is whether, given the lack of protected civic space, we should act at all, and when should we risk using dialogic politics instead of win-win or win-lose politics.

When are dialogic politics practical in organizational life? In some circumstances, at least initially, until the tradition and environment are reformed, effectively acting and learning with others may require more win-win deal-making and win-lose forcing politics than dialogic politics.

Win-win politics can be very effective where there is little protected civic space for framing issues such that the ethical dimensions are included. With win-win politics, the issues can be discussed in terms of wins for the organization and wins for individuals without even mentioning the ethical.

If we know how to make win-win deals—and if there's time for it, if the key people in authority are reasonable, and it's either a positive-sum situation or can be turned into one, then there's a relatively high chance of success. If, on the other hand, one doesn't know how to make win-win deals, there isn't time, the authority figures are unreasonable, and the situation is zero or negative sum, then the chances of success with win-win politics are much lower.

If it is unlikely that win-win politics can work, then we can try win-lose politics. As illustrated in chapters 4 and 11, win-lose politics can be very effective and safe in overcoming individual and environmental obstacles to ethical organization behavior.

The practical ethics choice simultaneously depends upon personal courage to be with a transcendent concern for the ethical, to be as a part of an organizational community, and to be as an individual against others and the organization when necessary. My personal opinion is that in all but the most extreme and unusual circumstance, one should first try to be a triple- or double-loop dialogic citizen. If that doesn't succeed, win-win politics can often be effective for the ethical, the organization, and other individuals. However, if that is unlikely to be effective, then there may be no other practical ethics choice than win-lose politics and having the courage to be as an individual and as a part in alliance with some and against others.

For example, Boisjoly had successfully led change dialogically within Morton Thiokol, but the day before the scheduled launch, NASA effectively pressured Morton Thiokol to reverse its dialogically developed recommendation not to launch. With such time pressures, the day before scheduled launch, and such pressure from NASA, the only solution that might have saved the lives of the Challenger crew and the subsequent negative repercussions to the organizations, managers, and engineers involved, may have been for Boisjoly or someone else to either secretly threaten to or actually blow the whistle to the press against his own managers, his own organization, and NASA.

To a large extent the choice depends upon personal courage. Being willing to stand up for what one believes and raise ethical issues appears to be an honorable course, but the negative consequences can be severe. In extremely constrained circumstances, if one's goals are to serve the ethical and to remain an effective member of the organization, then one of the secret win-lose methods may be unavoidable.

The circumstances include ourselves, others, our organization traditions, our organization environments, and our cross-cultural differences. If there is an implicitly characteristic organization ethics action-learning philosophy, perhaps it is some version of William James' 1907 *Pragmatism*. James explains our situation as follows:

> What we were discussing was the idea of a world growing not integrally but piecemeal by the contributions of its several parts. Take the hypothesis seriously and as a live one. Suppose that the world's author put the case to you before creation, saying: "I am going to make a world not certain to be saved, a world the perfection of which shall be conditional merely, the condition being that each several agent does its own 'level best.' I offer you the chance of taking part in such a world. Its safety, you see, is unwarranted. It is a real adventure, with real danger, yet it may win through. It is a social

scheme of co-operative work genuinely to be done. Will you join the procession? Will you trust yourself and trust the other agents enough to face the risk?" . . . It is then perfectly possible to accept sincerely a drastic kind of a universe from which the element of "seriousness" is not to be expelled. Who so does so is, it seems to me, a genuine pragmatist. He is willing to live on a scheme of uncertified possibilities which he trusts; willing to pay with his own person, if need be, for the realization of the ideals which he frames. What now actually are the other forces which he trusts to co-operate with him, in a universe of such a type? They are at least his fellow men, in the stage of being which our actual universe has reached. (James, 1907, pp. 290, 297)

There are realistic alternative approaches to practical ethics in organizational life. They require thought and consideration, choosing the appropriate path of action—and, depending upon the organizational circumstances including ourselves and our abilities to discern them, the courage pragmatically to be, interactively, as an individual, as a part, and transcendentally. As Goethe observed, "the world only goes forward because of those who oppose it." In order to go forward toward more ethical organizational life, ethical understanding is not enough. To quote Aristotle once again, "The student of ethics must apply himself to politics."

Appendix:
Varieties of Dialectic
Change Processes

The origin of the word dialectic is in classical Greek language and philosophy. Dialectic is the classical Greek word that was translated into French and now also into English as dialogue and dialog. Within organization studies broadly construed dialectic change has often been interpreted somewhat vaguely as change that emerges through conflict among differences.

While there are many different types of dialectic change processes, much of the organization studies and management literature has treated dialectics as if there was only one type of dialectic, Churchman's (1966, 1968, 1971) thesis-antithesis-synthesis formulation of the Hegelian dialectic change process (Cosier, 1981a, 1981b; Mitroff and Mason, 1981; Chanin and Shapiro, 1985; Schweiger, Sandberg, and Ragan, 1986; Schweiger and Sandberg, 1989; Schweiger, Sandberg, and Rechner, 1989). This interpretation of Churchman's interpretation of Hegel's dialectic method that is referred to in the management literature as "Hegelian dialectical inquiry" may be effective and useful in some circumstances, but it is neither Hegelian (Mueller, 1958; Bernstein, 1971) nor classical Socratic (Nielsen, 1990) dialectic method.

The objective of this appendix is to open up the area of dialectic change theory to include varieties of dialectics (e.g., Bernstein, 1971, 1985) beyond management's interpretation of Churchman's process. Different types of dialectic change processes underlie different types of action-learning methods, including several of those considered in this book. Six types of dialectic change processes are considered here in the context of a case study: Socrates' iteration, Hegel's aufheben,

219

Kierkegaard's opbyggelig, Marx's relentless criticism, Argyris's and Schon's action-science, and management's strategic dialectical inquiry (e.g., Schweiger, Sandberg, and Rechner, 1989).

It is important to recognize that there are many different types of dialectic change processes for at least three reasons. First, from an understanding perspective, it may be interesting to recognize that there are different types of dialectic change processes that can be studied. Second, from an action-intervention perspective for organization ethics change and development work, different types of dialectic change processes sometimes operate simultaneously. We can have some choice about which dialectic processes to work and cocreate with. Third, also from an action perspective, effective ethics intervention can depend on an appropriate match between action approach and the type or types of dialectics that are operating and/or dominating in a particular situation.

This appendix is developed as follows: First, the different types of dialectic change processes are identified. Second, the different processes are compared across the dimensions of (1) types of phenomena in conflict, (2) emotionality of conflicts, and (3) types of conflict resolution processes. Throughout the discussion the different types of dialectic processes are illustrated in the case of Cadburys in the period 1975–1985 as it addressed a worker displacement issue (Dellheim, 1987; Child, 1987; Child, Smith and Rowlinson, 1990) (see table A-1).

As discussed in chapter 8, Adrian Cadbury considered this issue both an ethics and productivity problem. He explains:

> The . . . aspect of ethics in business decisions I want to discuss concerns our reponsibility for the level of employment; what can or should companies do about the provision of jobs? . . . The company's prime responsibility to everyone who has a stake in it is to retain its competitive edge, even if this means a loss of jobs in the short run. Where companies do have a social responsibility, however, is in how we manage that situation, how we smooth the path of technological change. Companies are responsible for the timing of such changes and we are in a position to involve those who will be affected by the way in which those changes are introduced. (1987, p. 72)

STRATEGIC DIALECTICAL INQUIRY

Classical Socratic dialectic differs from strategic dialectical inquiry. As illustrated in chapter 6, in classical Socratic dialectic, transformation emerges though a systematic examination of the positives and negatives of one alternative that, iteratively and sequentially, is then transformed into improved alternatives. Better alternatives are generated from a search that iteratively tries to maintain the positives while

Table A-1.   Cadburys History

1824   Cadburys founded. One of original group of Quaker companies with Price-Waterhouse, Barclays Bank, Lloyds Bank, J. Walter Thompson, Lever Brothers, etc.

1824–1977   Cooperative, consensus-building employee relations with gradual technological change with bursts of larger technological change, but almost no strikes.

- Employee welfare: First or one of first organizations to give employees job security, profit sharing, pensions, medical care, good housing, adult education, women managers, and participative management; unions recognized and supported.
- Technological changes from hand production (1824) to flow-line mass production to integrated and computerized single production lines to integrated, computer-controlled production plants (1983).

1969–1976   Change from specialization to related diversification strategy begun with acquisition of Schweppes.

1976   Announcement of respecialization and productivity improvement strategy change.

1977   Industrial engineers meet and recommend gradual labor intensification and stretching strategy with punctuated bursts as needed. Recommend against radical automation.

1978   Will Jones (personnel managing director) and George Pierce (technical director) and group of managers decide on radical automation strategy as vehicle for breaking works council system and Cadburys' "democratic consensus" tradition.

1977–1979   Adversarial, coercive change and strikes during tenure of Will Jones.

- 1979 destruction of works council (employee-management decisionmaking).
- 1979 unilateral management decision on new shift system.
- Major strike, only strike in Cadburys history to involve all production workers.

1980–1983   Adrian Cadbury replaces personnel director and technical director and begins reconstructive dialog (Kierkegaard method) with employees.

- Reconstruction of works council as decentralized factory management committee with work site consultation councils, and functional management groups, briefing groups.
- Productivity increases 50 percent, labor costs increase by 33 percent.
- Redundancies (reductions in force) voluntary, high redundancy payments, 2.5 times higher than statutory requirements, retraining, transfers.
- Profitability, market share, cooperative employee relations tradition restored and improved.

trying to reduce the negatives of previous alternatives until no further improved alternative can be generated. This is an oversimplified description of the Socratic dialectic change process. Some professors use variations of this method in management case teaching.

Socratic case teaching is different from comparing two students' alternative solutions. With Socratic method the class considers the positives and negatives of an alternative (not assigned a student's name such as "Joe's solution"). Then, the class as a group tries to develop a series of improved alternatives that retain positives and reduce negatives of previous alternatives until no further improvements can be made. In the theory of Socratic method, it does not matter what alternative the group starts with. Postmodernists have some valid criticisms about that aspect (Derrida, 1977, 1981). Individual advocacy and identification with a position is less important than the quality of cooperative participation in the dialogic (the Greek word is dialectic) process. This method is very different from the win-lose debate method often used in management classes. "Compared to consensus groups, groups using dialectical inquiry and devil's advocacy made significantly higher quality decisions" (Schweiger, Sandberg, and Rechner, 1989). Similarly, in another study, "groups using dialectical inquiry (DI) or devil's advocacy (DA) make better strategic decisions than groups using a consensus (C) approach" (Schweiger and Sandberg, 1989).

The focus of these studies was on internal organization decision-making processes; they did not consider dialectic relationships between external environments and internal development processes. These studies are experimentally structured so that they do not include consideration of the problems that other dialectic approaches focus on, for example, negative biases within internal traditions or negative external environments that threaten to disrupt positive internal development relationships.

What the strategic management literature alternately calls dialectic method and Hegelian dialectic method is an over-simplification of both dialectic method and Hegelian method. Within the strategic management research cited earlier, Hegelian dialectic in interpreted incorrectly as adversarial debate between two alternatives followed by consensus integration. For Example, Schweiger, Sandberg, and Rechner (1989) experimentally operationalize dialectical inquiry as follows: "Dialectical inquiry manipulation. In this approach, two different recommendations based on contrary assumptions are developed from the same data. The two recommendations and the assumptions underlying each are subjected to in-depth, critical evaluation through a debate between two advocate subgroups. The two subgroups then work together to develop a recommendation based on the assumptions that have survived debate" (Schweiger, Sandberg, and Rechner, 1989, pp. 755–756).

Chanin and Shapiro summarize the area as follows:

Following a scheme suggested by Churchman's (1966, 1971) interpretation of Hegelian dialectics, Mason (1969) proposed the dialectical inquiry system

(DI) as a new problem solving approach to strategic planning and policy development. Essentially, DI involves a decision making process utilizing a confrontation of thesis (plan) and antithesis (counterplan) in a structured debate and a synthesis (integrated plan) of the opposing views. The synthesis constitutes a new conception of the world, or "Weltanschauung," that is, a higher level understanding of the problems, issues, premises, and assumptions facing decision makers in the strategic planning process. Constructive debate—explicit statement and examination of the underlying assumptions of two polarized opposites (plan vs. counterplan)—is hypothesized to improve the planning process by creating an awareness of the complexity and interdependence of the issues involved in strategic planning. (1985, p. 663)

That method may indeed improve the planning process, but it is neither Socratic nor Hegelian dialectic.

Hegel did not use the language or ideas of thesis/plan, antithesis/counterplan, synthesis. His language was affirmation, negation, transformation (Mueller, 1958; Bernstein, 1971). Instead of a plan or counterplan, an alternative is a social movement or an idea embedded within and linked to its social tradition—not the simpler idea of a decision alternative independent of a social tradition. Some aspects of an alternative are affirmed, some aspects of it are negated, and a transformed alternative emerges that includes some of the affirmed aspects without some of the negated aspects. Both the idea alternative and the social tradition within which the idea is embedded are transformed. The emerged transformation is not necessarily an improvement or progress.

Unlike what has been called Hegelian dialectic in strategic management, it is difficult to manipulate experimentally the affirmation, negation, and transformation change process of ideas embedded within and linked to social traditions that players are organically part of and tied to. Case study and participative field experimentation are more appropriate research forms for true Hegelian dialectic change process research than laboratory experimentation or simulation.

DIMENSIONS OF DIALECTIC CHANGE PROCESSES

Dialectic change processes differ with respect to (1) types of phenomena in conflict, (2) emotionality of conflicts, (3) types of change they are concerned with, (4) types of conflict resolution processes, and (5) different priority foci on learning and/or action. There are many different types of dialectic processes that can operate simultaneously, sequentially, interdependently, and/or independently.

For example, depending upon the type of dialectic process considered, the conflicts can be civil, friendly, and/or adversarial. The conflicts can be among ideas, feelings, consciousnesses, schemata, individuals, groups, traditions, and/or cultures. The changes that occur can be tactical, strategic, structural, positive, negative, neutral, and even independent of value considerations. Different types of dialectic processes have different priority orientations as ways of learning and ways of acting. Dialectic processes differ with respect to the types of conflict resolution processes, for example, iteration (Socrates), aufheben (Hegel), opbyggelig (Kierkegaard), relentless criticism (Marx), action-science (Argyris-Schon), strategic dialectical inquiry (e.g., Schweiger, Sandberg, and Rechner, 1989), and so forth.

Theories and methods of dialectic change processes were developed in related historical sequence. However, at any one time, different people and organizations can implicitly and explicitly practice dialectic methods that were articulated in a wide variety of historical periods. Historical development is not necessarily the same as contingency or normative development.

That is, in any historical period, such as the late twentieth century, and in any particular type of situation, such as a specific organizational ethics situation, implicitly and explicitly, there can be widely different models of dialectic change processes operating individually and simultaneously. As mentioned earlier, when several different types or at least strains of dialectic change processes are operating simultaneously, there are sometimes opportunities to choose which types to work and co-create with.

Following is a comparison of six dialectic change processes along three dimensions: (1) types of phenomena in conflict, (2) emotionality of conflicts, and (3) types of conflict resolution processes. (See table A-2 for a summary of the similarities and differences among the processes.) Six types of dialectic processes are compared: Socrates' iteration (Lawrence, 1984; Gadamer, 1989a; Nielsen, 1990); Hegel's aufheben (1807; Bernstein, 1971); Kierkegaard's opbyggelig (upbuilding) (1846; Nielsen, 1996); Marx's relentless criticism (1967; Bernstein, 1971); Argyris and Schon's action-science (1974, 1988; Argyris, Putnam, and Smith, 1985); and strategic dialectical inquiry (e.g., Schweiger, Sandberg, and Rechner, 1989).

While they are compared for the most part in historical order, the types of situations to which they refer can occur and have occurred in a wide range of historical periods and organizational situations.

TYPES OF PHENOMENA IN CONFLICT

In Socratic dialog, Argyris and Schon double-loop action-learning, and strategic dialectical inquiry processes, the type of phenomena in con-

Table A-2. Dialectic Change Processes

Process	Phenomena in Conflict	Emotionality of Conflicts	Affirmation, Negation, Transformation Process
Socratic Iteration	ideas	friendly	affirmation of positive aspects of alternative, negation of negative aspects of alternative, iterative transformation and generation of new alternatives until positives can't be increased and negatives can't be reduced
Hegelian Aufheben	ideas embedded within and organic to social groups	does not consider	evolving affirmation of positive aspect of socially embedded idea, negation of negative aspect of socially embedded idea, transformed socially embedded idea and transformed social group
Kierkegaardian Upbuilding	positive aspects of local tradition vs. negative aspects of more macro "crowd" environment	friendly, respectful	affirmation of positive aspect of local tradition, negation of negative aspect of more macro "crowd" environment, experiment-informed, transformed action and transformed local tradition
Marxian Relentless Criticism	social groups	adversarial	negate oppressive groups, affirm freedom/liberation, transformation to democratic community
Argyris and Schon Action-Science	ideas	civil	affirmation of positive aspects of advocated action, negation of negative aspects of advocated action, experiment-informed transformation toward improved and modified action
Strategic Mgt. Dialectical Inquiry	plan vs. counterplan	civil	affirmation of positive aspects of plan and counterplan, negation of negative aspects of plan and counterplan, transformed synthesis plan

flict are ideas. The partners in the conversation compare, and in Argyris and Scon and strategic dialectical inquiry even advocate, different ideas, but people and groups are not in conflict with each other. (table A-2.)

For example, in the Cadburys case (Smith, Child, and Rowlinson, 1990), the organization changed its strategy from specialization to related diversification and its technology to massive factory automation. In a discussion among headquarters engineers, the idea of adopting radical automation technology was in conflict with the idea of continuing incremental technological change. In this type of dialectic, apparently the engineers did not take the conflict between technological ideas personally, particularly since they were not worried about losing their jobs in the technological change. However, another type of dialectic was also operating in the organization; some of the factory managers were in more personal conflict with the technical director because they were concerned about unemployment for their workers and themselves.

As described in chapter 8, in Kierkegaard dialectic (Nielsen, 1996) there is also a different type of conflict operating. Kierkegaard explicitly focuses on conflicts between (1) individuals who are able and willing to remember traditional local-level ideals and (2) a more macro external "crowd" consciousness that is not concerned with such ideals. For example, continuing with the Cadburys case, there was a conflict between (1) plant managers, shop stewards, and workers who were able and willing to remember the Cadburys' tradition of technological advancement combined with employee welfare and consensus decisionmaking, and (2) a "crowd" consciousness that was afraid that if Cadburys did not rapidly and radically change its technology to automation and its strategy to related diversification, it would be overwhelmed by foreign multinationals, as had a few other British food companies and industries such as the automobile industry. In Kierkegaard's terminology, this type of "crowd" consciousness would consider the Cadburys tradition of employee welfare and consensus decisionmaking during periods of national-level industrial turmoil old fashioned and unrealistic.

Like Kierkegaard, Hegel was concerned with "social" conflict, but of a different type. Hegel's dialectic focused on conflicts between ideas that were organic to different social groups. For Hegel, the phenomena of conflict are (1) idea A that is organic to social group A and (2) idea B that is organic to social group B. This is quite different from what has been called "strategic dialectical inquiry." For example, in the Cadburys case, in this type of dialectic, there might be a conflict over appropriate distribution of economic profit/surplus between greater returns to shareholders as a reward for capital risk and job security for employees who sincerely consider the benefits to the organization of different types of technological changes (see table).

Kierkegaard explicitly reacted to and criticized the Hegelian dialectic. He criticized Hegel for underestimating the role of local responsibility and individuals for action and learning beyond narrow social group-based schemata and framing. For example, in Kierkegaardian conflict, it is the responsibility of individuals to look for, see, and transcend soley self-concerned group interests and consider transcendent tradition-based ideals that people from different groups can, at least to some extent, discuss, further develop, and co-create with.

In the Cadburys case, the interests of the manager of factory 1, the manager of factory 2, the workers in factory 1, the workers in factory 2, the shop steward of factory 1, the shop steward of factory 2, family shareowners, and public shareowners are not identical. Nonetheless, if Kierkegaardian dialectic is operating, there can be discussion of a transcendent traditional organizational ideal concerning simultaneous consensus decisionmaking, employee welfare, and technological advancement. For Kierkegaard, it is the responsibility of individuals to try to work with this type of dialectic and consider the interests of their particular social group in some balance and integration with tradition based transcendent ideals. However, if an organization, unlike Cadburys, had a very weak and inconsistent tradition of concern for consensus decisionmaking or employee welfare, there would be little opportunity to work with this type of dialectic.

Marx's dialectic conflict is more similar to Hegel's than Kierkegaard's, except that Marx goes further in a sense than Hegel. The types of conflicts Marx is concerned with are between not just the ideas that are organic to social groups, but the social groups themselves. In a Marxian conflict situation, the ideas of the social groups are inseparable from the social groups. When social ideas are in conflict, social groups are in conflict. In this type of actual or self-fulfilling situation, there is no opportunity for Kierkegaardian cooperative and peaceful change between the conflicts of ideas and the groups they are entangled with.

In a situation where a Marxian conflict is dominating, and/or where people choose to work with Marxian processes, it is very difficult if not impossible for individuals to do effective action-learning simultaneously from inside and transcendent of the fighting social groups they are grounded in.

EMOTIONALITY OF CONFLICTS

In Argyris-Schon action-science and strategic management dialectical inquiry situations, when ideas are in conflict, the people discussing the ideas are able to remain civil, detached, professional, not fearful, anxious, or angry. While there probably are situations where such cool detachment is possible, such as the technological discussion among headquarters engineers at Cadburys, it was not the case among the factory workers and managers, or between some of the factory managers and the technical director and the human resources vice president who were pushing the radical and rapid automation strategy. In contrast, with the Kierkegaardian dialectic, friendly and respectful emotions are in important part of the approach. Adrian Cadbury appeared to be able to maintain such friendly affect.

Hegelian dialectic does not specifically address the emotionality of the conflicts. For Hegel, what was important was the conflicts between the socially embedded ideas, not the individual or social groups themselves.

The emotionality is quite different in the Marxian dialectic. When social ideas are in conflict, social groups are in conflict, so conflicts are adversarial and angry, even violent. As the Cadburys situation degenerated into a strike, and polarization developed between management and labor, both the shop stewards and the human resources vice president appeared to take an angry, adversarial, and antagonist approach toward each other. The interpretative schema changed from "we" to "us versus them."

TYPES OF CONFLICT RESOLUTION PROCESSES

In Socratic dialectic change process there is a logos of affirmation, negation, transformation. More specifically, the I affirms the Other's initial opinion as much as possible in relation to the perspective of the issue under discussion. The reasons why that position might be correct are considered. Then there is a negation moment: The contradictions within and disadvantages of a position are considered. The process of affirmation and negation is repeated. The I invites the Others to similarly generate and sequentially consider additional alternatives that sequentially retain positives and reduce negatives of earlier alternatives. As mentioned earlier, in Socratic theory it does not matter which alternative a group starts with. Through sequential improvement, the final solution should be the same regardless of the starting point. Consequently, it is less important to advocate an individual position than it is to cooperate in the dialogic process.

This has never been tested in a laboratory experiment. However, it is a common occurrence in Socratic case teaching where the same case is considered by different classes who start the case from different positions but end in very similar places.

This process of affirmation and negation continues until further consideration of alternatives does not result in significant improvement or reduction of negatives and internal contradictions. A transformation outcome emerges. That is, in Socratic dialog, the partners in the conversation search together as thoroughly as possible for the appropriate decision/action in a context that transcends individual interests. There is a sincere intention of mutual searching for the appropriate, while recognizing the possibility that on some or even key material criteria, some individuals might not "win" with respect to their solely individual interests. The transcendent has a higher priority than individual winning narrowly construed.

If enough of this type of dialectic is operating in a situation, and if at least some of the players try to work with this process, the various parties to the action-learning would consider the positives and negatives of various alternatives. The parties would generate iteratively alternatives that retain positives and reduce negatives. However, they would consider alternatives independently of the tradition of the organization. That is, in Socratic type dialectic, the parties do not consider the embedded social tradition as a partner in mutual action-learning. In the evolving classical Greek world, differences within Greek culture occupied the dialog space much more than cross-cultural differences between, for example, Greek and Persian culture. In the Greek dialectic, culture was like the unseen air that was not explicitly and comparatively considered. The Cadburys headquarters engineers appeared to consider in more or less a Socratic fashion the technological change issue independently of the Cadburys tradition of consensus decisionmaking and employee welfare.

Argyris and Schon double-loop action-science dialectic process is somewhat similar to Socratic dialectic except in two important processes. First, it includes experimentation in the affirmation, negation, and transformation process. Second, it includes more advocacy. That is, in Argyris and Schon dialectic process, the various parties to the action-learning advocate positions while simultaneously holding them open to mutual questioning. Argyris and Schon advocate and inquire while the Socratic leader facilitates and leads the dialogic process.

Argyris and Schon action-learning process is also different from Socratic and strategic dialectical inquiry in that it includes experimentation as a source and method of learning about potential transformations that retain positives and reduce negatives. The experiment was not a part of classical Greek dialectic. The idea of controlled experimentation is a modern idea, not introduced into the sciences until the seventeenth century and not introduced into the social sciences until the late nineteenth and twentieth centuries (James, 1892, 1907). For example, the first course in psychology taught at Harvard University in 1883, which also included the idea of experimentation as a social and behavioral science learning method, was taught by the philosopher William James (1892).

In Argyris and Schon dialectic, various parties in the action-learning would not only mutually consider positives and negatives of alternatives as in Socratic dialectic. They would advocate alternatives and then, on the basis of mutual criticism and experimentation, would advocate a transformed solution that had better combinations of positives and negatives. As with Socratic and strategic dialectical inquiry dialectic, the organization's tradition would not have been explicitly included and would not have been relevant as a partner in the dialectic process.

For example, as described in chapter 6, Robert Daniels, the manufacturing manager of the Cadburys confectionary division, appeared to try to work with an Argyris and Schon double-loop action-learning dialectic. He advocated that instead of the radical labor elimination automation approach advocated by the technical director and the human resources vice president, Cadburys adopt a labor intensification approach where output would gradually be expanded with current or gradually reduced numbers of workers though gradual technological advancement and productivity improvement. He advocated this position without reference to the Cadburys tradition of employee welfare. In addition, he instituted an experiment to test this approach with a joint productivity committee of workers, engineers, and managers. The experiment succeeded.

Nonetheless, the technical director and the human resources vice president were committed to the radical automation approach and rejected Daniels' approach even though the experiment was successful. It takes two to double-loop. Apparently, while Daniels was able to advocate, inquire, and listen to the results of the experiment, his immediate superiors were not so open (Smith, Child, and Rowlinson, 1990).

In strategic dialectical inquiry, members of one subgroup are assigned a plan, while members of a different subgroup are assigned a counterplan. In the first moment of the process, one subgroup advocates its plan. In the second moment of the process, the other subgroup advocates its counterplan. In the third moment of the process, the two different subgroups hold open to mutual questioning their initial plan in an attempt to develop a third, better, synthesis plan. This method was not used by anyone at Cadburys.

The Kierkegaardian dialectic change process is an explicit reaction to and criticism of Hegelian dialectic (Nielsen, 1996a). Kierkegaard explicitly criticized Hegel for overemphasizing social determinism and underestimating the dialectic role of local responsibility and individuals relative to a more macro social movement. Kierkegaardian process explicitly focuses on conflicts between (1) individuals who are able and willing to remember what a local tradition's ideals are and (2) a "crowd" conciousness that conveniently does not or might not remember shared ideals.

Kierkegaard dialectic affirms personal respect and friendliness toward the Other and relevant ideas within a local tradition. The I's first motion toward the Other is emotive, respectful, friendly, warm. In addition, the I affirms that the I and the Other share and value a common tradition, consciousness, and tradition-embedded ideals.

More specifically, the I frames the conversation as a request for help in addressing a specific case related to an ideal in "our" tradition that may be threatened by a negative "crowd" environment. Further, the I affirms at least the possibility that "we" have addressed past similar issues consistently with shared ideals.

There is also a key negation moment in this process. The I and the Other consider how "we" have failed in the past to act in ways consistent with shared local tradition ideals by being overly influenced by a negative "crowd" environment. More specifically, the I asks the Other for help in considering how "we" have concretely addressed similar issues in the past in ways that were not only consistent, but times when "we" allowed ourselves to be overly influenced by negative external environments.

The transformation process is also different from Socratic, Hegelian, Argyris-Schon, and strategic dialectical inquiry transformations. Kierkegaard focuses on positive biases within a local tradition in relation to negative biases within a more macro "crowd" environment. More specifically, the I asks the Other for help in cocreating with internal traditional ideals in addressing problems related to negative external environments. There is evolving and continuing experimentation. Transformation occurs as "upbuilding" development, and cocreation proceeds. The present situation is addressed in the context of shared historical ideals. The organization, the "we," and the individuals involved develop, upbuild, and cocreate from and within the context and framework of a tradition.

For example, in the Cadburys case, after some Hegelian-Marxian labor class versus management class-based adversarial dialectic, with a bitter strike, elimination of the works council, lower productivity, and lower profitability, Adrian Cadbury intervened. The human resources vice president and the technical director who had pushed and implemented the radical automation strategy were replaced. Management and labor shifted to a more Kierkegaardian dialectic.

In an affirmation moment, top management and union leaders affirmed personal respect for one another. In addition, relevant aspects of the Cadburys cooperative tradition with respect to consensus decisionmaking, employee welfare, and technological advancement were affirmed.

There was also a key negation moment in this process. Managers, workers, and union representatives considered how "we" had failed in the recent past to act in ways consistent with "our" shared traditional ideals. "We" were overly influenced by a "crowd" consciousness of fear of industrial sector takeover, as well as a national climate of adversarial and destructive management-labor conflict.

The destructive Marxian dialectic appeared to play itself out in that both Cadburys' economic situation deteriorated and Cadburys family members became distressed at the erosion of cooperation within Cadburys. Kierkegaardian dialectic emerged in the change process as managers, engineers, workers, and shop stewards cocreated with "our" historical, positive, local Cadburys tradition in the present. More specifically, managers, workers, engineers, and shop stewards developed and experimented with more incremental technological changes that were informed by the traditional ideals of consensus decisionmaking, employee welfare, and technological advancement. The subsequent strategy change from related diversification to respecialization and from radical automation to incremental technological change was addressed in the context of traditional Cadburys ideals. Apparently, the change to working with this type of dialectic change process and strategy was successful (Smith, Child and Rowlinson, 1990). However, in another type of organization without historical tradition of simultaneous consensus decisionmaking, employee welfare, and technological advancement, an attempt to work with a Kierkegaardian dialectic probably would not have been successful, since a key element of such a dialectic, a strong tradition, would have been missing.

CONCLUSION

As illustrated in the Cadburys case, there are other types of dialectic change processes in addition to strategic management's interpretation of Churchman's interpretation of Hegel's dialectic method. For example, the headquarters engineers appeared to be working with a Socratic dialectic. In contrast, for a while, and as destructive conflicts escalated within Cadburys, the technical director and the human resources vice president on the one side, and the shop stewards and the workers on the other side, appeared to be engaged in self-fulfilling destructive interactions that included elements of Hegelian and Marxian dialectics.

In contrast to the technical director and the human resources vice president, the manufacturing manager of the confectionary division tried to work with a more constructive Argyris and Schon action-science dialectic. While this approach met with some success at the divisional level, it was blocked at the corporate level by the—at least for the moment—more powerful technical director and human resources vice president. After the negative consequences of the strategy change to related diversification and radical automation strategy became apparent, the organization was able to work with the more cooperative and friendly Kierkegaardian dialectic, but only after replacing the technical director and the human resources vice president.

What can be learned from this case example and theoretical exploration? First, there were several different types of dialectics operating beyond strategic management's dialectical inquiry. Dialectics is more complex than the strategic management literature suggests. Churchman (1966, 1968, 1971) made an important contribution by introducing the idea of dialectic into management and organization studies literature. However, the thesis-antithesis-synthesis model that is the foundation for dialectical inquiry research is much more strategic management than either Churchman or Hegel.

There are many different types of dialectic change processes beyond Churchman's thesis-antithesis-synthesis, including, for example, Socratic logos, Hegelian aufheben, Kierkegaardian upbuilding, Marxian relentless criticism, and Argyis and Schon action-science. Within the context of the Cadburys case, dialectic change processes were compared with respect to differences among: phenomena in conflict, emotionality of conflicts, and different affirmation-negation-transformation change processes.

Second, several different types of dialectic processes were operating simultaneously. This suggests that dialectics is even more complex than there being multiple types of dialectics. The multiple types of dialectic processes can operate simultaneously and can be entangled.

Third, there appears to be some choice available with respect to which dialectic processes we can choose to work and co-create with in our organization change and development efforts. To some extent, we can choose to work with more cooperative and peaceful change and transformation processes.

Fourth, there may be contextual and timing limitations with respect to how effective we can be in choosing to work with streams of dialectic processes that are not well-matched with situational opportunities. For example, even though the manufacturing manager was able to work with Argyris and Schon double-loop dialectic at the divisional level, this dialectic process was blocked, at least for a while, at the corporate level.

Similarly, Adrian Cadbury was able to work with Kierkegaardian dialectics after more destructive dialectics appeared to play themselves out. It might not have been possible to work with the more cooperative Kierkegaardian dialectic until both top managers and top labour leaders had become acquainted personally with destructive labor relations and strikes that they had not previously experienced at Cadburys. Sometimes, we may have to experience personally constructive (Weick, 1979) and destructive (Bateson, 1972) reciprocal interactions before we are able and willing to choose to work with more cooperative dialectic processes.

The relative effectiveness and appropriateness of all these change processes in management and organization ethics contexts can be compared and evaluated. However, the research methodology may have to change. Since the dialectical inquiry change model was based on strategic management's consideration of individual positions and counterpositions held independently of embedded traditions, it was possible to use laboratory experimentation. It is difficult to simulate in a laboratory the powerful organization social traditions that are key factors in most of the Hegelian and post-Hegelian dialectic change models. Case studies, participant observation, and field action-research methods are more appropriate.

Furthermore, since we think we know, and as the Cadburys case illustrates, if at least strains of various types of dialectic processes are operating simultaneously in a situation, then we have some ability to choose which processes to work with and co-create with. The action part of the action-learning relationship suggests, for example, that we look at regression equations somewhat differently. Instead of solely looking for which variables explain the most variance, the normative component of philosophy and ethics-based dialectic scholarship suggests that we also look at which variables we should try to work with.

We might choose to work with a factor such as an embedded organization tradition even if it explained less variance than another variable because of combined philosophical, ethical, and effectiveness reasons. Philosophical perspectives and methods can provide managers with options that are informed by ethical concerns, increasing organizational and managerial degrees of freedom. Mutual informing between philosophy-based dialectic change processes and management-organization studies scholarship may result in benefits similar to the very fruitful, older, and more mature research stream of behavioral science-informed management and organzation studies scholarship.

REFERENCES

Ackerman, R. W., and R. A. Bauer. 1976. *Corporate Social Performance.* Reston, Va.: Reston.

Adams, S. 1984. *Roche versus Adams.* London: Jonathan Cape.

American Broadcasting Company and G. Englund. 1988. *The Challenger.* Broadcast by American Broadcasting Company and produced by George Englund Productions and King Phoenix Productions; written by George Englund; transcript by George Englund.

American Company Shop Committee Plans. 1919. New York: The Bureau of Industrial Research.

Amjad, M. 1988. Lecture and discussion given in Pakistan management development course taught by the author and organized by Arthur D. Little, Inc., and the U.S. A.I.D. Mr. M. Amjad is chief executive officer of Chaudhry Textile Mills, Ltd. Mr. M. Amjad was also interviewed by the author.

Amnesty International. 1995. Amnesty International Report. London: Amnesty International Publications.

Arendt, H. 1964. *Eichmann in Jerusalem.* New York: Schocken.

Arendt, H. 1978. *The Life of the Mind.* Ed. Mary McCarthy. New York: Harcourt Brace Jovanovich.

Argyris, C. 1962. *Interpersonal Competence and Organizational Effectiveness.* Homewood, Ill.: Dorsey.

Argyris, C. 1965. *Organizations and Innovation.* Homewood, Ill.: Irwin.

Argyris, C. 1970. *Intervention Theory and Method.* Reading, Mass.: Addison-Wesley.

Argyris, C. 1976. Leadership, Learning, and Changing the Status Quo. *Organizational Dynamics*, Winter: 29–43.

Argyris, C. 1990. *Overcoming Organizational Defenses: Facilitating Organizational Learning.* Boston: Allyn and Bacon.

Argyris, C. 1992. *On Organizational Learning.* Cambridge, Mass.: Basil Blackwell.

Argyris, C., R. Putnam, and D. M. Smith. 1985. *Action Science*. San Francisco: Jossey-Bass.

Argyris, C., and D. A. Schon. 1974. *Theory in Practice: Increasing Professional Effectiveness*. San Francisco: Jossey-Bass.

Argyris, C., and D. A. Schon. 1988. Reciprocal integrity: creating conditions that encourage personal and organizational integrity. In S. Srivastva et al. (1988), *Executive Integrity*. San Francisco: Jossey-Bass. Pp. 197–222.

Argyris, D. 1985. The ethnographic approach to intervention and fundamental change. In C. Argyris, R. Putnam, and D. M. Smith. 1985. *Action Science*. San Francisco: Jossey-Bass. Pp. 158–189.

Aristotle. 1941. *The Basic Works of Aristotle*. Ed. R. McKeon. New York: Random House.

Aristotle. 1955. *The Nicomachean ethics*. Trans. J. A. K. Thomson. New York: Penguin.

Automobile Engineer, 1985. Lecture/discussion at Boston College by engineer who prefers to remain anonymous.

Axelrod, R. 1984. *The Evolution of Cooperation*. New York: Basic Books.

Ayer, A. J. 1936. *Language, Truth and Logic*. New York: Dover.

Baier, K. 1958. *The Moral Point of View*. Ithaca, N.Y.: Cornell University Press.

Bailey, J. 1993. Browning-Ferris bucks Mob, warily hauls New York City trash. *The Wall Street Journal*, Nov. 8, pp. 1, A6.

Bank Board Member. 1993. Interview with board member who prefers to remain anonymous.

Barnard, C. I. 1938. *The Functions of the Executive*. Cambridge, Mass.: Harvard University Press.

Bartunek, J. M. 1984. Changing interpretive schemes and organizational restructuring: the example of a religious order. *Administrative Science Quarterly* 29(2):355–372.

Bartunek, J. M. 1988. The dynamics of personal and organizational reframing. In R. E. Quinn, and K. S. Cameron, eds., *Paradox and transformation: Towards a Theory of Change in Organization and Management*. Cambridge, Mass.: Ballinger. Pp. 137–162.

Bartunek, J. M. 1993a. The multiple cognition and conflicts associated with second-order organizational change. In J. K. Murnighan, ed., *Social Psychology in Organizations: Advances in Theory and Research*. Englewood Cliffs, N. J.: Prentice-Hall. Pp. 322–349.

Bartunek, J. M. 1993b. Organizational aspects of the Harvard alcohol project. In T. E. Backer, and E. M. Rogers, eds., *Organizational Aspects of Health Communications Campaigns: What Works*. Newbury Park: Sage. Pp. 203–213.

Bartunek, J. M., M. K. and Moch. 1987. First-order, second-order, and third-order change and organization development interventions: a cognitive approach. *Journal of Applied Behavioral Science* 23(3):483–500.

Bass, B. M. 1985. *Leadership and Performance Beyond Expectations*. New York: The Free Press.

Bass, B. M., and V. J. Shackleton. 1979. Industrial democracy and participative management: a case for a synthesis. *Academy of Management Review* 4(3):393–404.

Bauer, R. A. 1973. Conversation with Richard P. Neilsen.

Bateson, G. 1972. *Steps to an Ecology of Mind.* New York: Ballantine Books.

Benson, G. C. 1989. Ethics codes. *Journal of Business Ethics* 8(4):309–315.

Bentham, J. [1789] 1897. *An Introduction to the Principles of Morals and Legislation.* Oxford: Clarendon.

Berger, P. L., and T. Luckmann. 1966. *The Social Construction of Reality.* New York: Doubleday–Anchor.

Bernstein, R. J. 1971. *Praxis and Action.* Philadelphia: University of Pennsylvania Press.

Bernstein, R. J. 1985. *Beyond Objectivism and Relativism: Science, Hermeneutics, and Praxis,* Philadelphia: University of Pennsylvania Press.

Bird, F., F. Westley, and J. A. Waters. 1989. The uses of moral talk: why do managers talk ethics? *Journal of Business Ethics* 8(1):75–89.

Boisjoly, R. P., E. F. Curtis, and E. Mellican. 1989. Roger Boisjoly and the Challenger disaster. *Journal of Business Ethics* 8(2):217–230.

Bok, S. 1980. Whistleblowing and professional responsibility, *New York University Education Quarterly* 2(4):2–7.

Bond, K. M. 1989. *Bibliography of Business Ethics and Business Moral Values.* Omaha, Neb.: Creighton University.

Boston Banker. 1992. Interview with Boston banker who prefers to remain anonymous.

Boulding, K. 1978. *Stable Peace.* Austin: University of Texas Press.

Bowditch, J. L., and A. Buono. 1982. *Quality of Work Life Assessment.* Boston: Auburn House.

Bowie, N. E., and R. E. Freeman, eds. 1992. *Ethics and Agency Theory: An Introduction.* New York: Oxford University Press.

Brady, N. 1986. Aesthetic components of management ethics. *Academy of Management Review* 11(2):337–344.

Brauchli, M. W. 1994. Indonesia is striving to prosper in freedom but is still repressive. *The Wall Street Journal,* Oct. 11, pp. 1, 13.

Braybrooke, D. E. 1987. Social contract theory's fanciest flight. *Ethics* 97(4):750–764.

Brinton, H. 1952. *Friends for 300 Years.* New York: Harper and Brothers.

Broker. 1989. Lecture and discussion at Boston College by broker who prefers to remain anonymous.

Bronner, E. 1995. Doctors ensnared in torture dilemma. *The Boston Globe,* Jan. 16, pp. 41–42.

Buber, M. 1937. *I and Thou.* Edinburgh: T. and T. Clark

Burkert, W. 1985. *Greek Religion.* Cambridge, Mass.: Harvard University Press.

Burns, J. M. 1978. *Leadership.* New York: Harper and Row.

Buono, A. F., and J. L. Bowditch. 1989. *The Human Side of Mergers and Acquistions.* San Francisco: Jossey-Bass.

Business Roundtable. 1988. *Corporate Ethics.* Business Roundtable.

Cadbury, A. 1964. Appraisal of course-signposts to the future. In T. Wylie, ed., *International Industrial Relations*. Birmingham: College of Advanced Technology.

Cadbury, A. 1983. Cadbury Schweppes: more than chocolate and tonic. *Harvard Business Review,* Jan.–Feb.: 133–144.

Cadbury, A. 1985. Quaker values in business. Paper presented Oct. 22 at Gresham College.

Cadbury, A. 1987. Ethical managers make their own rules. *Havard Business Review,* Sept.–Oct.: 69–73.

Cadbury, A. 1989. Conversation: an interview with Sir Adrian Cadbury. *Organization Dynamics,* Winter: 39–58.

Cadbury, A. 1990. Foreword, In C. Smith, J. Child, and M. Rowlinson, 1990, *Reshaping Work: the Cadbury Experience*. Cambridge: Cambridge University Press, pp. ix-xiii.

Cadbury, E. 1912. *Experiments in Industrial Organization*. London: Longmans, Green.

Cadbury, E. 1914. Some principles of industrial organization: the case for and against Scientific management. *Sociological Review* 7(1):96–115.

Cadbury, E., and G. Shann. 1907. *Sweating*. London: Longmans, Green.

Campbell, D. T., and J. C. Stanley. 1963. *Experimental and Quasi-Experimental Design for Research*. Chicago: Rand-McNally.

Camus, A. 1946. *The Outsider*. London: Hamilton.

Carley, W. M. 1991. Artificial heart valves that fail are linked to falsified records. *The Wall Street Journal,* Nov. 7, pp. 1, A6.

Carlzon, J. 1987. *Moments of Truth*. Cambridge, Mass.: Ballinger.

Cavanagh, G., D. Moberg, and M. Velasquez. 1981. The ethics of organizational politics. *Academy of Management Review* 6(3):363–374.

Chandler, A. D. 1977. *The Visible Hand*. Cambridge, Mass.: Harvard University Press.

Chanin, M. N., and H. J. Shapiro. 1985. Dialectical inquiry in strategic planning: extending the boundaries. *Academy of Management Review* 10(4): 663–675.

Chappell, T. 1993. *The Soul of a Business: Managing for Profit and the Common Good*. New York: Bantam.

Child, J. 1964. Quaker employers and industrial relations. *Sociological Review* 12(3):293–315.

Child, J., and C. Smith. 1987. The context and process of organizational transformation: Cadbury Limited in its sector. *Journal of Management Studies* 24(6):565–591.

Chronicle of Higher Education. Tenure critic protects by shaving his head. Nov. 3, p. A4.

Churchman, C. W. 1966. Hegelian inquiring systems. Working paper no. 49. University of California, Berkeley. Space Sciences Laboratory, Social Sciences Project.

Churchman, C. W. 1968. *The Systems Approach*. New York: Dell.

Churchman, C. W. 1971. *The Design of Inquiring Systems: Basic Concepts of Systems and Organization*. New York: Basic Books.

Clarke, L. 1988. Explaining choices among technological risks. *Social Problems* 35(1):22–35.

Coch, L., and P. R. French. 1948. Overcoming resistance to change. *Human Relations* 1(1):112–132.

Crosier, R. A. 1981a. Dialectical inquiry in strategic planning: a case of premature aceptance? *Academy of Management Review* 6(4):643–648.

Crosier, R. A. 1981b. Further thoughts on dialectical inquiry: a rejoinder to Mitroff and Mason. *Academy of Management Review* 6(4):653–654.

Cowell, A. 1993a. Accused Olivetti chief surrenders and is freed under house arrest. *The New York Times,* Nov. 3, p. A16.

Cowell, A. 1993b. Head of Olivetti faces charges in bribe inquiry. *The New York Times,* Oct. 31, p. 7.

Cowell, A. 1993c. Italy's scandal lays bare a bankruptcy of politics. *International Herald Tribune,* March 4, pp. 1, 6.

Cyert, R., and J. March. 1963. *A Behavioral Theory of the Firm.* Englewood Cliffs, N.J.: Prentice-Hall.

Dean, J. 1976. *Blind Ambition: The White House Years.* New York: Simon and Schuster.

Dellheim, C. 1987. The creation of a company culture: Cadburys. *The American Historical Review* 92(1):13–44.

Derrida, J. 1981. Three questions to Hans-Georg Gadamer. Interpreting signatures (Nietzsche/Heidegger): two questions. In D. P. Michelfelder and R. E. Palmer. 1989. *Dialogue and Deconstruction: The Gadamer-Derrida Encounter.* Albany: State University of New York Press. Pp. 52–55.

Derrida, J. 1988. *Limited INC.* Evanston, Ill.: Northwestern University Press.

Donaldson, T. 1989. *The Ethics of International Business.* New York: Oxford University Press.

Donaldson, T. 1992. The language of international corporate ethics. *Business Ethics Quarterly* 2(3):271–282.

Drucker, P. 1980. *Managing in Turbulant Times.* New York: Harper and Row.

Eliot, T. S. 1944. *Four Quartets.* London: Faber and Faber.

Emden, P. H. 1940. *Quakers in Commerce.* London: Sampson Low, Marston and Co.

Emerson, H. 1919. Society of industrial engineers. Unpublished notes, In W. F. Muhs. 1982. Worker participation in the progressive era: an assessment by Harrington Emerson. *Academy of Management Review* 7(1):99–102.

Emerson, H. 1920. Resolved: that workers should participate in the management. In W. F. Muhs, (1982). Worker participation in the progressive era: an assessment by Harrington Emerson. *Academy of Management Review* 7(1):99–102.

Emerson, R. W. [1850] 1895. *Representative Men: Seven Lectures.* Philadelphia: Henry Altemus.

Endo, S. 1972. *The Sea and the Poison.* New York: Taplinger.

Environmental Protection Agency Investigators. 1988. Interview with two EPA investigators who prefer to remain anonymous.

Ethics Resource Center. 1988. Xerox programs in business ethics and corporate responsibility. Business Roundtable. *Corporate Ethics.* New York: Business Roundtable.

Ewing, D. W. 1977. *Freedom Inside the Organization.* New York: McGraw-Hill.

Ewing, D. W. 1983a. Case of the rogue division. *Harvard Business Review* 61(May–June):166–168.

Ewing, D. W. 1983b. *Do It My Way or You're Fired.* New York: John Wiley.

Ewing, D. W. 1983c. How to negotiate with employee objectors. *Harvard Business Review,* Jan.–Feb.: 103–110.

Ewing, D. W. 1989. *Justice on the job: Resolving Grievances in the Nonunion Workplace.* Boston: Harvard Business School Press.

Fama, E. F. 1980. Agency Problems and the theory of the firm. *Journal of Political Economy* 88:288–307.

Fisher, R., and W. Ury. 1991. *Getting to Yes: Negotiating Agreement Without Giving In.* New York: Penguin Books.

Fitzgerald, A. E. 1977. *The High Priests of Waste.* New York: Norton.

Fleischacker, S. 1994. *The Ethics of Culture.* Ithaca, N.Y.: Cornell University Press.

Forman, C., and L. Bannon. 1993. A corruption scandal leaves Italy's leaders weakened and scorned. *The Wall Street Journal,* March 1, pp. 1, A8.

Foucault, M. 1972. *Power/Knowledge.* Ed. Colin Gordon. New York: Pantheon.

Freeman, R. E. 1984. *Strategic Management: A Stakeholder Approach.* Boston: Pitman.

Freeman, R. E., and D. R. Gilbert. 1988. *Corporate Strategy and the Search For Ethics.* Englewood Cliffs, N. J.: Prentice-Hall.

French, P. 1979. The corporation as a moral person. *American Philosophical Quarterly* 5(3):207–215.

French, W., and C. H. Bell. 1973. *Organization Development.* Englewood Cliffs, N.J.: Prentice-Hall.

Gadamer, H.-G. 1989a. *Truth and Method.* New York: Crossroad.

Gadamer, H.-G. 1989b. Text and interpretation. Reply to Jacques Derrida. Letter to Dallmayr. Destruktion and Deconstruction. Hermeneutics and Logocentrism. In D. P. Michelfelder and R. E. Palmer, *Dialogue and deconstruction: The Gadamer-Derrida Encounter.* Albany: State University of New York Press. Pp. 55–58.

Gardiner, A. G. 1923. *Life of George Cadbury.* London: Cassell.

Gauthier, D. 1986. *Morals by Agreement.* Oxford: Clarendon Press.

Geary vs. U.S. Steel Corporation. 319 A. 2d 174, Supreme Court of Pa.

Geertz, C. 1973. *The Interpretation of Cultures.* New York: Basic Books.

Geertz, C. 1983. *Local Knowledge.* New York: Basic Books.

General Motors Manager. 1989. Lecture and discussion at Boston College by General Motors manager who prefers to remain anonymous.

Gerlin, A. 1995. Deals on the side: How a Penny buyer made up to $1.5 million on vendors' kickbacks. *The Wall Street Journal,* Feb. 7, pp. 1, 16.

Geuss, R. 1981. *The Idea of a Critical Theory.* Cambridge: Cambridge University Press.

Gillette Executive. 1986. Presentation and discussion at Boston College management class by an executive who prefers to remain anonymous.

Gilligan, C. 1982. *In a Different Voice: Psychological Theory and Women's Development.* Cambridge, Mass.: Harvard University Press.

Goodpaster, K. E., and J. B. Mathews. 1982. Can a Corporation Have a Conscience? *Harvard Business Review,* Jan.–Feb., 132–141.

Gilmore, D. 1988. *The Last Leopard: A Life of Giuseppe Tomasi di Lampedusa.* New York: Pantheon.

Gioia, D. A. 1992. Pinto fires and personal ethics: a script analysis of missed opportunities. *Journal of Business Ethics* 11(5):379–389.

Glaberson, W. B. 1985. Did Searle close its eyes to a health hazard? *Business Week,* Oct. 14, pp. 120–122.

Goethe, J. W. 1948. *The Permanent Goethe.* Ed., Thomas Mann. New York: The Dial Press.

Gosselin, P. G. 1993. NIH aide fasts in protest. *The Boston Globe,* May 12, p.3.

Greenleaf, R. K. 1977a. Overcome evil with good. *Friends Journal,* May 15, pp. 292–296.

Greenleaf, R. K. 1977b, *Servant Leadership,* New York: Paulist Press.

Greenleaf, R. K. 1989. Conversation with the author.

Gronn, P. C. 1983. Talk as the work: the accomplishment of school administration. *Administrative Science Quarterly* 23(1):1–21.

Grubb, I. 1929. *Quakerism and Industry Before 1800.* London: William and Norgate.

Grunwald, W., and W. F. Bernthal. 1983. Controversy in German management: the Harzburg model experience. *Academy of Management Review* 8(2): 233–241.

Gummere, A. 1922. *The Journal and Essays of John Woolman.* London: Macmillan.

Guthrie, K. S. 1919. *Pythagoras Source Book and Library.* N.J.: Alpine.

Guyon, J. 1988. GE Chairman Welch, though much praised, starts to draw critics. *The Wall Street Journal,* Aug. 4, pp. 1, 8.

Habermas, J. 1971. *Knowledge and Human Interests.* Boston: Beacon Press.

Habermas, J. 1979. *Communication and the Evolution of Society.* Boston: Beacon Press.

Habermas, J. [1983] 1990. *Moral consciousness and Communicative Action.* Cambridge, Mass.: The MIT Press.

Hare, R. M. [1952] 1961. *The Language of Morals.* Oxford: Clarendon Press.

Hare, R. M. 1963. *Freedom and Reason.* Oxford: Oxford University Press.

Hays, T. C. 1994. Changes at IBM. *The Wall Street Journal,* Oct. 6, pp. 1, 6.

Harmon, M. 1981. *Action Theory for Public Administration.* New York: Longman.

Hegel, G. W. F. [1807] 1977. *Phenomenology of Spirit.* Oxford: Oxford University Press.

Hegel, G. W. F. [1821] 1953. *Philosophy of Right.* Trans. with notes by T. M. Knox. Oxford: Clarendon Press.

Hegel, G. W. F. [1837] 1975. *Lectures on the Philosophy of World History.* Translated by H. B. Nisbet. Cambridge: Cambridge University Press.

Heidegger, M. [1927] 1962. *Being and Time.* New York: Harper and Row.

Herling, J. 1962. *The Great Price Conspiracy*. Washington, D.C.: Luce.

Hersey, R. B. 1924. Rests authorized and unathorized. *Journal of Personnel Research* 4(1):39–45.

Hill, M. A. 1979, ed. *Hannah Arendt: The Recovery of the Public World*. New York: St. Martin's Press.

Hilts, P. J. 1994. Panel finds wide debate in '40s on the ethics of radiation tests. *New York Times,* Oct. 12, pp. 1, A14.

Hinshaw, D. 1951. *Rufus Jones: Master Quaker*. New York: G. P. Putnam's Sons.

Hirsch, J. S. 1991. Procter & Gamble calls in the law to track news leak. *The Wall Street Journal,* Aug. 12, p. 1.

Hirschman, A. O. 1970. *Exit, Voice, and Loyalty: Responses to Decline in Firms, Organizations, and States*. Cambridge: Harvard University Press.

Hobbes, T. [1651] 1960. *Leviathan*. Oxford: Basil Blackwell.

Hodgkin, J. E. 1918. *Quakerism and Industry: Being the Full Record of a Conference of Employers, Chiefly Members of the Society of Friends, held at Woodbrooke, Birmingham, 11th–14th, 1918 together with the report issued by the conference*. Darlington: The North of England Newspaper Co., Ltd., Priestgate.

Hooper, L., and M. W. Miller. 1992. IBM shares fall 11% as firm says it will cut 25,000 jobs and may trim dividend. *Wall Street Journal,* Dec. 16, p. 3.

Hotel Executive. 1988. Lecture and discussion given in Pakistan management development class by hotel executive who wishes to remain anonymous.

Husserl, E. 1962. *Ideas*. New York: Collier.

Husserl, E. 1965. *Phenomenology and the Crisis of Philosophy*. New York: Harper Torchbooks.

Hyatt, J. C., and A. K. Naj. 1992. GE is no place for autocrats, Welch decrees. *The Wall Street Journal,* March 3, p. B1.

Industrial democracy in a textile plant. 1919. *Textile World,* June 14, p. 78.

Jacobs, J. 1992. *Systems of Survival: A Dialogue on the Moral Foundations of Commerce and Business*. New York: Random House.

Jacobs, M. A. 1994. Riding crop and slurs: how Wall Street dealt with a sex-bias case. *The Wall Street Journal,* June, 9, pp. 1, 6.

James, S. V. 1963, *A People Among Peoples: Quaker benevolence in eighteenth-century America,* Cambridge: Harvard University Press.

James, W. 1892, 1984, *Psychology: Briefer Course,* Cambridge: Harvard University Press.

James, W. 1907, *Pragmatism: A new name for some old ways of thinking,* New York: Longmans, Green and Co.

James, W. 1902, *Varieties of Religious Experience,* New York: Longmans, Green and Co.

Jaspers, K. 1948, *Philosophy,* Heidelberg-Berlin: Springer-Verlag.

Jensen, M. C. and W. H. Meckling, 1975, Theory of the firm: managerial behavior, agency costs and ownership structure, *Journal of Financial Economics,* 3, 305–360.

Jones, R. M. 1941, *Spirit in Man*. Palo Alto, California: Stanford University Press.

References 243

Jones, R. M. 1947, Our day in the German Gestapo, *Friends Intelligencer,*
August 2, pp. 6–23.

Jowett, B. 1903, *The Four Socratic Dialogues of Plato.* Translated into English
with analyses and introductions. Oxford: The Clarendon Press.

Kant, I. [1765] 1959. *Foundation of a Metaphysics of Morals.* Trans. L. W. Beck.
New York: Bobbs-Merrill.

Kearney, R. 1984. Dialogue with Jacques Derrida. In *Dialogues with Contemporary Continental Thinkers.* Manchester: Manchester University Press.

Kegan, R. 1982. *The Evolving Self.* Cambridge, Mass.: Harvard University
Press.

Keneally, T. 1982. *Schindler's List.* New York: Simon and Schuster.

Kennedy, J. H., and M. Brelis. 1992. Ex-GE official says firm fixed diamond
prices. *The Boston Globe,* April 23, pp. 37–38.

Kierkegaard, S. [1843] 1941. *Fear and Trembling. The sickness unto Death.*
Trans. W. Lowrie. Princeton, N.J.: Princeton University Press.

Kierkegaard, S. [1843] 1944. *Either/Or.* Trans. D. F. and L. Swenson and
W. Lowrie. Princeton, N.J.: Princeton University Press.

Kierkegaard, S. [1847] 1946. *Works of Love.* Trans. D. F. Swenson. Princeton,
N.J.: Princeton University Press.

Kierkegaard, S. [1847] 1956. *Purity of Heart.* Trans. D. Steere. New York:
Harper and Row.

Kierkegaard, S. [1846] 1962. *The Present Age.* Trans. Alexander Dru. New
York: Harper Torchbook's.

Kierkegaard, S. [1845] 1967. *Stages on Life's Way,* Trans. W. Lowrie. New
York: Schocken Books.

Kierkegaard, S. [1846] 1968. *Concluding Unscientific Postscript to the Philosophical Fragments.* Trans. D. F. Swenson. Princeton, N.J.: Princeton University Press.

Kohlberg, L. 1968. *International Encyclopedia of the Social Sciences.* Vol. 10,
Moral Development. Ed. David L. Sills. New York: Macmillan and The
Free Press.

Kohlberg, L. 1969. *Stages in the Development of moral thought and action,* N.Y.:
Holt, Rinehart & Winston.

Kohlberg, L. 1981. *Eassays on Moral Development.* San Francisco: Harper and
Row.

Kohlberg, L. 1983. *Moral Stages: A Current Formulation and Response to Critics,*
New York: Karger.

Kramer, J. 1996. Bad Blood. *The New Yorker.* Oct. 11, pp. 74–95.

Krieger, J. 1987. The United Kingdom: symbiosis or division? In G. C. Lodge
and E. F. Vogel, eds., *Ideology and National Competitiveness: An Analysis of
Nine Countries.* Boston: Harvard Business School Press. Pp. 29–55.

Kuhn, T. 1962. *The Structure of Scientific Revolutions.* Chicago: University of
Chicago Press.

Kunen, J. S. 1994. *Reckless Disregard: Corporate Greed, Government Indiffer-
ence, and the Kentucky School Bus Crash.* New York: Simon and Schuster.

Ladwig, F. 1986. Personal conversation with and letter to Richard P. Nielsen.

Lampedusa, G. di. 1961. *The Leopard.* Trans. Archibald Colquhoun. New
York: Signet.

Latin American Banker. 1993. Interview with Latin American banker who prefers to remain anonymous.

Lawrence, F. 1981. Translator's introduction. In H. G. Gadamer. 1981. *Reason in the Age of Science*. Cambridge: MIT Press. Pp. ix–xxxiii.

Lawrence, F. 1984. Language as horizon. In F. Lawrence, ed. 1984. *The Beginning and the Beyond*. Chico, Ca.: The Scholars Press. Pp. 13–35.

Ledvinka, J., and V. G. Scarpello. 1991. *Federal Regulation of Personnel and Human Resource Management*. Boston: PWS-Kent.

Leitch, J. 1919. *Man to Man: The Story of Industrial Democracy*. New York: Forbes.

Lewin, K. 1948. Action Research and Minority Problems. In K. Lewin, ed. *Resolving Social Conflicts*. New York: Harper and Row. Pp. 123–137.

Lewin, K., R. Lippitt, and R. K. White. 1939. Patterns of aggressive behavior in experimentally created social climates. *Journal of Social Psychology* 10(3):271–299.

Likert, R. 1960. *New Patterns of Management*. New York: McGraw-Hill.

Likert, R. 1967. *The Human Organization*. New York: McGraw-Hill.

Liebowitz, A. G. 1991. The Polariod due process system as an approach for intergrating ethic into the organization. Address given at Boston College Faculty Workshop on integrating ethics into the organization, Feb. 15, 1991. Ms. Liebowitz is responsible for managing the Polaroid due process system.

Lifton, R. J. 1987. *The Nazi Doctors*. New York: Basic Books.

Lindblom, C. E. 1977. *Politics and Markets: The World's Political-Economic Systems*. New York: Basic Books.

Lindblom, C. E., and D. K. Cohen. 1979. *Usable Knowledge: Social Science and Social Problem Solving*. New Haven, Conn.: Yale University Press.

Lobkowicz, N. 1967. *Theory and Practice: History of a Concept from Aristotle to Marx*. Notre Dame, Ind.: University of Notre Dame Press.

Loevinger, J. 1976. *Ego Development*. San Francisco: Jossey-Bass.

Loevinger, J. 1978. *Measuring Ego Development*. San Francisco: Jossey-Bass.

Lowrie, W. [1942] 1970. *A Short Life of Kierkegaard*. Princeton, N.J.: Princeton University Press.

Lyotard, J.-F. 1984. *The Postmodern Condition: A Report on Knowledge*. Trans. Geoff Bennington and Brian Massumi. Minneapolis: University of Minnesota Press.

Maccoby, M. 1976. *The Gamesman*. New York: Simon and Schuster.

March, J., and H. Simon. 1958. *Organizations*. New York: John Wiley.

Marcuse, H. 1964. *One-Dimensional Man*. Boston: Beacon Press.

Marketing Director. 1986. Conversation with and letter to author.

Maritain, J. 1954. *Creative Intuition in Art and Poetry*. Cleveland, Ohio: Meridian.

Marx, K. 1959. *Basic Writings on Politics and Philosophy*. Ed. L. S. Feuer. New York: Anchor Books.

Marx, K. 1967. *Writings of the Young Marx on Philosophy and Society*, Ed. L. D. Easton and K. H. Guddat. Garden City, N.Y.: Anchor Books.

Marx, K. 1967. *Capital*. 3 vol. Ed. F. Engels. Trans. S. Moore and E. Aveling. New York: International Publishers, 1967.

Mason, R. O. 1969. A Dialectical Approach to Strategic Planning, *Management Science* 15(2):403–414.

Mayo, E. 1923. The irrational factor in society, *Journal of Personnel Research* 1(3):419–426.

Mayo, E. 1930a. Changing methods in industry. *Personnel Journal* 8(3):326–332.

Mayo, E. 1930b. The human effect of mechanization. *American Economic Review* 20(1):156–176.

Mayo, E. 1930c. *A New Approach to Industrial Relations*. Boston: Harvard Business School Press.

Mayo, E. 1930d. The Western Electric Company experiment, *Human Factor* 6(1):1–2.

Mayo, E. 1933. *The Human Problems of an Industrial Civilization*. New York: Macmillan.

McCann, T. 1976. *An American Company*. New York: Crown.

McCann, T. 1984. Lecture and discussion at Boston College.

McConnel, M. 1987. *Challenger, A Major Malfunction: A True Story of Politics, Greed, and the Wrong Stuff*. Garden City, N.Y.: Doubleday.

McCormick, J. 1992. Can't see the forest for the sleaze. *The New York Times*, Jan. 23, p. 37.

McCoy, C. S., and F. N. Twining. 1988. The corporate values program at Champion International Corporation. Business Roundtable. *Corporate Ethics*. New York: Business Roundtable.

McGregor, D. 1960. *The Human Side of Enterprise*. New York: McGraw-Hill.

Milgrim, S. 1974. *Obedience to Authority*. New York: Harper and Row.

Miller, A. 1949. *Death of a Salesman*. New York: Viking.

Mills, C. W. 1959. *The Sociological Imagination*. Oxford: Oxford University Press.

Minkes, A. L., and C. S. Nuttall. 1985. *Business Behaviour and Management Structure*. London: Croom Helm.

Mitchell, R., and M. Oneal. 1944. Managing by values: is Levi Strauss' approach visionary—or flaky? *Business Week*, Aug. 1, pp. 46–52.

Mitroff, I., and R. O. Mason. 1981. The metaphysics of policy and planning: a reply to Cosier. *Academy of Management Review* 6(4):649–651.

Monan, J. D. 1968. *Moral Knowledge and Its Methodology in Aristotle*. Oxford: Clarendon Press.

Moore, G. E. 1903. *Principia Ethica*. Cambridge: Cambridge University Press.

Mueller, G. E. 1958. The Hegel legend of "Thesis-Antithesis-Synthesis." *Journal of the History of Ideas* 19(2):411–414.

Muhs, W. F. 1982. Worker participation in the progressive era: an assessment by Harrington Emerson. *Academy of Management Review* 7(1):99–102.

Naj, A. K. 1992. Internal Suspicions: GE's drive to purge fraud is hampered by workers' mistrust. *The Wall Street Journal*, Aug. 22, pp. 1,6.

Nash, G. B., and J. R. Soderland. 1991. *Freedom By Degrees: Emancipation in Pennsylvania and Its Aftermath*. New York: Oxford University Press.

Neuffer, E. 1988. GE manager sentenced for bribery. *The Boston Globe*, July 26, p. 67.

Nicklin, J. L. 1995. When a university does business with members of its board. *The Chronicle of Higher Education,* Jan. 6, pp. A39–A40.

Nielsen, R. P. 1973. Communicating with and motivating high fatalists. *The American Journal of Economics and Sociology* 32(3):337–350.

Nielsen, R. P. 1979. Stages in moving toward cooperative problem solving labor relations and a case study. *Human Resource Management* 18(4):29–40.

Nielsen, R. P. 1981. Toward a method for building consensus during strategic planning. *Sloan Management Review* 22(4):29–40.

Nielsen, R. P. 1982. Book review/essay of D. B. Windsor. *The Quaker Enterprise: Friends in Business. The Academy of Management Review* 8(3):506–508.

Nielsen, R. P. 1983. Training programs: pulling them into sync with your company's strategic planning. *Personnel* 60(3):19–26.

Nielsen, R. P. 1984. Arendt's action philosophy and the manager as Eichmann, Richard III, Faust, or Institution Citizen. *California Management Review* 26(3):191–201.

Nielsen, R. P. 1986. Piggybacking strategies for nonprofits: a shared costs approach. *Strategic Management Journal* 7(3):201–215.

Nielsen, R. P. 1988. Limitations of ethical reasoning as an action strategy. *Journal of Business Ethics* 7(10):725–733.

Nielsen, R. P. 1989a. Changing unethical organizational behavior. *Academy of Management Executive* 3(2):123–130.

Nielsen, R. P. 1989b. Cooperative strategy. *Strategic Management Journal* 9(5):475–492.

Nielsen, R. P. 1990a. Dialogic leadership as ethics action (praxis) method. *Journal of Business Ethics* 9:765–783.

Nielsen, R. P. 1990b. Discussions with Cadbury family members.

Nielsen, R. P. 1993a. Woolman's "I Am We" triple-loop, action-learning: origin and application in organization ethics. *Journal of Applied Behavioral Science* 29(1):117–138.

Nielsen, R. P. 1993b. Triple-loop action-learning as human resources management method. *Research in International Human Resources Management.* Greenwich, Conn: JAI Press. Pp. 75–93.

Nielsen, R. P. 1993c. Varieties of postmodernism as moments in ethics action-learning, *Business Ethics Quarterly* 3(3):251–269.

Nielsen, R. P. 1993d. Organizational ethics from a perspective of action (praxis). *Business Ethics Quarterly* 3(2):131–151.

Nielsen, R. P. 1996a. Upbuilding dialog as organization ethics method: Kierkegaard triple-loop action-learning, *Organization Science,* in press.

Nielsen, R. P. 1996b. Varieties of dialectic change processes. *Journal of Management Inquiry* 5(3): in press.

Nielsen, R. P. and Bartunek, J. M. 1996. Opening narrow, routinized schemata to ethical stakeholder consciousness and action. Paper presented to Academy of Management, August.

Nietzsche, F. [1878] 1969. *Ecce Homo.* Trans. W. Kaufmann and R. J. Holingdale. New York: Random House.

Nietzsche, F. [1887] 1969. *The Genealogy of Morals.* Trans. W. Kaufmann and R. J. Holingdale. New York: Random House.

Northrup, H. R., and J. A. Larson. 1979. *The Impact of the AT&T–EEO Consent Decree.* Philadelphia: University of Pennsylvania, Industrial Research Unit, The Wharton School.

Organization Development Manager. 1992. Case presentation to a Boston College human resources management course by a computer software company organization development manager who prefers to remain anonymous.

Ouspensky, P. 1949. *In Search of the Miraculous.* New York: Harcourt.

Parfit, D. 1984. *Reasons and Persons.* Oxford: Oxford University Press.

Pasztor, A. 1985. Electrical contractors reel under that they rigged bids. *The Wall Street Journal,* Nov. 29, pp. 1, 14.

Pennock, G. A. 1930. Test studies in industrial research at Hawthorne. *Research Studies in Employee Effectiveness in Industrial Relations.* New York: Western Electric Co.

Peters, M., and V. Robinson. 1984. The origins and status of action research. *Journal of Applied Behavioral Science* 20(2):113–124.

Peters, T. 1987. Foreword to J. Carlzon. 1987. *Moments of Truth.* Cambridge, Mass.: Ballinger–Harper and Row.

Pfeffer, J. 1981. *Power in Organizations.* Marshfield, Mass.: Pitman.

Pickett, C. E. 1953. *For More Than Bread: An Autobiographical Account of Twenty-Two Years' Work with the American Friends Service Committee.* Boston: Little Brown.

Planty-Bonjour, G. 1983. Hegel's concept of action as unity of poiesis and praxis. In L. S. Stepelevich, and D. Lamb. *Hegel's Philosophy of Action.* The Hegel Society of Great Britain and the Hegel Society of America. Papers delivered at the 1981 Oxford Conference, Atlantic Highlands, N.J.: Humanities Press. Pp. 19–30.

Plato. 1903. *The Four Socratic Dialogues of Plato.* Trans. B. Jowett. Oxford: Clarendon Press.

Polaroid Executive. 1986. Guest speaker at Boston College management class who prefers to remain anonymous.

Pound, E., and D. Rogers. 1992. The money trail: U.S. firms are linked to an Israeli general at heart of a scandal. *The Wall Street Journal.* Jan. 20, pp. 1, A4.

Pound, E. T. 1985. Investigators detect pattern of kickbacks for defense business. *The Wall Street Journal,* Nov. 14, pp. 1, 25.

Program Manager. 1986. Personal interview with program manager who prefers to remain anonymous.

Putnam, M. 1930. A plan for improving employee relations on the basis of data obtained for employees. In *Research Studies in Employee Effectiveness in Industrial Relations.* New York: Western Electric Co. Pp. 74–92.

Quine, W. V. 1960. *Word and Object.* Cambridge: M.I.T. Press.

Raiffa, H. 1982. *The Art and Science of Negotiation.* Cambridge: Harvard University Press.

Raistrick, A. 1950. *Quakers in Science and Industry.* New York: Kelly.

Rawe, D. 1991. P&G calls in police to probe journal leak. *Cincinnati Post,* Aug. 11, p. 7C.

Real Estate Manager. 1986. Personal interview with manager who prefers to remain anonymous.

Reinhold, R. 1986. Astronauts' chief says NASA risked life for schedule. *The New York Times,* June 10, pp. 1, 36.

Report of the Presidential Commission on the Space Shuttle "Challenger" Accident. 1986. Washington, D.C.: U.S. Government Printing Office.

Research Manager. 1986. Interview with research manager who prefers to remain anonymous.

Ricoeur, P. 1991. *From Text to Action: Essays in Hermeneutics.* Evanston, Ill.: Northwestern University Press.

Roethlisberger, F. J. 1941. *Management and Morale.* Cambridge, Mass.: Harvard University Press.

Roethlisberger, F. J., and W. J. Dickson. 1934. *Management and the Worker: Technical versus Social Organization in an Industrial Plant.* Boston: Division of Research, Harvard Business School.

Rogers, B. 1986. *The IBM Way.* New York: Harper and Row.

Rorty, R. 1982. *Consequences of Pragmatism.* Minneapolis: University of Minnesota Press.

Rorty, R. 1991. *Essays on Heidegger and Others: Philosophical Papers, Volume 2.* Cambridge: Cambridge University Press.

Rorty, R. 1995. Feminism, ideology, and deconstruction: a pragmatist view. In S. Zizek, ed., *Mapping Ideology.* London: Verso.

Rowlinson, M. 1987. Cadbury's New Factory System. Ph.D. diss. University of Aston.

Ryan, W. 1976. *Blaming the Victim.* New York: Random House.

Safire, W. 1991. At P&G: It Sinks. *The New York Times,* Sept. 5, p. A19.

Schein, E., and W. Bennis. *Personal and Organizational Change Through Group Methods.* New York: John Wiley.

Schon, D. A. 1983. *The Reflective Practitioner.* New York: Basic Books.

Schweiger, D. M., and W. R. Sandberg. 1989. The utilization of individual capabilities in group approaches to strategic decision making. *Strategic Management Journal* 10(1):31–43.

Schweiger, D. M., W. R. Sandberg, and J. W. Ragan. 1986. Group approaches for improving strategic decision making: a comparative analysis of dialectical inquiry, devil's advocacy, and consensus. *Academy of Management Journal* 29(1):51–71.

Schweiger, D. M., W. R. Sandberg, and P. L. Rechner. 1989. Experiential effects of dialectical inquiry, devil's advocacy, and consensus approaches to strategic decision making. *Academy of Management Journal* 32(4):745–722.

Schwenk, C. R., and R. A. Cosier. 1980. Effects of the expert, devil's advocate and dialectical inquiry methods on prediction performance. *Organizational Behavior and Human Performance* 26(3):409–424.

Shakespeare, W. 1974. *The Riverside Shakespeare.* Boston: Houghton Mifflin.

Simon, H. A. 1983. *Reason in Human Affairs*. Palo Alto, Ca.: Stanford University Press.

Smart. J. J. C. 1984. *Ethics, Persuasion and Truth*. London: Routledge & Keegan Paul.

Smith, C., J. Child, and M. Rowlinson. 1990. *Reshaping Work: The Cadbury Experience*. Cambridge: Cambridge University Press.

Solomon, C. 1993. What really pollutes? Study of a refinery proves an eye-opener. *The Wall Street Journal*, March 29, pp. 1, A6.

Solomon, R. C. 1989. Business and the humanities: an Aristotelian approach to business ethics. *Ruffin Lectures in Business Ethics*. Charlottesville, Va.: Olsson Center for Applied Ethics, University of Virginia.

State Banker. 1994. Interview with state banker who prefers to remain anonymous.

Steere, D. 1949, Translator's introduction to Soren Kierkegaard's *Works of Love*. Princeton,N.J.: Princeton University Press.

Steere, D. 1956. Translator's introduction to S. Kierkegaard's *Purity of Heart*. New York: Harper and Row. Pp. 9–24.

Steere, D. 1957. *Work and Contemplation*. New York: Harper and Brothers.

Steere, D. 1988. Personal conversation with author.

Sterngold, J. 1992. Another scandal in Japan, this time involving billions, *New York Times*, p. E3.

Stevenson, C. 1960. *Ethics and Language*. New Haven, Conn.: Yale University Press.

Strauss, L. 1989. *Political Philosophy: Ten Essays*. Detroit, Mich.: Wayne State University Press.

Strauss, L., and J. Cropsey. 1987. *History of Political Philosophy*. Chicago: University of Chicago Press.

Stricharhuk, G. 1988. Ex-foreman may win millions for his tale about cheating at GE. *The Wall Street Journal*, June 23, pp. 1, 12.

Summers, C. W. 1980. Protecting all employees against unjust dismissal. *Harvard Business Review*, Jan.–Feb., pp. 132, 139.

Swasy, A. 1993. *Soap Opera: The Inside Story of Procter & Gamble* New York: Random House.

Taylor, F. W. 1911. *Shop Management*. New York: Harper and Brothers.

Telecommunications Company Executive. 1986. Lecture given at Boston College by executive who prefers to remain anonymous.

Tillich, P. 1952. *The Courage to Be*. New Haven, Conn.: Yale University Press.

Toffler, B. L. 1986. *Tough Choices: Managers Talk Ethics*. New York: John Wiley.

Tolles, F. B. 1948. *Meeting House and Counting House: The Quaker Merchants of Colonial Philadelphia, 1682–1763*. New York: W. W. Norton.

Torbert, W. R. 1972. *Learning From Experience: Towards Consciousness*. New York: Columbia University Press.

Torbert, W. R. 1976. *Creating a Community of Inquiry*. London: John Wiley.

Torbert, W. R. 1987. *Managing the Corporate Dream: Restructuring for Long-Term Success*. Homewood, Ill.: Dow-Jones, Irwin.

Torbert, W. R. 1989. Leading organizational transformation. In R. Woodman and W. Pasmore, eds., *Research in Organizational Change and Development.* Greenwich, Conn.: JAI Press.

Torbert, W. R. 1994. The good life: good money, good work, good friends, good questions. *Journal of Management Inquiry* 3(1):58–66.

Toulmin, S. 1961. *An Examination of the Place of Reason in Ethics.* Cambridge: Cambridge University Press.

Trahair, R. 1984. *The Humanist Temper: The Life and Work of Elton Mayo.* New Brunswick, N.J.: Transaction Books.

Trevino, L. K. 1986. Ethical decision-making in organizations: a person-situation interactionist model. *Academy of Management Review* 11(3):601–617.

Trevino, L. K. 1990. A cultural perspective on changing and developing organizational ethics. *Research in Organizational Change and Development,* pp. 195–230.

Vaccaro, V. 1981. Cost-benefit analysis and public policy formulation. In N. Bowie, ed., *Ethical Issues in Government.* San Antonio, Tex.: Temple University Press. Pp. 146–162.

Vanesse, R. 1991. The Champion International organizational development approach for intergrating ethics into the organization. Address given at Boston College faculty workshop on intergrating ethics into the organization, February 15, 1991. Mr. Vanesse is a divisional organizational development manager at Champion International, Inc.

Vaughan, D. 1990. Autonomy, interdependence, and social control: NASA and the Space Shuttle *Challenger, Administrative Science Quarterly* 35(2): 225–257.

Vaughan, D. 1996. *The Challenger Launch Decision.* Chicago: University of Chicago Press.

Velasquez, M. 1983. Why corporations are not morally responsible for anything they do. *Business and Professional Ethics Journal* 2(3):1–23.

Vining, E. G. 1958. *Friend of Life: The Biography of Rufus M. Jones.* Philadelphia: Lippincott.

Walters, K. D. 1975. Your employee's right to blow the whistle. *Harvard Business Review,* July–Aug., pp. 26–34.

Wang Executive. 1989. Lecture and discussion at Boston College by Wang executive who prefers to remain anonymous.

Waters, J. A. 1978. Catch 20.5: corporate morality as an organizational phenomenon. *Organizational Dynamics,* Spring: 3–9.

Weber, M. [1904] 1930. *The Protestant Work Ethic and the Spirit of Capitalism.* Trans. Talcott Parsons with foreword by R. H. Tawney. New York: Charles Scribner's Sons.

Weick, K. E. 1979. *The Social Psychology of Organizing.* New York: Random House.

West Coast Banker. 1995. Interview with West Coast banker who prefers to remain anonymous.

Westin, A. F. 1981. What can and should be done to protect whistleblowers in industry? In A. F. Westin, ed., *Whistleblowing, Loyalty and Dissent in the Corporation.* New York: McGraw-Hill. Pp. 131–165.

Westin, A. F. 1981, ed. *Whistleblowing, Loyalty and Dissent in the Corporation*. New York: McGraw-Hill.

White, S. K. 1991. *Political Theory and Postmodernism*. Cambridge: Cambridge University Press.

Whittier, J. G. 1871. *The Journal of John Woolman With An Introduction by John G. Whittier*, Boston: Houghton, Osgood and Company.

Whyte, W. H. 1956. *The Organization Man*. New York: Simon and Schuster.

Whyte, W. H., and E. Hamilton. 1964. *Action-Research for Management*, Homewood, Ill.: Irwin-Dorsey.

Wiener, N. 1954. *The Human Use of Human Beings*. Garden City, N.Y.: Anchor Books.

Williams, B. 1985. *Ethics and the Limits of Philosophy*. Cambridge, Mass.: Harvard University Press.

Wilson, S. 1955. *The Man in the Gray Flannel Suit*. New York: Simon and Schuster.

Wilson, W. [1919] 1964. Industrial democracy. In S. Haber, ed., *Efficiency and Uplift*, Chicago: University Chicago Press.

Windsor, D. B. 1980. *The Quaker Enterprise: Friends in Business*. London: Frederick Muller Limited.

Wolfe, D. 1919. Successful industrial democracy, *Industrial Management* 58(1):67–71.

Woodward, R., and C. Bernstein. 1974. *All the President's Men*. New York: Simon and Schuster.

Woolman, J. [1774] 1818. *The Works of John Woolman in Two Parts*. 5th. ed. Philadelphia: Benjamin and Thomas Kite.

Young-Bruehl, E. 1982. *Hannah Arendt: For Love of the World*. New Haven, Conn.: Yale University Press.

Yoshino, M. Y., and T. Lifson. 1986. *The Invisible Link: Japan's Sogo Shosha and the Organization of Trade*. Cambridge: MIT Press.

Zaleznik, A. 1984. Foreword to R. C. S. Trahair. 1984, *The Humanist Temper: The Life and Work of Elton Mayo*. New Brunswick, N.J.: Transaction Books.

Zuckoff, M. 1995. Three ex-Bard executives guilty in health fraud. *The Boston Globe*, July 25, pp. 1, 21.

Zuckoff, M., and J. H. Kennedy. 1993. Heart catheter became killer. *The Boston Globe*, Oct. 31, pp. 1, 28.